Shakespeare's Creation

Shakespeare's Creation
The Language of Magic and Play

Kirby Farrell

The University of Massachusetts Press   Amherst   1975

822.33
D
F245a
1976

Library of Congress Cataloging in Publication Data
Farrell, Kirby, 1942–
  Shakespeare's creation.
  Includes bibliographical references and index.
  1. Shakespeare, William, 1564–1616—Criticism
and interpretation I. Title.
PR2976.F3 822.3'3 75-8447
ISBN 0-87023-184-7

For Helena and Joseph Farrell

Contents

Preface

This is a book about Shakespeare's conception of creation. More exactly, it explores a conflict between visionary and more rational uses of imagination. Early commentators such as Nicholas Rowe associated the visionary in Shakespeare with "Magick." In his essay on Falstaff, Maurice Morgann identifies poetry itself with magic:

> True *Poesy* is *magic*, not nature; an effect from causes hidden or unknown. To the Magician I prescribed no laws . . . his power is his law. Him, who neither imitates, nor is within reach of imitation, no precedent can or ought to bind, no limits to contain. . . . —But whither am I going! This copious and delightful topic has drawn me far beyond my design. . . .

My own argument uses the concepts of magical thinking and play. As Johan Huizinga's *Homo Ludens* demonstrates, "magic" and "play" have far more precise meanings—and more in common—than we popularly suppose. Lest they be thought phantoms of the critic's heat-oppressèd brain, I will venture no quick definitions of these terms here. Let me say, however, that the secret of Shakespeare's creative genius does not lurk between these covers. Nor is this a study of the Renaissance beliefs in ghosts, witches, and the occult arts surveyed in R. H. West's *The Invisible World*.

Part One of this book examines magic and play in the structure of Shakespeare's sonnets and drama. It begins with an analysis of certain sonnets as acts of "magical" praise, and means of evoking wonder from the audience. In Part Two the emphasis shifts to Shakespeare's exploration of his characters' creative faculties and the complex moral consequences of their imaginative behavior.

For Maurice Morgann, "this copious and delightful topic" is a siren luring him from his "design." My own design is more vulnerable than I could wish. But I found I could not lash myself to the mast, as it were, and still confront the Shakespeare Coleridge called "myriad-minded." In recent years some commentators have begun to harken with new understanding to the siren Morgann heard, and this book owes much to their efforts. In footnotes, however, I have felt able to credit only my most outstanding debts. If I have been a borrower, hopefully in my turn I may a lender be as well. One who deserves particular mention in any case is Sigurd Burckhardt, whose thinking provided an early catalyst to my own. In his essay "The Poet as Fool and Priest" Burckhardt discerns a twofold rhythm of creation in Shakespeare: the voice of the fool mocks and disrupts stale conventional meanings, whereupon other, priestlike voices may be free to bring about renewal. It is a simple but powerful insight. In extending its implications to new problems of course I alone am responsible for failings.

And faults there are. Rather than do the reader's ear violence by a further report against myself, however, let me instead pay thanks to some friends and colleagues whose imaginative sympathy and sharp physic sustained the book during some desperate sea-changes: John Blanpied, James Calderwood, Maurice Charney, Linda Flower and Tim Flower, David Kalstone, Arthur Kinney, Simon Lesser, and Thomas Van Laan. To these, to some inspiring students, and to my wife Susan, who weathered the book's creation with special grace, I feel grateful in a richly inarticulate way.

Quotations follow Peter Alexander's edition of Shakespeare (New York, 1952). Line references for prose passages are sometimes approximate.

Part One

Word is a shadow of deed.
—*Democritus*

This is the monstruosity in
love, lady, that the will is
infinite and the execution
confin'd, that the desire is
boundless and the act a slave
to limit. —*Troilus and Cressida*

       . . . but you are the
music
While the music lasts.
— T. S. Eliot

Introduction

It is customary to introduce a new study of Shakespeare by apologizing for its inadequacy—partly to propitiate nemesis. For even more than most art, Shakespeare's seems always to exceed the grasp of each critical apparatus brought to it. Nor will the chapters that follow prove the ultimate exception. But I mean these opening remarks to be more than a flourish of modesty.

Shakespeare's art and the vast commentary upon it present an awesome sum of meanings. Certain plays—*Hamlet* is one—are famous for the diverse and irreconcilable interpretations they continue to generate year after year. Of late a single critic has given us a frankly pluralistic study of Iago which offers "some approaches to the illusion of his motivation." The book deploys no less than five different, equally sensible critical vocabularies to "approach" what is, after all, only one of many problems in but a single play. Moreover, these five methods are "merely the ones most obviously invited by the text."[1] Theoretically, it would seem, Shakespeare could sustain infinite investigation. I deliberately put the matter in a strong form because for my purposes here the important question is not which partisan or partial interpretations have merit, but rather how do we respond to the larger prospect of indeterminacy?

Basically the answer is twofold. On the one hand, we may believe that Shakespeare's mysteriousness is finally unimportant or even illusory. We may militantly conclude that certain viewpoints are true and sufficient. Or if skeptical, we might reason that ideally, given unlimited time and new historical data, for example, the properly uncanny critic could arrive at truth: an answer to the question of *Hamlet* or, to be more boldly wishful, a resolution to the mystery of Shakespeare's disposition toward politics or sex or religion.

Alternately we might argue that no absolute resolution is possible. In this view Shakespeare deliberately made his art insoluble, striving to fashion an imaginary world as awesomely irreducible as the real one. However lucid in its particulars, such a world requires a continuing act of interpretation from us. *King Lear* resists the satisfying summaries which we can make (and feel) at the close of *The True Chronicle History of King Leir*, in which vice is punished and virtue rewarded. We may comprehend individual actions in *Hamlet* yet be unable to articulate any definitive meaning for the destiny the play as a whole depicts. Because we cannot exhaust it, we say the play "lives." Taking this standpoint, we would sympathize with Caroline Spurgeon's impulse to preface her famous study of Shakespeare's imagery by applauding "the richest experience and the most profound and soaring imagination known to man." Such art, rather like a cockatrice, the spectator cannot contemplate for long "without being reduced to a condition of complete humility."[2] To put it more positively, such art stirs us to wonder.

It will be seen that the alternatives I have sketched above imply two different attitudes toward the artist's role. The first and more common of these envisions art as rationally clarifying an intelligible world, or imparting God's truth to men. In its most openly didactic form this model of the artist's role escapes Platonic and Christian hostility toward art as irrational and a peril to men's souls. Renaissance literary criticism advanced such a model in a variety of guises, and I suspect that most medieval and Renaissance dramatists would have considered their work included (and justified) under one or another of its rubrics.[3] The second, more complex view of art is not so easily described. Nevertheless I believe it is closer to Shakespeare's own.

Shakespeare gave a lifetime to creation, and we have come to perceive that the joys and stresses of the artist's role are everywhere replicated in his art. When Coleridge identified Prospero as a figure of the playwright ("the very Shakespeare himself, as it were, of the tempest") he was innocently venturing toward a critical perspective which in recent years has begun to find direct formulation.[4] In no other dramatist of the period do we encounter anything like Shakespeare's ongoing exploration of the relation between art and life. In the old *King Leir* characters may speak ambiguously of life in theatrical terms:

When will this Scene of sadnesse haue an end,
And pleasant acts insue, to move delight?[5]

The effect, however, is limited—almost incidental. By contrast, Shakespeare's art again and again calls attention to itself *as art*, questioning its own nature and meaning. At the close of *Love's Labour's Lost*, for example, Berowne observes that

Our wooing doth not end like an old play:
Jack hath not Jill. These ladies' courtesy
Might well have made our sport a comedy.

[5.2.862–64]

If the play "doth not end like an old play," we are left to wonder how does it end? In a sense Berowne is disowning the literally "art-ful" behavior of the characters up to this point, welcoming uncomfortably spontaneous life into the play. What follows, he implies, will be more authentic—indeed more real—than what is past. At the same time on another level Shakespeare seems to be suggesting that his play itself is closer to life than conventional, pat comedy can be.

Hamlet admires the art of the "mousetrap" play as "an honest method," and desperately searches for an analogous method by which to shape his own life and recreate corrupted Denmark. His tragedy is his failure to achieve an adequate "art":

Being thus benetted round with villainies—
Ere I could make a prologue to my brains,
They had begun the play.

[5.2.29]

Hamlet's concern with the uses and "honesty" of art almost inevitably stirs us to consider the nature of the art we behold on the stage before us, the play *Hamlet*. From one perspective, against the backdrop of the play of life, the Prince dramatizes a question which must have been significant to Shakespeare himself: What does it mean to create?

While *Hamlet* is especially self-conscious and complex, it is by no means freakish in its concern with art and creation. It will be useful therefore to begin by considering some Sonnets, whose smaller proportions will enable me to make plain some of the more elusive and complex features of Shakespeare's creation.

I. Which Wondrous Scope: Creation as Praise

Conventions and Wonder

By Shakespeare's time the sonnet had become an extravagantly conventionalized form, bristling with artifice and witty permutations of traditional themes. Wyatt's unoriginal image of the poet as a galley "charged with forgetfulness" and "despairing of port" was still in service half a century later, when in one of his *Tears of Fancy* sonnets (1593) Thomas Watson lamented

> That like a mastless ship at seas I wander,
> For want of her to guide my heart that pineth. . . .

In the *Emarcidulf* sequence of "E. C." (1595) the lover's heart is at one point "like a ship on Neptune's back," "Long tossed betwixt fair hope and foul despair." In Richard Lynche's *Delia* (1596) the ship is the poet's mind,

> But beauty was the rock that my ship split,
> Which since hath made a shipwreck of my joy. . . .

The most mediocre sonneteers appear merely to shuffle emblematic Cupids and forsaken shepherds from one poem to another. When Richard Lynche invokes the beloved's "hard heart" or the hope of "sweet reward," we scarcely register such lifeless phrases at all. Significantly, the inadequacy of poetry to express love—an old theme—itself became a perfunctory device in casual references to "these rude unpolished rhymes."

It is this highly conventionalized art which of course provoked the negative strategy of many Shakespeare sonnets. In Sonnet 130, for example, the poet challenges the adequacy of such art. He

6

vows that "My mistress' eyes are nothing like the sun," and goes on to negate, one after another, a host of lifeless tropes. Despite the amusing satire ("If hairs be wires, black wires grow on her head"), the poem argues a serious point also: conventional poetry breeds "false compare"—in effect, lies.

Sonnet 130 turns on a witty paradox. By denying conventional praises to his beloved the poet might appear to belittle her. Whereas the final couplet confounds any such expectations by vowing

> And yet, by heaven, I think my love as rare
> As any she belied with false compare.

Whether the "love" referred to is the poet's affection or the beloved herself, "rare" here means uncommonly valuable. But as the rhyme words emphasize, the couplet also implies that the beloved is incomparable—presumably beyond all such conventional comparisons. While there is no denying the poem's humorous qualities, we may also appreciate the poet's wish to make us wonder at his beloved. We may understand "rare" in the sense of wonderful.

Sonnet 130 praises the beloved by forcing us to recognize the inadequacy of our customary means of conceiving her. It invokes the beloved only by means of negation; it identifies what is *not* true. The poet seeks to dramatize her extra-ordinary worth. She is beyond us, "inconceivable." As in the Renaissance use of the term *admiratio*, "rare" suggest the miraculous and transcendent. Apart from its negative strategy, the sonnet also arouses wonder in us through its paradoxes. Its ridicule of "false compare" is actually a vow of love as well. Our response is meant to be at once amusement and "serious" admiration.

But there is a further—and crucial—paradox in the sonnet's theme. For the poem maintains that the beloved is most individual and most real when she is not directly conceived, but wondered at. As in all paradoxes, the contradiction here is only apparent. The poet allows only two possibilities for awareness. Either the mind is rigidly conventional and hence false to reality, or it is in a state of awe, open to reality but beyond words. Wonder need not preclude meaning absolutely—after all, the sonnet does express the poet's love and the beloved's worth. We *feel* we know what the poem means. But we cannot reduce that meaning to any glib verbal formula. In Sonnet 130 this paradox—that we know most truly by not knowing—is lighthearted and relatively simple: a stroke of wit.

Nevertheless, the notion has profound implications everywhere in Shakespeare's art.

The Problem of Praise

In the vow which concludes Sonnet 18 the poet-lover swears that

> So long as men can breathe or eyes can see,
> So long lives this, and this gives life to thee.

By "this" we understand the poet to mean his art, the poem our "eyes can see" before us on the page. To come to terms with the couplet's literally incredible claims, we try to regard them as metaphors. For the verb "lives" we substitute "exists." As long as an audience can experience whatever the sonnet signifies, then it will exist not only as an artifact, but also "as if" it lives. Specifically we say that the sonnet "lives" by meaning. Logically and almost as effortlessly we take "this gives life to thee" to mean something like "this sonnet, my art, will represent you to hearers forever."

Such a response accords poetry an honorific, metaphorical immortality. Presumably the sonnet "gives life" by memorializing the beloved, or at least the poet's affection for the beloved, representing one or both in verse by some mimetic technique. The problem is that even if the sonnet did make an attempt to describe the poet's specific emotion or beloved, we would still have to concede that they "lived" only in a manner of speaking. We would still be making the poet's vow metaphorical in order to placate or hoodwink our common sense.

We respond to the vow's fantastic hyperbole by trying to make "sense" of it so that we may believe. We recreate the vow as a noble figurative statement which we can define in terms of familiar notions about the immortality of art, although such notions were even in Shakespeare's day genteel and sentimental conventions. And we do recreate the vow. Insofar as we produce metaphors to force the couplet to match our expectations of what sense is, we are making our own art of it. And to the extent that our manipulations falsify the sonnet and leave us either ruefully unconvinced or patronizing toward its "immortality," we are making bad art.[1]

Confronted by the couplet we try to comprehend it, to "grasp" and thereby possess it as a meaning. The sonnet itself we conceive as a problem for which we can and should manufacture a solution. By no accident, our problem corresponds to the one the poet poses for himself at the outset. As in Sonnet 130, he questions how to create "honest" art. Contemplating the act of praise, he asks:

> Shall I compare thee to a summer's day?

In the strictest sense of "compare" his question poses an equation, a metaphor in fact: "Shall I make a poem saying you are [like] a summer's day?" In his answer, the poem itself, he not only repudiates the proposed metaphor, but also denies the integrity of any "made-up" identity:

> Shall I compare thee to a summer's day?
> Thou art more lovely and more temperate.
> Rough winds do shake the darling buds of May,
> And summer's lease hath all too short a date.
> Sometime too hot the eye of heaven shines,
> And often is his gold complexion dimm'd;
> And every fair from fair some time declines,
> By chance, or nature's changing course, untrimm'd;
> But thy eternal summer shall not fade
> Nor lose possession of that fair thou ow'st;
> Nor shall death brag thou wand'rest in his shade,
> When in eternal lines to time thou grow'st.
> > So long as men can breathe or eyes can see,
> > So long lives this, and this gives life to thee.

Enacting the summer's day, the poet aggressively conventional-izes it. Whether witty literary devices such as "the eye of heaven" and "his gold complexion," or such forthright epithets as "lovely" and "darling," the conventions represent a summer's day and in turn the beloved in a manner so approximate and stylized that it calls attention to itself as a crude poetical apparatus. Rightly we recognize the "summer's day" to be a sequence of polite clichés.

Considered as a meaning, then, the metaphor "you are [like] a summer's day" could only be a decorous fib or distortion. Nor does it help matters that the poet vehemently repudiates the

9

cliches. It is as if he has offered us a flagrantly untrustworthy likeness of his beloved, then made a show of denying its adequacy. Such a tactic would be rhetorical and, however gallant, flattery of the sort scorned elsewhere in the Sonnets. How then are we to respond?

Magical Language

The answer I propose requires that we let the sonnet be exactly what the couplet says: not an artifact to be transformed into "sense," but an *action*, the willful gesture "this," which "so long as men *can* breathe or eyes *can* see" does literally "live" in the present tense as a vow we ourselves are making. Like the poet, that is, we must accomplish the sonnet as enacted praise. In uttering the sonnet our voice and the poet's merge into one, simultaneous and out of time. The poem comes to be an incantation, an action of the will. The beloved, the poet-lover, and we ourselves momentarily become the palpable words on our tongues which do, as the vow stipulates, have life.

As praise, the sonnet conjures. It "names" the poet's love and beloved into existence. For such praise celebrates the poet's love-making as, literally, love-creating or *poiesis*. To appreciate how "in eternal lines" the beloved "grow'st to time" or comes into being, we must understand *poiesis* to mean more than a mere significa-tion of things—*mimesis* in our sophisticated sense. Shakespeare, I think, recognized in the creative act the drastic ambiguities con-tained in the word "conceive." *Poiesis* not only represents reality, but somehow forms or imagines it into being.

As a vow the sonnet owes its force not to logic, but to strong emotion. It enacts love. Saying its words, we come to feel love or, more precisely, to *wish* love into being. Our passionate action is the sonnet's life. That is, the poem facilitates magical thinking.

Formally, magic is a medium for obtaining or controlling super-natural power. In a primitive society, for example, it may express itself as a belief in the ability of charmed objects or words to bring about wished-for events, or to avert danger. However, magical attitudes are far more subtly pervasive than formal examples—or even the complacent label "superstition"—might suggest. Funda-

10

mentally magical thinking presupposes that inner experience such as wishes, fears, ideas and visions may be as real as external phenomena, and be able to influence them. A wish, say, may seem to influence events in the objective world. Ordinary wishful thinking is magical to the extent it is purposive or believed able to influence real circumstances. In childhood magical thinking is usually as forthright as it is egocentric, as in the fairy-tale theme that the will to believe by itself can make dreams "come true" or supersede reality. In adult behavior such attitudes take subtler forms. When people speak of sheer spiritual or mental force overcoming natural limits—in sickness, for instance, or in gamblers' convictions about feeling or thinking lucky—we may look for an underlying magical assumption. On a more exalted plane, such thinking may contemplate a universe created by the spiritual force of God's love, which in turn the spirit of prayer may sway, with concrete earthly results.[2]

It will be useful to return to Sonnet 18 by way of some lines in Sonnet 136 which offer a relatively forthright example of magical creation in Shakespeare. The poet-lover urges his beloved to swear an oath:

> If thy soul check thee that I come so near,
> Swear to thy blind soul that I was thy Will,
> And will, thy soul knows, is admitted there.

As a pun, the name "Will" is at the same time "will," the beloved's volition and sexual appetite. Clever as it promises to be as an assertion of the unity of lover and beloved, the pun nevertheless becomes a linguistic act not merely beguiling in its effects, but magical. For the poet subsequently vows that

> Will will fulfil the treasure of thy love,
> Ay, fill it full with wills, and my will one.

The statement enacts an oath. Given the pun, however, the statement simultaneously *enacts* what it *means:* it is a vow pledging the efficacy of will or a vow. *Will* will fulfill thy love.

On the one hand, the simultaneity of the pun's meanings creates an evanescent identity for the poet by making "Will" mean more than we can comprehend. By the end of the second line "will" has come to "be" each of the other three words in these lines with the same sound—and each of those three itself has multiple meanings that, all told, sail off into indeterminacy. On the other hand, that simultaneity suspends time as well as logic. For when we respond, laboring rationally to grasp the pun's manifold identities, we must make out each sense sequentially, even as we experience a vivid sense of the word's latent unity. What's more, no gift of time would ever enable us to discover a final meaning for each "will." We would have to put an arbitrary limit on its implications. Nor is "will" the only ambiguous word. Among others, we would have to contend with "ay," at once signifying immediate assent, the pronoun "I," and "forever."

The effect, then, is to force us to relinquish our grasp on the sonnet, to open us to wonder. Exactly what the final "will" is we can only intuit. In a closing vow the poet bids and implores the beloved to

> Make but my name thy love, and love that still,
> And then thou lov'st me, for my name is Will.

However much a rational joke, by now "will" fairly dazzles in our minds, full of meaning yet mysterious.[3] The name of the poet has somehow become the poet himself and the beloved's love as well. The couplet vows, finally, that the beloved's "naming" vow will, in the act, create.

Art as Magical Creation

As praise, we noted, Sonnet 18 conjures. The poet "names" his beloved as an identity akin to "Will," suspended beyond our grasp. Such praise is no conventional hyperbole.[4] For the sonnet vehemently denies all fixed identities as mutable and magically impotent. The poet refuses to answer his initial question by reducing his beloved to the witty designation "incomparable." If we are to *enact* the poem's praise, we must experience wonder. Hence the sonnet must make us feel the inadequacy of all designation. Calling the beloved "incomparable," as the cliché has it, we specify a value we can grasp. We become a bad artist like the poet's rival, death, who captures love and shamelessly "brags" of his possession.

Strictly speaking, a comparison asserts an identity. We might ordinarily expect "a summer's day" to be a conventional enough "name" for the beloved, which all hearers would corroborate. In the octet, however, the poet denies the truth of the identity "thou

= a summer's day." Furthermore, the mutable nature of a summer's day *itself* dramatizes the mutable nature of its own designation "a summer's day." Linguistically, the situation is akin to
"Will will . . . "—a vow vowing that a vow will work. The poet's
very elaboration of what a summer's day *is* denies identity. For "a
summer's day" turns out to entail a list of clarifying names strung
together by "ands," a list of conventions at once arbitrary and
theoretically endless. Nor can we fasten upon an opposite of the
repudiated qualities. The poet copes with the inadequacy of the
named qualities by assertions such as "thou art *more* lovely and
more temperate." How short is "all too short"? and how often is
"sometime"?

At the close of the octet the upshot of all this comes with the
assertion that

> every fair from fair some time declines,
> By chance, or nature's changing course, untrimm'd.

Not only does every "fair" in the actual world change, but
further—and as we shall see, no less important—its conventional
identity, the name or sign "fair" treacherously varies from an
absolute "fair." I am taking the second "fair" to be the word, the
standard of identity by which things exist for us as themselves.
"Every beauty and designation of beauty," the poet avows,
"comes sometimes to corruption." Every identity is vulnerable to
distortions because of the inherently unstable nature of meanings.
Names are conventions—agreed upon—and hence they depend on
points of view doomed by time to change and aberrancy. Words
become trite and lose their literalness, their magical efficacy. The
declining "fair" becomes "untrimm'd"—not only divested of its
superficial beauty, but also "untrimm'd" in the sense of "unstable
in its identity." And "untrimm'd" now "by nature's changing
course," "every fair" is susceptible to death and "wand'rest in his
shade."

Naming, then, is a treacherous endeavor. That the poet forces
words to reveal their ambiguity, as in "fair," itself warns us about
the fickleness of coventional identity. Life changes and undergoes
death when named "life" and distinguished from "not-life." Such
discrete naming not only falsifies, but is the effectual "cause" of
change and destruction. Time exists because we name "now"
distinct from "then," and both distinct from "always," so that the
issue in the sonnet is not simply that conventional names cannot
apprehend the beloved's being, but that they *must* not.[5] Therefore the poet creates magical names, and we must share his vows,

realizing his words as living praise. Otherwise, if we make the negations such as "more" and "all too short" and "sometime" into hyperbole—into some*thing* we can seize upon—we reduce the sonnet to a critical problem, an ingenious compliment, lifeless and false.

Relinquishing conventional perceptions we might be expected to feel confusion or even anxiety. After all, we do seek meanings, only to have the poet's verbal strategy intervene. What enables us to experience wonder is the poet's art.[6] To be sure, the sonnet's formal structure dictates a physically coherent act. Whatever our motives, we are apt to delight in simply saying the verse over. But out of that inarticulate feel for the sonnet as a verbal shape emerges our sense of its praise.

Addressing the beloved as "thou," the poet puts himself and us into a ceremonial act. At the same time, by denying that "thou = a summer's day," our praise effects an extra-logical identity: all the irreducible meanings we experience by naming the beloved as "eternal summer" in "eternal lines." The identity disrupted in the octet comes to be ineffable in the sestet's affirmation. The beloved *becomes* the sonnet's "eternal lines," and in uttering them we ourselves do also. For a moment we may forget ourselves. "Who" the beloved or poet is comes to seem a mental quibble. The uncertain "I" of the opening problem resolves itself into a conviction of love. With the bonds of identity loosened, the poet, beloved, and we ourselves momentarily fuse in what Sonnet 116 would call a marriage of true minds. Our self-conscious will to manipulate the world through words dissolves in the action of love-making, even as the tentative "shall" of the opening question becomes the uncompromising vow "shall" in the sestet, and the "fair" which time threatens to corrupt becomes the enacted, timeless "fair thou ow'st," an identity which is liberating and seemingly inviolate.[7]

Wonder and Madness

Wonder depends on a verbal strategy. Emphasizing conceptual conventions as the basis of reality, the poet sets about confounding conventions.[8] By redefining or contextualizing meanings—exposing the inadequacy of a concept by suddenly placing it in a

14

wider context—the poet induces wonder in us. It is worth observing that the contextualizing process has a vivid analogue in illustrations of infinite regression. Witness a child's awe at a picture-book on whose cover a child sits reading a picture-book on whose cover a child sits reading, and so forth: a world within a world, *ad infinitum*.

As I noted earlier, any frustration of customary awareness potentially jeopardizes the integrity of the world and the self. By changing the world into words pressed beyond their simple meanings, the poet risks chaos. Without rational, public reality for corroboration, he must conceive his beloved as the crucial locus of all order. In the experience of wonder the beloved ultimately displaces the world itself. As Sonnet 112 describes it,

> You are so strongly in my purpose bred
> That all the world besides methinks are dead.

The couplet celebrates that venerable refrain, the world well lost. Yet however nice a compliment it appears, it locates a fearful hazard latent in all magical thinking. For at the extreme the poet commits himself to isolation, his "purpose" or will so wholly given over to his beloved that his self virtually becomes "you," transcended yet lost, at once all and nothing. Like "grow'st" in Sonnet 18, "bred" claims life for the beloved, life conceived and ongoing in the poet's will, but forcibly maneuvered by the rhyme "bred-dead" into opposition and intimate connection with death. The poet has abandoned to death "all the world" which "are" (the plural insists) other selves: all the voices and relations which ordinarily safeguard the personality.

Not surprisingly, then, in a sonnet such as 105 the poet-lover endeavors to "name" his art itself magically in an effort to secure the certain existence of the beloved and self.

> Let not my love be called idolatry,
> Nor my beloved as an idol show,
> Since all alike my songs and praises be
> To one, of one, still such, and ever so.
> Kind is my love to-day, to-morrow kind,
> Still constant in a wondrous excellence,
> Therefore my verse to constancy confined,
> One thing expressing, leaves out difference.
> Fair, kind, and true, is all my argument,
> Fair, kind, and true, varying to other words,
> And in this change is my invention spent,

> Three themes in one, which wondrous scope affords.
> Fair, kind, and true, have often lived alone.
> Which three till now, never kept seat in one.

(I have used the punctuation of the 1609 quarto.)
Given the imperious negation,

> Let not my love be called idolatry,

and the feint at paradox in "since," which we can grasp only in the unlikely sense of "just because" or "although," the sonnet directs us at the outset toward indefinable meanings. In a line such as

> To one, of one, still such, and ever so,

"still such, and ever so" means something like "always one" and negates time and difference—just as the repetition of "one," culminating in "one thing expressing," does. In the enactment, the riddling repetitions and the unspecific demonstratives "such" and "so" generate more meanings than we can at once cope with. And so we relinquish such discriminate meanings, feeling their ineffable sense—love—even as the sonnet itself,

> One thing expressing, leaves out difference.

Saying the verse, we simultaneously enact what it means.
Now if, as the poet maintains,

> Fair, kind, and true, is all my argument,

the concluding couplet and the sonnet as a whole pose a dilemma. For "fair, kind, and true" to express "one thing" and "keep seat in one," we would have to take them in a trite sentimental sense signifying a sort of reflex approval. By repeating the formula "fair, kind, and true" throughout the sestet, however, we may find that the words begin to seem strange, as if we have never noticed them before and they have only begun to exist for us. Once stripped of their merely honorific sense, "fair, kind, and true" become complicated words. Their permutable connotations defy immediate summary. Now the whole verbal structure of the poem seems to resonate. In the vow that

> Fair, kind, and true, is all my argument,

the comfortable promise of limits and "mere" sense vanishes from the word "all," and it may startle us.

Presumably by disrupting the ordinary sense of "fair, kind, and true," the sonnet could engender consternation as readily as "wondrous excellence." What accounts for the poet's buoyant tone is a reassuring paradox. For all their threatening multiplicity, "fair, kind, and true" do in fact share a common "seat"—an ineffable root meaning akin to "rightful" or "just." Even signifying one love, one beloved, the three words "have often lived alone" as conventional terms with discrete meanings, torn by "difference" and so exposed to change and death. But "now," the couplet vows, in this present celebration of love, those fickle identities "keep seat" in an incorruptible one, "rightful love," beyond thoughtless public use.

In another sense "fair, kind, and true have often lived alone" as the three persons of the poet's problematical love situation, now brought together in his words at least. This meaning, of course, adds a wily joke to the sum of the couplet's significance.

As a whole, the enacted sonnet conceives a mysterious root integrity beyond the lifeless or promiscuous meanings words have in ordinary use. Experienced through praise alone, such a root meaning confutes the world of apparent change, the rational world under the sway of death. For all the verbal sophistication of the poet's argument, the notion of an immutable unity behind words leads toward historically religious conceptions of sacramental language. As Saint John vows, "In the beginning was the Word." Christianity, however, expressly controls sacramental language through a priesthood and publicly sanctioned ritual. Moreover, the Church has discouraged and often enough punished private meddling in the realm of the ineffable.

The point is that Sonnet 105 cheerfully celebrates a world of "wondrous excellence" and "wondrous scope," which, as the word "excellence" itself bears out (from the Latin *excellere*, to raise [oneself] out of, to surpass), opposes the rational world of limits. Just this, potential abandonment of the regulated, lawful reality of man's public compact with God, generates the poet's concern with "idolatry."

From the willful negation "let not my love," which communicates with no specific agency, to the final "one," which the poet "confines" in drastic singularity by refusing even to rhyme it, the sonnet maintains the concept of identity in strenuous paradoxes. Despite its incantatory conviction, the poem creates disturbingly unmanageable identities for the lovers. That the poet's confidence derives partly from verbal manipulation itself proves troubling.

But beyond that, as mystics have traditionally warned, the ineffable holds its own perils. For as a disposition of the self away from the rational world, love risks self-obsession or dissolution in the infinite. Consequently the sonnet seeks not only to justify praise against charges of idolatry by "naming" itself an expression of lawful wonder, but also to reassure us of the sure integrity as well as isolation in love's "one-ness." Both functions of "naming" figure in the couplet. For the "seat" which "fair, kind, and true" keep is not simply a common base of meaning, but in another sense of the word "seat" a source of authority as well. Specifically "seat" may designate a throne, as in *Richard II*. As metonymy for kingship it betokens the basis of God's law on earth.

As an obsessive infatuation with forms, "lust" in Sonnet 129 stands in the same relation to "idolatry" as love does to praise in Sonnet 105. Defining "lust" the poet defines idolatry, enacting the corruption of the word "love." For whereas "love" unifies fragments of meaning which "till now never kept seat in one," "lust in action" literally "wastes" itself in a chaos of brawling synonyms and clichés that plunges furiously from line to line in a rhetorical act of madness:

> Th' expense of spirit in a waste of shame
> Is lust in action, and till action, lust
> Is perjur'd, murd'rous, bloody full of blame,
> Savage, extreme, rude, cruel, not to trust,
> Enjoyed no sooner but despised straight,
> Past reason hunted, and no sooner had
> Past reason hated as a swallowed bait,
> On purpose laid to make the taker mad.
> Made in pursuit and in possession so,
> Had, having, and in quest, to have extreme,
> A bliss in proof and proved a very woe,
> Before a joy proposed behind a dream,
>> All this the world well knows yet none knows well
>> To shun the heaven that leads men to this hell.

Unlike true praise, language which orients the self toward "wondrous" love, the idolatrous language of love disperses the self in a frantic profusion of names for lust. None of the names can be more than arbitrary, for in that twelve-line opening sentence no hierarchy governs the syntax. Grasping at forms of the verb of possession,

> Had, having, and in quest, to have extreme,

the poet makes words act out the monotonous, insatiable craving that they simultaneously mean. And the structure of the definition similarly dramatizes such a fruitless "quest" in its string of static appositives without verbs or development. The language mimics lust.

In its shifting and collapsing identities,

> A bliss in proof and proved a very woe,
> Before a joy proposed behind a dream,

lust is hellish, sound and fury exhausting "spirit" to no end.[9] Reminding us that words and syntax stand between us and the things they designate, the definition of lust makes us feel how close to madness the self is when "past reason" and bereft of inexpressible "constancy" (Sonnet 105) and even the imperfect corroboration which other voices ordinarily provide in speech. Significantly, the first twelve lines point to no beloved. In fact, no personal identities appear at all: no "I" or "thee." Instead we have only the reposeless nightmare of lust to experience.

Didactic as the couplet sounds, we should resist the impulse to make sense of it as a self-congratulating homily. In the context of the other sonnets we should hear in the couplet a vow:

> All this the world well knows yet none knows well
> To shun the heaven that leads men to this hell.

Indirectly, by negating lust, the "world's" false love, the couplet affirms the sonnet as an act of praise. By treating "lust" as a conventional name for all the world's love, then "shunning" it, the poet points toward his own beloved and singular love. In a sense the couplet acknowledges "the world well lost" (as in Sonnet 112) to be a trite vow, and now redefines it, pressing it to an illimitable extreme, where all the world's love stands revealed as lust, and the poet's love can be absolute anew.[10]

II. Incense in Sense: Magical and Dramatic Creation in the Sonnets

Critics have tended to approach the Sonnets as exercises of wit or, more commonly, as parts of a more or less autobiographical drama. In the latter view the poems *represent* experiences of love: "The interplay of mixed feelings in the sonnets on the woman, on time and poetry, and on the rival poet, are conflicts understood and expressed with a confident wit." The same critic detects a failure to understand mixed feelings in the poems to the youth, so that "when Shakespeare thus unlocks his heart, it is to reveal its stores in disarray. In only a few of the poems to the youth are these stored experiences ordered into a work of art." From this standpoint the Sonnets present characters and, latently at least, a plot. As in drama there are emotions and motives to explore, and relationships to fathom.[1]

At first glance this view of the Sonnets in no way accords with the account of them I have offered so far. Where I have shown the poet striving to create an incantatory transcendence, this view perceives the poet unlocking his heart "to reveal its stores in disarray." Where we have felt it necessary to regard certain sonnets as creative *acts*, this view takes them to be aesthetic artifacts, accounts of passionate experience, an order of information. In what follows I wish to demonstrate that both of these viewpoints are appropriate to the Sonnets.

The Power of Negative Creation

The poet's magic, I have been saying, depends on a verbal strategy. He sets about rationally confounding rationality by emphasizing, then negating, conventional perceptions. The resulting dissociation we experience as wonder, a moment of transcendence. Magic, then, proceeds by negation. Because the poet *is* manifestly invoking a meaning, however indefinable, it is useful to think of this process as "negative creation."[2] In Sonnet 106, for example, the poet "names" his beloved obliquely, through the agency of all the tributes paid to love in ages past:

> When in the chronicle of wasted time
> I see descriptions of the fairest wights,
> And beauty making beautiful old rhyme
> In praise of ladies dead and lovely knights,
> Then, in the blazon of sweet beauty's best,
> Of hand, of foot, of lip, of eye, of brow,
> I see their antique pen would have express'd
> Even such beauty as you master now.

The octet protects its meaning from reduction by deflecting us toward the past, specifically to the province of the late medieval Romance. In the sestet Romance conventions promise (or threaten) to capture the reality of the beloved:

> So all their praises are but prophecies
> Of this our time, all you prefiguring.

So a delicate negation intercedes to make past praises an illimitable name:

> And for they looked but with divining eyes,
> They had skill enough your worth to sing.

The couplet's sudden paradox clinches our astonishment:

> For we, which now behold these present days,
> Have eyes to wonder, but lack tongues to praise.

In the immediate enactment of the sonnet we ourselves become its voice. And we do have "eyes to wonder," but also "tongues to praise," so that the poem does celebrate the beloved, seeming to speak in spite of itself.

Wonder is a paradoxical condition. In Sonnet 106, for example, the truest praise seems to negate praise. The poet-lover appears to speak with uncanny efficacy because he speaks in spite of himself. Considered as praise of the paradoxical *condition* of wonder, one of the most enigmatic sonnets, 94, becomes clearer:

> They that have power to hurt and will do none,
> That do not do the thing they most do show,

> Who, moving others, are themselves as stone,
> Unmoved, cold, and to temptation slow—
> They rightly do inherit Heaven's graces,
> And husband nature's riches from expense;
> They are the lords and owners of their faces,
> Others but stewards of their excellence.
> The summer's flow'r is to the summer sweet
> Though to itself it only live and die;
> But if that flow'r with base infection meet,
> The basest weed outbraves his dignity.
>> For sweetest things turn sourest by their deeds:
>> Lilies that fester smell far worse than weeds.

The octet celebrates both lover and beloved. For sacramental language gives "power" to those who praise, though they may be "unmoved" or absolute in their love. Like the poet specifically, they "do show" what visionary love exempts them from having to "do" in the mutable world. They conserve mortality "from expense," as Sonnet 18 swears the poet-lover does, and as 129 warns that lust (an "expense of spirit in a waste of shame") does not. Open to awe, granted access to feelings and will which are ordinarily repressed, lover and beloved "are the lords and owners of their faces."

The sestet, by contrast, describes existence untouched by wonder. However praiseworthy in the context of youth ("summer's flow'r is to the summer sweet"), youthful beauty is nonetheless particularly vulnerable to "base infection" when confined in a conventional identity ("to itself it only live and die"). Not disposed toward visionary love, that is, such a youth knows no true intimacy. Rather, he is oriented toward the "summer" world of "deeds," the world of selfish, ephemeral acts (and forms) which Sonnet 129 calls lust. Arousing love but to no end, such a beloved offends "far worse" than mere "weeds," whose overtly meretricious natures neither invite nor betray praise.

Some lilies "do" fester. "They that have power," those conceived in praise, they "will do none." Unlike "summer's flow'r," a pretty *thing*, they have an existence beyond comparisons (as opposed to lilies / weeds), in paradox, and immutable.

> They rightly do inherit heaven's graces,

for after all, to signify them the octet calls upon the concept of the "unmoved mover," an ancient notion which has long served to point the baffled mind toward God. The concept could as well apply to the poet's own negative creation which, "moving others," remains static and "unmoved." In quite a specific way, then, the poet establishes "they that have power" not simply beyond corruption, but in the human state closest to God's.

The Sacramental Context

Original sin describes in a manageable scheme how our first parents arrived at self-consciousness. For Genesis is a tale of man's seduction out of a natural state of wonder or praise. "Ye shall be as gods," vows the serpent, "knowing good and evil." He coaxes the pair to digest not just an apple, but the notion of a conscious identity also. He urges a role upon them: they shall be *as* gods. The actual sin, alas, creates nothing very godly. The promised wisdom turns out to be a pitiful awareness of nakedness and weakness and a need to hide. "And they heard the voice of the Lord God walking in the garden. . . ."

Surely the authors betray some complicated sympathy, however much doctrine denies it, when Adam answers that disembodied, accusing voice without a moment's quibbling, and nevertheless suffers his curse. Be that as it may, God's curse fatefully defines man, and not as a god at all: "For dust thou art, and unto dust shalt thou return." Death happens, that is, because God vows man was and will be "dust." The divine word binds the world. Only now does Adam name the woman, his helpmate, "Eve." The sequence of events dramatizes the awful connection Shakespeare himself espied between names and dust, identity and death.

Time and theological sophistication have obscured the Indo-European root sense of the word "grace"—to praise aloud. Yet Adam's fall from grace *is* a loss of his state of praise. Before the Fall man communicated directly with God. In the aftermath, by contrast, praise became prayer. By means of *poiesis*, his love-making, the poet seeks to undo cursed self-consciousness and thereby recreate that lost condition.[3] He enters into a sacramental role such as the archaic poet or *vates* embraced. It is a bold step. Hence the peculiarly nervous confidence in the tone Sidney takes in his *Defence of Poesy* when justifying the artist as a literal "lord of creation."

Himself an initiate, at pains to sound judicious and even pious,

Sidney touches upon Genesis as the source of that self-consciousness which has tormented men since Adam, the artist in particular:

> Neither let it be deemed too saucy a comparison to balance the highest point of man's wit with the efficacy of nature; but rather give right honor to the heavenly Maker of that maker [the poet], who, having made man to his own likeness, set him beyond and over all the works of that second nature. Which in nothing he showeth so much as in poetry, when with the force of a divine breath he bringeth things forth far surpassing her doings, with no small argument to the incredulous of that first accursed fall of Adam,—since our erected wit maketh us know what perfection is, and yet our infected will keepeth us from reaching unto it. But these arguments will by few by understood, and by fewer granted; thus much I hope will be given me, that the Greeks with some probability of reason gave him the name ['poet'] above all names of learning.[4]

At this distance we can only guess how artful or genuinely defensive Sidney means to be in his disclaimer that "these arguments will by few be understood." In the nice parallel between "erected" wit and "infected" will we do observe the artist at work. But for all that, the passage recognizes the supra-mundane powers of language ("the force of a divine breath") and the problematical relation of wit and will which threatens those powers.

Self-consciousness, Sidney sees, is a disconnection between "erected wit," which forcefully "maketh us know what perfection is," and our "infected will which keepeth us from reaching unto it." (We might recall the "base infection" menacing the summer's flower in Sonnet 94.) As the metaphors "erected" and "infected" themselves suggest, wit comes to judge us in all our flawed mortality. As "what I should be" becomes an identity constant and apart from "what I am," we begin to exist (at root, as Heidegger points out, to "ex-ist" or be outside of oneself). Conscious of our selves, apart from our selves, we become aware of volition as a series of acts, and eventually the word "act" acquires the duplicity it has, say, in theatrical vocabulary. Identity loses its absoluteness, and we become conscious of roles. A disconnection between wit and feeling may haunt us, and a sense of estrangement from others.

Wonder promises to make us coherent once more. All will come whole, Sonnet 108 assures us, because words have an intrinsic ritual efficacy:

What's in the brain that ink may character
Which hath not figur'd to thee my true spirit?
What's new to speak, what new to register,
That may express my love or thy dear merit?
Nothing, sweet boy; but yet, like prayers divine,
I must each day say o'er the very same;
Counting no old thing old, thou mine, I thine,
Even as when first I hallowed thy fair name.
So that eternal love in love's fresh case
Weighs not the dust and injury of age,
Nor gives to necessary wrinkles place,
But makes antiquity for aye his page;
    Finding the first conceit of love there bred,
    Where time and outward form would show it dead.

Saying is believing, so the argument goes. The word controls the world, and gives no "place" to signs of necessity. The poet says his verse, "the very same," again and again, "like prayers divine," hallowing the beloved's "fair name" with his priestly litany. His sacramental words, "love's fresh case," sustain "eternal love." Nevertheless, the word's power depends upon magical belief or a facsimile of magic, and that presents a serious liability.

The Limits of Wonder

The trouble with magic is that men die. We change, become corrupt, and do cease to be. And awareness impinges on the poet.[5] Though few of the Sonnets so nearly concede the triumph of mutability as does the elegiac 73 ("That time of year thou may'st in me behold"), no art can ever fully secure wonder against its menace. For one thing, the creation of wonder is an action existing in time, not an artifact. After many a vow the act itself may well come to be perfunctory. For in our fallen state the "infected" will is forever reducing life to habit and manageable stereotypes. The truest poetry cannot endlessly satisfy our "erected" awareness of perfection, especially given the contingencies of ominously

    reckoning Time, whose millioned accidents
Creep in 'twixt vows and change decrees of kings

and poets alike (Sonnet 115). Should the capacity for wonder be impaired or lost, praise comes to seem merely a strategy. Moreover, because the poet must incorporate mutability into his art in order to negate and in turn transcend it, we are left with reminders of mortality and disorder if the poem's spell fails. In that event we are apt to see ourselves reciting the verse as a speech and implicitly acting a role. Instead of losing ourselves in a celebration of love, we may be nagged by the consciousness that we are feigning our involvement in praise. The sonnet then appears no more than an artifact. We may begin to listen for personal voices in the sonnet, and to regard it as a dramatic situation which we merely observe.

Such a discovery of duplicity in magical thinking is reflected in Shakespeare's awareness of role-playing in the plays. And the threat of such a discovery haunts the Sonnets. At the close of Sonnet 125, for example, as if denying Satan, the poet struggles to banish baleful self-consciousness as a perjured witness to his love:

> Hence, thou suborn'd informer! A true soul
> When most impeach'd, stands least in thy control.

Significantly, the metaphorical context is a court of law, and the dispute about the true governance ("control") of the soul.

But beyond the conflict between wit and will is the basic peril of mutability. If reality, especially the beloved, may become corrupt, as inconstant as the "millioned accidents" of time itself, then vows are vain. In the exclamatory paradoxes of Sonnet 95:

> How sweet and lovely dost thou make the shame
> Which, like a canker in the fragrant rose,
> Doth spot the beauty of thy budding name!
> O, in what sweets dost thou thy sins enclose!
> That tongue that tells the story of thy days,
> Making lascivious comments on thy sport,
> Cannot dispraise but in a kind of praise:
> Naming thy name blesses an ill report.
> O, what a mansion have those vices got
> Which for their habitation chose out thee,
> Where beauty's veil doth cover every blot,
> And all things turn to fair that eyes can see!
> > Take heed, dear heart, of this large privilege;
> > The hardest knife ill-us'd doth lose his edge.

"Naming thy name," the poet's ritual resource, "blesses an ill report." For the beloved's name is "a kind of praise" which can overwhelm rational, social discourse. On one level, then, the argument appears to perform a version of "the world well lost." The poet discounts other, critical "tongues." Indeed, the beloved's name grows ("budding") as in Sonnet 18, with a vital life of its own.

Only the couplet qualifies such praise. The "knife ill-used" I take to be the poet, specifically the language upon which he stakes his being.[6] As an admonition the warning goes something like this: If your promiscuous (mutable) nature continues to blunt the precision of my words by being too inconsistent for them to "name" you justly, the knife of language will lose its integrity, its ability to cut through the chaos of appearances to absolute love. Put another way, the more "real" or imperfect the ideal beloved comes to be, the more incoherent and vulnerable and even ambivalent the poet-lover must be.

Poetic Creation as Drama

Should wonder cease, the poet must rely upon his fragile wit to relate him to his beloved as his love has done. He must struggle to *know*, despite the illusions and alienation knowing fosters. Hence the poet resists—sometimes with great poignancy—the onset of self-consciousness. As in Sonnet 93, he may apprehensively cry

> How like Eve's apple doth thy beauty grow,
> If thy sweet virtue answer not thy show!

Even such a gentle sonnet as 35 sustains within it some surprisingly unruly ambivalence:

> No more be griev'd at that which thou hast done:
> Roses have thorns, and silver fountains mud;
> Clouds and eclipses stain both moon and sun,
> And loathsome canker lives in sweetest bud.
> All men make faults, and even I in this,
> Authorizing thy trespass with compare,
> Myself corrupting, salving thy amiss,
> Excusing thy sins more than thy sins are;
> For to thy sensual fault I bring in sense—

> Thy adverse party is thy advocate—
> And 'gainst myself a lawful plea commence;
> Such civil war is in my love and hate
>> That I an accessory needs must be
>> To that sweet thief which sourly robs from me.

"No more be grieved"—like the lyrical song "Fear no more the heat o' the sun" in *Cymbeline*, the sonnet takes a wistful, comforting tone toward the troubling faults of mortality. The poet wishes to overrule the wit in us which judges not only the world's imperfection, but mortal love as well. What mitigates the conflict between "wit" and the world is the stereotyped nature of the corruption which gets into the poem: the "staining" clouds and perfunctory "loathsome canker," for example. In effect, the poet's voice and art mediate the conflict between ideal and actual love, protecting his beloved and in turn his own feeling of love from judgment. Rather than exaltation, we experience a disturbing dissociation between the serene voice we hear and the turmoil it describes, the "civil war" of "love and hate."

We are listening, I would contend, to an incipient role. Even self-betrayal, the poem argues, is more tolerable than loss of the beloved. Significantly, self-betrayal is not purely a function of the poet's character, although of course that does matter. In truth, the poet's mode of loving, his art, abets his self-betrayal. Always he lives as a potential "accessory" to crimes against his self. Just as his love-making proceeds by verbal means, so the poet does live, as it turns out, "in a manner of speaking." Passionately invested, his words always threaten to supplant the experiential world and dictate feeling though authentic feeling fail.

The "sense" the poet brings to his beloved's "sensual fault" corresponds in a way to the wisdom which the double-talking serpent promised Adam and "the woman." By means of paradox the poet can make some poignantly provisional "sense" of his beloved's nature. Yet that sense enhances neither his identity nor his power. It divides him between "love and hate." Paradox may fix his relation to his faithless beloved in spite of mutability and "sins," but it cannot wholly nullify their threat.

Alternately, the punning "incense" ("in sense") which the poet brings also promises to remedy the beloved's fault, but by ritualizing it. Yet magical creation must be absolute and wholehearted. It cannot rationalize or "make sense" of an actual "amiss" as well. And in the absence of profound vows the sonnet itself corroborates the lapse of unifying praise which the poet depicts in his "warring" will.

In the belief that there can be "sense" in "incense" and "incense" in "in sense" a crucial liability lies. The poet commits himself in frail language, which in the end cannot ever disarm time and death, and which may in fact facilitate self-betrayal, the "fault" of "authorizing thy trespass with compare, / Myself corrupting." By excusing the beloved in the comparison to roses, whose thorns or sins are natural, art corrupts the poet and the meaning of "trespass." The poet's ambivalence, then, extends to his art. Already of course we have encountered misgivings about art or "compare" in the question which begins Sonnet 18, "Shall I compare thee. . . ?" The couplet before us plays out one consequence of that question:

> Such civil war is in my love and hate
> That I an accessory needs must be
> To that sweet thief which sourly robs from me.

No intransigent vow sounds in these lines, no illimitable naming of the beloved. Nor does a selfless incantation hold sway, disposing our own voices to merge in its enactment. On the contrary, we hear and may well be tempted to extrapolate the lineaments of a character and a dramatic situation. We are directed not away from the world, but toward it. The "sense" of art creates—I am tempted to say perpetrates—a laborious tranquillity which orders the surface of the poem, but it does not fully efface the shadows of deception and suffering beneath. We can observe, then, an overt conflict between magical and dramatic modes of creation in the poem. It will be seen that without discounting thematic concerns *within* the Sonnets, our effort all along has been to elucidate this conflict in the drama of poetic creation *itself*.

Parody and Negative Creation

In his *Defence of Poesy*, contemplating creativity and the relation of art to nature, Sidney expansively declares that

> There is no art delivered unto mankind that hath not the
> works of nature for his principal object, without which they

could not consist, and on which they so depend as they become actors and players, as it were, of what nature will have set forth. . . . Only the poet, disdaining to be tied to any such subjection, lifted up with the vigor of his own invention, doth grow, in effect, into another nature, in making things either better than nature bringeth forth, or, quite anew, forms such as never were in nature . . . so as he goeth hand in hand with nature, not enclosed within the narrow warrant of her gifts, but freely ranging within the zodiac of his own wit.[7]

It is a charmed vision, buoyed up by the vigor of its own invention, innocent of any tragic sense of human limits. As such, it is a young man's vision, heedless of the tyranny of time and convention. Without contradiction the poet can go "hand in hand" with the same nature he disdains to be tied to. Without penalty he may usurp nature's authority as playwright, and as "another nature" himself dictate roles for art to act.

Sidney's theatrical metaphor echoes in Sonnet 53:

> What is your substance, whereof are you made,
> That millions of strange shadows on you tend?
> Since every one hath, every one, one shade,
> And you, but one, can every shadow lend.
> Describe Adonis, and the counterfeit
> Is poorly imitated after you;
> On Helen's cheek all art of beauty set,
> And you in Grecian tires are painted new.
> Speak of the spring and foison of the year:
> The one doth shadow of your beauty show
> The other as your bounty doth appear,
> And you in every blessed shape we know.
>   In all external grace you have some part,
>   But you like none, none you, for constant heart.

The poem's essential vocabulary ("shadows" and "counterfeit," for example) consists of synonyms for "actor."[8] Self-consciously the poet envisions as actors all the customary concepts by which we are able to conceive the beloved. "What is your actual nature," the poet asks, "if all conceptions of you are merely poor models of an ideal [like] you?"[9] The answer, of course, is that the beloved's "substance" must be indefinable. And therefore wonder becomes the sole means of creating relations between true natures. Knowing by any other means is mere art. As the couplet vows:

In all external grace you have some part,
But you like none, none you, for constant heart.

In all conventional beauty or praise ("grace") the beloved has a "part" or role. What we know, illimitable nature, reciprocally figures in the "shape" (art) by which we know it. But for a "constant" heart disposed absolutely in love—for the poet, who can create an ungraspable relation—the beloved never becomes merely identical with the superficial "part" he or she acts. For "the counterfeit is poorly imitated after you." For the poet, who alone among artisans rivals nature, the beloved exists at one remove from "external" conceptions, just as an actor exists within and yet behind his role: "like none," beyond art or "compare."

Latent in this sonnet, as in Sidney's sanguine argument, is a troubling idea: that we conceive the world by means of artifices ordinarily "tied to" nature, but in the poet's use potentially dissociated from and substantial as, nature. The word rivals the world, so to speak. As in Sonnet 129, the disproportion between the poet's argument and his final affirmation shows how radical his love is. In order to effect absoluteness the last line must reject all that precedes it: all the known world. So long as praise orients the poet's constant heart, loving wonder ensues. Should praise fail, however, and those "millions of strange shadows" cease to "tend on" or serve an ideal beloved, that disconnection of art and nature would assume the aspect of madness. In the language of the plays, life becomes a pageant of dreams, full of comic miracles or tragic horror.

In this perspective the Sonnets are a sort of tragicomedy. However wretched, the poet clings to the beloved by labors of will and syntax. He does not actually suffer a catastrophic loss. Yet fear of a fall from grace or praise underlies his dependence on the beloved and the mistrust of art which sounds throughout the sequence. "Thou art all my art," the poet vows in Sonnet 78, as if to deny altogether his reliance on the fickle medium of language. He fears that "every alien pen hath got my use" (78), implicitly lamenting that even indefinable love has a corporeal "use" which can be grasped and thereby deadened. Elsewhere, as in Sonnet 82, art appears as "gross painting" and "strained touches" of rhetoric.

The danger posed by "every alien pen" is selfish mimicry. Loveless imitations of the poet's art debase it, reducing its praise to flattery, its meanings to ornamental clichés. Such mimicry can only be sterile. Where in Sonnet 53 the poet decisively repudiates the adequacy even of his own art, imitators would vainly admire the forms they contrive. As we have seen, the poet's defense is to repudiate art. What remains to be pointed out is that when his magic loses its efficacy, the poet turns to another mode of negative creation: parody. In some ways the transition is almost inevitable. For parody implicitly presents what is *not* true, what is *not* sufficient. Only indirectly, if at all, does it name what *is* true. It tends to expose the limitations of things without specifying the ideal which motivates it.

In Sonnet 130, for example, the poet adopts the posture or mask of a Petrarchan hack. At first he appears to "paint" his beloved by mocking the clichés of others. Once we become aware of the parodic spirit, however, we are no longer apt to trust *any* effort to grasp the beloved. Implicitly, that is, the poet demonstrates that all conventional art is "false compare." His own art, the poem itself, is presumably exceptional: but of course it refuses to capture his beloved. Nowhere does he offer to show us "true compare," no matter that it is his own goal.

Far more subtle than Sonnet 130 is Sonnet 94, which we have glanced at earlier. While I believe the poem does praise the condition of wonder, as we noted, it is difficult not to feel irony and parody in its ambiguities. (Like parody, irony is inherently negative inasmuch as it points to other, deeper meanings latent in the obvious one, but leaves them unspecified.) To put the case strongly: if Sonnet 94 "is praise, it is the most back-handed of compliments, for there is doubtful merit in being cold like a stone and in the narcissistic self-enjoyment of living and dying to oneself."[10] As William Empson has shown, such ambiguities lead to consideration of roles and the relationship between the poet and his formidable patron.[11]

Because they resist reduction, irony and parody give life to the preternaturally stylized vision of the Sonnets. In effect, they allow the poet to take the world seriously—to bring it into his art—while permitting him to maintain his detachment from it. In Sonnet 138, for instance, the accommodation with the world generates not selfless vows, but drama and a revealing model of Shakespeare's dramatic process:

> When my love swears that she is made of truth,
> I do believe her, though I know she lies,
> That she might think me some untutor'd youth,
> Unlearned in the world's false subtleties.
> Thus vainly thinking that she thinks me young,

Although she knows my days are past the best,
Simply I credit her false-speaking tongue;
On both sides thus is simple truth suppress'd.
But wherefore says she not she is unjust?
And wherefore say not I that I am old?
O, love's best habit is in seeming trust,
And age in love loves not to have years told.
    Therefore I lie with her, and she with me,
    And in our faults by lies we flattered be.

The lovers' sole relation is in the grossly mutable act of "lying together." Tacitly they cast one another in fictitious roles which permit them to play out their hearts' desires. The beloved vows she is the constant, ideal love which truth has "made," as if the identity fabricated by the word play ("maid of truth") can yet prove to be absolute. The poet responds with a vow full of stress:

    I do believe her, though I know she lies.

This is tantamount to saying, "Despite the threat presented by my beloved's deceptions (her lies = faithless words and sexuality), I willfully believe in her ineffable worth (made of truth)." Belief enables him to be an "untutor'd youth" again, innocent of "the world's false subleties" and presumably able to feel the magical potency of wonder. In the complex sense of the word "credits" the poet *praises* her lies. For lies paradoxically free the lovers from the corrupt conventional "reality" of the world. Fictions, the sonnet seems to proclaim, may preempt mundane reality. "Lies" may become a superior truth.

Life in this view is properly play. The lovers act as four personae "simply" yet obscurely related, in two incommensurate worlds. Lying together keeps "simple truth suppressed," just as in the sonnets of wondrous love-making verbal intercession suspends "simple" truth. Play liberates the lovers from an unbearable, fickle reality. Insofar as the poet recognizes the limits of the lovers' "lying," we might say he parodies a lover. For he repudiates the fraud and frailties of his love even as he affirms values beyond them. Insofar as he can accept the peculiar virtues of this sort of lying, we may justly regard his parody as a celebration of the imperfect world.

Like the lovers, we are left to sustain in the subtle equilibrium of playing all the conflicts which the act of lying implies. The multiple viewpoints play makes available, and their evident accommodation in the sly, tolerant voice of the sestet, act to forestall our judgment of the lovers. And so for us as well, praise has come to accept love's compromise with mortality. It is not an ideal solution, yet it releases the poet from the magic circle of his art. "Lying" enables him to *act* in the world (sexually and emotionally) even as it permits him to create the poem before us. With its embrace of masks and play, the ironic spirit of the poem allows the poet both to be and not to be "in" an insoluble reality: to engage the world and yet look beyond it.

Sonnet 138 brings magical creation as close to objective reality as sonnet form permits.[12] Beyond lies drama, where incantation may develop into, or give way before, the interplay of personal voices. It remained for the plays, with their greater resources, to realize more fully the expanding meanings of love and creation itself.

III. To Beguile Nature of Her Custom:
Drama as a Magical Action

Magical thinking figures not only in the Sonnets, but in the plays also. Few critics would demur if we referred to *A Midsummer Night's Dream* and *The Tempest*, say, as plays about magic. But can a play be a magical creation as we have seen certain of the Sonnets to be? That is, can a play somehow be *about* magic and, at the same time, *be* magical in its effects?

As I indicated earlier, Shakespeare commentary has traditionally had a didactic cast. In his edition of Shakespeare (1765) Dr. Johnson waxes impatient with the dramatist's ungraspable qualities, including his obsession with word play, the "fatal Cleopatra for which he lost the world, and was content to lose it." A quibble, Dr. Johnson argues, "has some malignant power over his mind. . . ." And Shakespeare's admirers

> have most reason to complain when he approaches nearest to his highest excellence. . . . He is not long soft and pathetick without some idle conceit, or contemptible equivocation. He no sooner begins to move, than he counteracts himself; and terror and pity, as they are rising in the mind, are checked and blasted by sudden frigidity.

Often the most uncritical critics of Shakespeare share Dr. Johnson's assumptions about unity—but are convinced that they themselves have found out that unity: "I believe that if *Hamlet* is read against a background of contemporary philosophy, it will come to life as a study in passion, rather obviously constructed to show the profound truth of its dominant idea."[1]

Far less common, and itself rather mysterious, is Keats's tribute to Shakespeare's quality of negative capability, "that is when a man is capable of being in uncertainties, Mysteries, doubts, without any irritable reaching after fact and reason. . . ."[2] Keats would probably sympathize with the warning of the witches in *Macbeth*, that "you all know security / Is mortals' chiefest enemy" (3.5.32–33).

Despite the witches, the mortal mind is perpetually ordering experience, turning uncertainty into security. As critics we are perhaps especially inclined to neglect experiences of wonder, and to concentrate instead upon what we *can* articulate. Nor is this merely an intellectual bias. As the popularity of melodrama attests, audiences are attracted to art they feel they can grasp and, in the end, master. Shakespeare himself of course often used old melodramas as sources for his plays. A familiar story such as the old *King Leir* might be said to orient spectators beholding *King Lear*, even as Shakespeare goes about complicating and transcending the old play's banal moral scheme. The point is that negative capability requires us to overcome our natural penchant for order so that we may be more deeply aware. I hope to show that the relation between security and negative capability is crucial in *The Winter's Tale*, one of Shakespeare's most magical plays: and crucial not only as a theme which the play explores, but also as a dimension of the play's structure itself.

Magic and Play

The Winter's Tale opens with reflections upon childhood as a lost paradise. The lifelong friends Polixenes and Leontes were

> Two lads that thought there was no more behind
> But such a day to-morrow as to-day,
> And to be boy eternal.
>
> [1.2.63–65]

Like the Fall, maturity brings men discoveries they may ever after long to forget; distinctions between life and death, good and evil, play and seriousness. Only when cursed from the Garden could Adam appreciate that he had been lord of creation, exempt from death and serious toil. He had been "in" nature and unaware; henceforth he would work at nature, under a compulsion "to till the ground from whence he was taken" (Genesis 3:23). Banished, he suffered alienation from God and nature, but also from himself. Defined by divine wrath ("dust thou art, and unto dust shalt thou return"), Adam's kind could not help yearning for their original condition, when man had no knowledge of himself.

Reminiscing, Polixenes fancies children absolved of identity:

> We were as twinn'd lambs, that did frisk
>   i' the sun,
> And bleat the one at th' other; what we changed
> Was innocence for innocence; we knew not
> The doctrine of ill-doing, nor dreamed
> That any did. . . .
>
> [i.2.67–71]

Life, he insists, was then pure play, unconscious of itself, natural even in its dreams. Despite its impersonally genteel pastoralism, his vision bespeaks a deeply felt conviction that an adult identity is a burden, defective yet inescapable. As "lambs" men may "bleat the one at th' other" without the intervention of language: life would be pure feeling, and feeling would be an order of communication as direct yet wordless as music. Free to "frisk i' the sun," life would be wholly play. At the start, then, *The Winter's Tale* asks, how may that lost condition be (re-)created?

When a child plays at being other than himself—a hero or locomotive or an animal perhaps—he delights in forgetting himself. Rapt in a play identity he is "beside" himself; time and other limits of ordinary life momentarily relent. By his action he acquires for himself the prerogatives of the being he impersonates— the strength and valor of the hero, the freedom of the bird, and so on. Yet the child's belief is complex. When all is said and done he knows he is impersonating, and in all likelihood takes particular pleasure in his freedom and power to do so.

Still, we consider that the child can more fully make believe than the adult. His personality is more labile, his inhibitions less formidable. Like Polixenes, we commonly envy the capacity to "frisk i' the sun" with self-abandonment. To be sure, play-trans-formation occurs only within a magic circle of belief: a mental sphere temporarily kept separate from mundane reality. Yet the child's lot looks blessed to us because he so easily passes into that circle, and so intensely involves himself in the wishes it actualizes, that he appears to have regained Eden.[3]

In archaic and primitive ritual men take vicarious identities, but the concept of illusion is formally indistinct.[4]

> The rite, or "ritual act" represents a cosmic happening, an event in the natural process . . . but here "representation" is really *identification*, the mystic repetition or *re-representation* of the event. The rite produces the effect which is then not so much *shown figuratively* as *actually reproduced* in the action. The function of the rite is far from being imitative; it causes the worshippers to participate in the sacred happening itself. As the Greeks would say, it is *methetic* rather than *mimetic*. It is a "helping-out of the action."

Professor Huizinga, however, stresses the ambiguous relationship between ritual forms and play:

> it remains an open question whether we do not come nearest the mental attitude [in] a ritual act, by adhering to this primary, universally understandable term "play". In play as we conceive it the distinction between belief and make-believe breaks down. The concept of play merges quite naturally with that of holiness. . . . Primitive, or let us say, archaic ritual is thus sacred play . . . in the sense Plato gave to it—an action accomplishing itself outside and above the necessities and seriousness of everyday life.[5]

The paradoxical qualities of the play attitude stand out in Joseph Campbell's account of the masked god in primitive festivals. The mask

> is revered and experienced as a veritable apparition of the mythical being that it represents—even though everyone knows that a man made the mask and that a man is wearing it. The one wearing it, furthermore, is identified with the god during the time of the ritual of which the mask is a part. He does not merely represent the god; he *is* the god. The literal fact is dismissed from the mind, and the presentation is allowed to work without correction upon the sentiments of of both the beholder and the actor. In other words, there has been a shift of view from the logic of the normal secular sphere, where things are understood to be distinct from one another, to a theatrical or play sphere, where they are accepted for what they are *experienced* as being. . . ."[6]

Campbell's passive verbs discreetly leave unclear how personally active the participant's role is. A logical distinction "is dismissed from the mind, and the presentation is allowed to work." Does the participant choose his behavior? or does he feel that the ceremony—specifically the *spirit* of the ceremony, even the god himself—draws him into its charmed sphere? In this crucial moment of transition the gods materialize; or skepticism does.

Anthropologists remind us that even among so-called primitive people there are religious skeptics for whom play's daemonic dimension remains merely make-believe. It is a measure of the enigmatic power of play that we can find a twentieth-century philosopher-artist such as José Ortega y Gasset arguing a tacitly magical view: that the theater can liberate the energies of play transfiguration, affording the spectator a sort of transcendence even as its fiction supersedes reality itself.[7] In *Idea del teatro* (1946) Ortega has Shakespeare in mind when he proposes that as spectators to Hamlet, say, we participate in a double vision. We appreciate the actor before us and also his imaginary character. However, "that which is not real, the unreal—Ophelia enclosed in the palace—has the power, the magical virtue of making that which is real disappear." The unreal promises to free us from the prison of our limited mortal selves; play promises to fulfill aspirations which otherwise may oppress us with a sense of inadequacy and alienation.

As Shakespeare does, Ortega compares play-transcendence to the consuming otherness of the dream. "We are," in Prospero's formula, "such stuff as dreams are made on." Like Time in *The Winter's Tale*, who invites us across a gulf of deepening unreality by vowing to "turn my glass, and give my scene such growing / As you had slept between" (4.1.15), drama may induce a shiver of wonder: "Is the dream in us, or are we in the dream?" In a companion essay, "Máscaras," Ortega cautions us not to discount primitive man's belief that "in sleep a reality of a superior order presents itself." Just as the actor "becomes" Hamlet during a performance, so the spectator "metamorphoses himself into a contemporary of Hamlet, participates in the life of the latter—he also, the public, is a player who *rises* above habitual being to an exceptional and imaginary state and participates in the world as it does not exist, in a world beyond, and in this sense *not only the dream*, but also the auditorium and the entire theater in the end become a phantasmagoria—beyond life."

This giddy perspective is worth sampling because it so distinctly echoes venerable magical themes. It rediscovers yet again play's power to reveal, as dream does, the tacitness of all reality. "The stage and the actor are the universal metaphor incarnate, and this is the theater: visible metaphor." On one level, that is, the theater dramatizes the structure of thought. As metaphor, one thing can "be" another or, more exactly, itself and something else as well. It takes some such expansion of strict logic to embrace the multiplicity of mental life. Memories, for example, even memories we have as much as forgotten, continue to exist, we feel, somewhere "in the back of" our minds. The past may seem to be present in memory as in dreams (or in collective memory: myth) even as, in the predictive (or in an earlier age, prophetic) imagination the future may seem latent yet real. The same ambiguous reality conditions the different, sometimes radically incompatible roles that form an individual's character or self. And ultimately of course play may actualize man's deepest being because it confers immediacy on parts of his nature that as a rule he can only intuit or honor as an abstraction such as "the unconscious." So that passing beyond himself, becoming a little "unreal," man paradoxically authenticates himself.

Especially given these magical implications, play may inspire ambivalence, skepticism, or outright hostility. Despite the conservatism of many play forms, the energies they tap are an irresistible source of creative or anarchic change. More concretely play often involves personal vulnerability, challenges, and dangers, calling as it does for self-surrender or self-surpassing behavior. As Shakespeare's tragedies witness, play may produce not an authenticating re-creation of man, but a vision of evil and limitless deception. And in an age of increasing self-consciousness and inquiry, charlatanism, one of the less apocalyptic kinds of evil, became (and continues to be) an obsessive theme. For charlatanism indirectly confirms man's ability to manipulate his own destiny, even as it calls into question the efficacy and purposes of play.[8] Let me return to *The Winter's Tale* by way of a dramatic form which gives some of these airy matters concrete shape.

The Masque as Rite

Shakespeare knew one form of theater which was eminently a rite: the masque.[9] For masques attempted to dissolve the distinction between spectators and actors, so that "the viewer became part of the spectacle. The end toward which the masque moved was to destroy any sense of theater and to include the whole court in the mimesis—in a sense, what the spectator watched he ultimately became."[10] Myth and reality appear to fuse. Yet clearly the masque is sophisticated theater. What meaning can ritual have in such a context?

Attending *Proteus and the Adamantine Rock* by one Francis Davison at Shrovetide in 1595, the court celebrated a triumph of man over mortality. In a speech extolling the Queen the masque's hero routs its villain, Proteus, whose mythological pedigree makes him "in a sense, the spirit of the masque, the embodiment of the idea of disguising. Yet to the Elizabethans, he is also the great enemy Mutability. . . ."[11] The sea god's defeat wins for the Queen and mankind the adamantine rock of the title, and in turn power over Proteus. Were it a play, *Proteus* would be about mortals overcoming divinity and death, and mastering the principle of impersonation. As a masque, however, it not only represents that triumph, but also makes its spectators part of it. The fiction acquires the reality of the Queen herself. To observe that immortal conquests are routinely remarkable in this genre unfortunately explains nothing. We are left asking how *Proteus* makes Elizabeth mightier than a god.

For the Shrovetide revels the gentlemen of Gray's Inn appointed a Lord of Misrule who styled himself "Prince of Purpoole." Captured by the Prince, Proteus has agreed to ransom himself by surrendering the adamantine rock, which gives its possessor control over the god's "wild Empire." Proteus sets one condition,

Which, as he thought, would never be perform'd;
That first the Prince should bring him to a power,
Which in attractive Vertue should surpass
The wondrous force of his iron-drawing Rock.

[181–4]

The masque proper opens with Proteus and the rock onstage, as it were, at the palace at Whitehall, the agreed place of the trial and, by no coincidence, the performance's necessary location. The Prince's Esquire engages Proteus in some prefatory debate, then "performs" the sea god's condition. He directs his smug adversary's attention outward, beyond the stage and the fictive world, toward the Queen. He "realizes" in the masque Elizabeth herself, more powerful than the lodestone, "true Adamant of hearts."

Stephen Orgel has tried to account for the potency of the hero's performance. The Esquire, he argues, demonstrates the superiority of spiritual qualities over the material forces Proteus stands for.

> But the sea god's defeat involves a more subtle distinction as well. He is a literalist; his faith is founded on a rock, his vision bounded by the properties of this world, which are after all only stage properties. He is helpless before a figure who can step outside that world and . . . see the properties of the rock as metaphorical rather than physical—a figure who knows he is an actor in a masque and is conscious of the . . . significance of the audience.

Because it is the nature of masques to recognize the audience, Orgel continues, a character's ignorance of the audience is a sort of moral blindness: he cannot appreciate the true nature of this world.

> In part, of course, Proteus loses in the trial through a lawyer's trick, a play on words. But in the world of the masque, the trope also expresses a literal truth; the metaphorical "Adamant of hearts," the Queen's "attractive vertue," has the same power as the lodestone. . . .[12]

Despite its incipient circularity, its tendency to explain the masque by appealing to the nature of masques, this seems a sensible account of *Proteus*. Yet while the argument does acknowledge the masque as a celebration, "a world purged of drama, of conflict," it nonetheless fights shy of the implications by trying to make sense of the Esquire's gratuitous triumph. However ostentatious its logical trappings, the Esquire's crucial speech depends little on reasoning:

> Proteus, stout Iron-Homager of your rock,
> Impresa of force, and Instruments of Wars,
> Hath praise indeed; yet place your praises right;
> For force to will, and wars to peace do yield.
> But that I'll give you. This I wou'd fain know,
> What can your iron do without arms of men?
> And arms of men from hearts of men do move:
> The hearts of men, that's it thence motion springs.
> Lo Proteus then, the attractive Rock of hearts . . .
> Your rock claims kindred of the Polar star,
> Because it draws the needle of the North;

Yet even that star gives place to Cynthia's rays
Whose drawing virtues govern and direct
The flots and re-flots of the Ocean. . . .
What excellencies are there in this frame,
Of all things which her Vertue doth not draw?

[229–78]

Though it appears aggressively forensic, the speech directs our wits toward thin air: toward word play, unanswerable questions, and obtrusively ingenious myth. If anything, its logic dissipates our common sense as we try to follow it. Yet we do *feel* the speech somehow does demonstrate the Queen's "Vertue."

Actually the Esquire's recitation reveals rather than persuades: it is sacramental. Beginning with the formulaic "lo Proteus then," its language becomes an operative gesture matching the physical one by which the Esquire invokes Elizabeth and fuses the court and the masque, the real and the unreal. His "action" depends no more on reasoning than does the priest's litany or Orpheus's song.

As in magical thinking, the masque conceives the *metaphorical* power of the Queen's "attractive Vertue" to be as substantial as the lodestone's *physical* counterpart. As an "Adamant of hearts" her spiritual force becomes a material force as well: a natural force. Like a natural power, the Esquire's name for her itself shapes the events while the performance lasts. Undeniably the magic derives from an illusion. The poet has created a perceptual situation in which abstract and concrete levels of thought temporarily coincide (as in the Roman mimes examined in the Appendix). Though the masque's revelation does turn on a conceptual puzzle, it leads us toward imagination and feeling, where the cumulative uncertainty of what we "fain wou'd know" has a definite yet indefinable resolution. We praise the Queen's "Vertue"; we feel it, and wish it to be.

Therefore the masque *must* disrupt our comfortable prejudices about human limits. The revelation of the Queen to Proteus and all the participants does more than signify the villain's "moral blindness."[13] For like Proteus, we too initially believe in a foreshortened reality. At the outset the masque-world appears equal to the actual world. But the Esquire exposes the limits of that world by pointing beyond it to the incontestable "force" of the Queen, and we feel we have been embracing an illusion. Fundamentally we have not been fooled. At bottom we know that the sensation of wonder is partly theater. Yet insofar as we have assented to the convention that the world of the performance is real, as in a play, we share the sea god's amazement at its sudden expansion when the Queen enters it.

In the masque's poetry an analogous disruption occurs when the expected sense of "attractive Vertue" expands into the conceit "the attractive Rock of hearts." Like Proteus, we are meant to be astonished as the usual bounds of meaning become fluid. Conventionalized as the stage prop before us, the imagined rock is readily graspable. The Queen's "adamantine heart," by contrast, requires a different order of understanding. The metaphor requires a leap of imagination to integrate things that appear radically unrelated.

As an artist might, the Esquire recreates the Queen's identity for us. As it turns out, her "Vertue" is not merely "power," a matter of measurable political force, but also "worth," which excites our emotional conviction and love. Entering into this praise of the Queen, we not only observe the triumph of her worth, but actually will it also. And this is the masque's magical promise, that spiritual power (Elizabeth's goodness and our praise of it) will oversway material power: that "force to will [does] yield" (232).

Proteus culminates in an act of social communion and harmony: the dance which unites spectators and actors. The dance expresses a liberation of feeling and a potential for transformation. The ceremony secures the Queen, the "heart" of the nation's governance, against the evils of time and change. The Queen supplants Proteus, confirming a new order in all things. The celebrants experience real wishes and mythical purpose combining. The ceremony fulfills the human wish to be at one with the forces of destiny, even as the dancers effect the commingling of mortals and divinity. Coming to life in the dance as in its aroused feeling, the court participates in an action of rebirth.

Why has Davison made the magical basis of his creation so covert? The answer points to a complex ambivalence about ritual art. In one respect the decorous pastoralism of *Proteus* disguises an impious desire: a wish that harks back to the serpent's treacherous blandishment that "ye shall be as gods." From an orthodox viewpoint that wish entails unlawful striving the devil would abet.[14]

But there is a more fundamental problem. The court must have been perfectly capable of understanding, if necessary, that its wonder originated in an illusion. To some discreet observers, in fact, the ceremony may well have seemed blasphemous or cynical political trumpery. Consequently the illusionistic—and manipulative—aspects of the masque needed to remain hidden. Were the magical process itself exposed, comprehended as a predictable *technique*, its efficacy would cease.

Because magic cannot permanently loose the bonds of mortality, but must always be reenacted and renewed, its creation may arouse fears which its limited potency cannot assuage. *Proteus* magnifies the Queen's identity, but also the potential menace of change and disorder and death. If its ceremony should fail to be sufficiently spellbinding—if it produces no love— it would leave its spectators contemplating the Queen's presumption in the face of the divine, and the fearful prospect of her death to come.

For the artist the creation of wonder involves serious risks. If he fails to sway feelings and belief, he appears a seducer, using artifice to project us toward troubling passions and loss of control. If he succeeds, time must sooner or later prove his triumph ephemeral in any event, provoking him to recreate it anew. To our eyes, after all, there is an element of politic and quixotic escapism in *Proteus*. Davison may be said to have overlooked or buried these difficulties, whereas Shakespeare's responses to them are implied everywhere in his art.

The Problem of Playing

The Winter's Tale shows us men yearning for the lost Eden of childhood—yearning to escape themselves. Polixenes recollects youth as an innocent state, unconscious of itself, bound neither by time nor by serious toil. As selfless "lambs," the two youths were paradoxically most themselves. They were "in" nature; now they rue their alienation. As we have seen, sacred rite goes about restoring its participants to grace. After the Fall man's immediate relation to God—praise—became a ritual form, prayer.

In the opening of the play the court stands alienated not only from nature, but also from the possibility of ritual. What blocks the characters is their self-consciousness, the peculiar "knowing" which the serpent advertised to Eve as wisdom. No longer directly open to their feelings and the objects of their love, as children may be, they appear transfixed by the *means* of knowing, preoccupied with the conventions of speech and comportment which mediate their relations with the world. Groping to express generosity, competing with Camillo in a subtle show of feeling, Archidamus lapses into incoherence and finally silence (1.1.11–15). Even while trying to make his gratitude vivid, Polixenes cannot help discoursing about *how* he is speaking:

> And therefore, like a cipher,
> Yet standing in rich place, I multiply
> With one "We thank you" many thousands moe
> That go before it.
>
> [1.2.6–9]

His verbal extravagance makes especially abstract the emotions he is presumably so desperate to actualize. Since this wit prevents him from truly expressing himself, he is in an ironic, even sinister way more of a "cipher" than he knows.

In the debate between the royal figures the limitations of customary means of expression come repeatedly to the fore. In the delicate challenges to Polixenes' motives for his departure there is much emphasis on "saying" and "swearing." The Queen herself exacerbates the mistrust of speech and appearances, though she means only to banter. She mimics Polixenes' "I may not [stay], verily."

> Verily!
> You put me off with limber vows; but I,
> Though you would seek t'unsphere the stars with oaths,
> Should yet say, "Sir, no going". Verily,
> You shall not go; a lady's "Verily" is
> As potent as a lord's.
>
> [1.2.46–51]

With its sly imitation of him, and its talk about talk, her playfulness is fraught with uncertainty. Repetition of "verily" calls into question the assurance of truth the word denotes. Her tone and feelings resist easy analysis. Certainly she mistrusts Polixenes' "art" in presenting himself, including his casual vows. She seems concerned as well about her own "potency" as a woman. Given the anxious undertone in the interview, Hermione inadvertently abets the chaos which overcomes her husband.

Through the serpent's so-called wisdom mankind discovered not only its dependence on speech but, more disastrously, that speech often deceives—as the serpent's did. Unwitting irony bedevils each of the speakers at Leontes' court. Archidamus, who boasts of his "understanding" (1.1.19), describes "great difference" between the two kings, and an affection "which cannot choose but branch now" (3 and 25). Ambiguity undermines his words with opposite, unwanted meanings. Expecting his understanding and not his heart to "instruct" his speech, Archidamus confutes himself. Hermione is not so blind, yet she seems willing to use ambiguities to express obliquely what might otherwise have to go unsaid. Her motives deserve closer attention.

Like Lear with Cordelia, Leontes vacillates between commands and entreaties. He turns most imperious when most in need of Hermione's help: "Tongue-tied, our Queen? Speak you" (1.2.27). He admires her ability to influence Polixenes ("Well said, Hermione"), yet he appears jealous of it as well ("At my request he would not [stay]"). In her manner of speaking Hermione tends to play the fool, quibbling and riddling ("My prisoner or my guest").[15] She uses the fool's license to exercise in play a sort of potency we gather she cannot openly wield. Hence her jests about fencing (33), "thwacking" Polixenes from the palace (37), and taking him prisoner (52–55). When she begins interrogating him about his boyhood, it is reasonable to see Polixenes' sally about original sin (76–80) as a gentle stroke of retaliation. For after all, she is out to bend his will to her purpose. Her response betrays hints of manipulation. She bids him say no more, "lest you say / Your queen and I are devils." In the same breath, however, she urges "Yet go on," promising that "th' offenses we have made you do we'll answer" (82–83). Offense or not, she is even now making him stay.

Curiously, Leontes praises Hermione's "art"—her powers of speech—rather than her person ("thou never spok'st to better purpose"). And she makes this an issue in her subsequent fishing for praises. In this speech she obliquely depicts herself as a spirited wild animal who would become "fat as tame things" with praise. In a prickly way she is conscious of serving her husband ("you may ride's"), but coaxes him to use kisses rather than spurs for incentive. She plays at bargaining her power for love, in sum, and to make clear her loyalty to love Shakespeare has her openly admit her feelings at last: "I long" (89–101). Like her wish for love, her pun on "Grace" puts her needs in the same Edenic context Polixenes has set forth.

Leontes' reply is revealing in its insecurity and doubleness: she had spoken well once before when

> Three crabbed months had sour'd themselves to death
> Ere I could make thee open thy white hand
> And clap thyself my love; then didst thou utter
> "I am yours forever."
>
> [102–5]

"Clap" can mean not only a clasp or vow to seal a bargain, but also prating or chatter. In addition, it has theatrical connotations, and suggests applause for his "performance" in courtship or love-making. In its lurking implications this is a speech about dominance and the fear of playing at love.

Hermione's "play" opens life to possibilities. For Leontes the upshot is an instant of wonder which releases not love but mad jealousy (108 ll.). He behaves as if he is only now awakening to the indeterminacy which shadows language and conventional gestures. He dreads that like an actor, "this entertainment/May a free face put on, derive a liberty/From heartiness" (110–12). He has lost sight of the consensus upon which conventions rely for their truth (at root the word means to agree or come together). Suddenly every gesture appears to him an act, even his own:

> Go play, boy, play; thy mother plays, and I
> Play too; but so disgrac'd a part, whose issue
> Will hiss me to my grave.
>
> [187–89]

There are multiple perspectives subsumed in this obsession with "play." Variously the word means: to amuse oneself, to deceive, to toy with, to be libidinous, to make believe, and to play-act. The word's riddling complexity makes vivid for us Leontes' sense of bewildered entrapment in an evil drama. But there is another torment implied too: to some extent he is aware of his own outrage as play-acting. Just as the world has turned into phantasms and masks, so the inner world of emotions seems to him tenuous, a storm of ugly energy signifying nothing. Imagination "communicat'st with dreams . . . And fellow'st nothing" (140–42). Instead of wonder—a meaning beyond appearances—he senses nothingness. And he cannot bear it. Hence the rich, self-intoxicating flood of metaphors and word play by which Shakespeare dramatizes Leontes' struggle to make himself real. We witness his interpretive creation (or re-creation) of life taking him further and further away from life, into the snares of destructive passion and madness itself.[16]

What Leontes cannot imagine is play as the experience of children or "twinn'd lambs," an Edenic state of praise or—to use Hermione's word—grace. Instead he conceives himself in a "*dis*grac'd part," in an endlessly treacherous drama. Subsequently he "begins to play in the sense of constructing an intensely moral drama in which he enacts the role of the deceived husband."[17] To create this paranoid, gratifyingly ordered "play," Leontes takes on a spuriously godlike role, bewitched by his new knowledge, defying Apollo—"There is no truth at all i' the Oracle" (3.2.140). In the process he looses death in his kingdom, beginning with the death of Mamillius, his son. When he questions the child about deception (1.2.161) and stresses their close resemblance—"they say we are / Almost alike as eggs" (130)—Leontes speaks as if addressing the child in himself. So that on one level the boy's death is virtually the death of the child in himself. One way of looking at Leontes' behavior, then, is to see it as an echo of the Fall. It plays out the anxiety in Polixenes' vision of childhood as paradise:

> What we chang'd
> Was innocence for innocence; we knew not
> The doctrine of ill-doing, nor dream'd
> That any did. Had we pursu'd that life,
> And our weak spirits ne'er been higher reared
> With stronger blood, we should have answer'd heaven
> Boldly "Not guilty", the imposition clear'd,
> Hereditary ours.
>
> [68–75]

At bottom the court's dilemma resembles Shakespeare's: how to create an unself-conscious vision of life. As Leontes' mad insight into playing reveals, the artist has reason to fear the deceptive "arts" of life. For masks and the gilded lie are his stock in trade. For better or worse his artifice stands between him and other men. Unavoidably illusion mediates his relation to the world. The artist, then, would appear to be as implicated in manipulation and alienation as the court figures. Ritual would answer some of Polixenes' yearning for lost grace. But the artist seems as removed from ritual as the troubled king. Were he to see through Leontes' eyes, all things would loom treacherous and mutable before him. Art would be an unceasing strife with Proteus, not a triumph over him.

Consider, for example, Davison's ceremonial victory, *Proteus.*

About the time the masque made its debut, Shakespeare produced *A Midsummer Night's Dream.* There, Davison's momentous trope, his "adamant of hearts," has a comic echo. In the dark, disorienting wood outside Athens, in a bemusing version of the pastoralism Davison so earnestly marshaled, Helena professes hopeless love to Demetrius:

> You draw me yet, you hardhearted adamant;
> But yet you draw not iron, for my heart
> Is true as steel. Leave you your power to draw
> And I shall have no power to follow you.
>
> [2.1.195–98]

As he does elsewhere in the play, Shakespeare burlesques a lover who behaves as if words have the love-making powers of magical praise. We share his mockery of Helena's adamantine invention; it delights us. Juxtaposed with its counterpart in *Proteus,* by contrast, it would nullify the effectiveness of the masque. Writing for an elite, private audience, with an actual queen among his props, Davison could afford to ignore critical attitudes which in the public theaters were rife.

The Elizabethans were much preoccupied with style.[18] A purely ritual art would involve no awareness of style *for its own sake.* What we call style was for archaic man an efficacious formula which, as we noted, reaccomplishes rather than represents an event. When style comes into its own as an abstract concept, we can speak of art in terms of technique. And techniques are vulnerable to imitation and debasement. Prodigal imitations of Marlowe's rhetoric, for instance, robbed it of its meaning and vitality. Thus when eventually Jonson made his confidence artist Volpone use the magnificent Marlovian manner to ravish the chaste Celia, the seduction's failure comically exposed a style so thoroughly used up that the foxiest of rascals could wring no more life from it.[19]

Jonson himself suffered the slings and arrows of outrageous parody, and learned to be defensive. His *Poetaster* opens with the machinations of Envy, whom "an armed Prologue" drives from the play with the admonition:

> know, 'tis a dangerous age:
> Wherein, who writes, had need present his *Scenes*
> Fortie-fold proofe against the coniuring meanes
> Of base detractors, and illiterate apes,
> That fill up roomes in faire and formall shapes.[20]

Like Shakespeare's plays-within-plays, Jonson's own parody of Marlowe in *Volpone* demonstrates the vulnerability of an aesthetic form once it has been isolated as a technique or artifact. Unlike ritual forms, such artifacts exist in time, defenseless against mockery and overexposure, as frail in their meanings as mortality itself. By the same token, this frailty may spur the artist to strive to transcend it: to make his art more richly complex and inimitable, as life itself is. In *The Winter's Tale* Shakespeare has Julio Romano reported as wishing "to beguile nature of her custom" (5.2.95). He would transform his art into nature.

Rather than deny self-consciousness, as Davison does, Shakespeare turns it into a liberating action. Rather than try to still our critical faculties, he arouses in us such an active contemplation of the relation between art and life that the two appear to merge. Leontes' references to "playing" provide a single brief example. For a character to view himself in the play of life was a common trick of Elizabethan dramatists. Yet Shakespeare alone explored its many consequences.

When Leontes imagines himself playing a "disgrac'd part, whose issue / Will hiss me to my grave" (1.2.188), he *dramatizes* a self-conscious perspective. He becomes an audience to himself, at once within and outside the play. As his soliloquy develops, he displaces our perspective as well, prompting us to view ourselves from without:

> many a man there is (even at this present,
> Now, while I speak this) holds his wife by th' arm,
> That little thinks she has been sluic'd in's absence.
> [190–94]

The effects of this shift in viewpoint are complex. We may uneasily realize how secure our spectator's role permits us to feel. Conceivably we may wonder if "even at this present,/Now" one or more of the women among us in the audience is disguising her true self. And our uncertainty may well deepen. For Leontes' lines forestall any complacent judgment of him as a mere lunatic and villain. They win him some sympathy from us, for he shows himself able to view things from our perspective as onlookers. He seems to struggle with plausibility as we do.

No longer can we readily resolve our feelings and appraisals of the play's action. Because Leontes (and his creator) are ironical toward his potentially "stagey" roles as cuckold and villain, we may wish to laugh at the play's artifice even as, on another level, the fate of its characters continues to involve us. If we try to grasp the implications of Leontes' speech about playing, we may become the more perplexed. We would find ourselves looking at ourselves as an audience looking at a play in which a real actor is looking at himself as a King who is discovering himself an "actor" in a "play" whose plot he can scarcely divine.[21]

The more conscious we become of the interplay of art and life, the less capable we feel of categorizing them. As so often in the play, artistic form induces an experience of paradox. We may well sympathize with Leontes' attempt to put art between himself and a situation too painful to bear:

> he shifts his vision . . . to a stage artifice which protects him from . . . total involvement. He attempts to achieve for himself the same double sense of commitment to real experience and of safety from real threat which every theater audience knows.[22]

At moments, that is, art consoles us. It distances us, casting life in manageable forms. At other moments, however, art seems disturbing; we doubt our ability to control it. The play's perspective puzzles amuse us yet underscore the inadequacy of our perceptions. One meaning of Leontes' "thy mother plays, and I / Play too" (187) is that his deluded contentment with life has been like a bad play, ludicrously unrelated to the reality of his wife's supposedly adulterous "playing." In passing we too may wonder if our picture of life is as artificial and false as a bad play.

When the play's conclusion focuses our perplexity on the resurrection of Hermione, we do feel a liberating wonderment. Unlike *Proteus*, naturally, *The Winter's Tale* cannot produce an actual queen onstage to ensure our belief. On the contrary, like the opening scenes, the statue scene guides us to appreciate its artifice. How, then, does our wonder come about? And how can the play be magical in its effects?

Living Art

To reveal the Queen, Paulina stages a sort of play-within-a-play, drawing a curtain to disclose her "statue." She uses certain conventions of art to prepare the beholders (onstage and in the audience) for a miraculous restoration. To those present, including us, she says, "I like your silence, the more it shows off / Your wonder" (5.3.21). Most awestruck of all is Leontes. Her words remind us that the King's present openness sharply contrasts with his tyrannical behavior at the beginning of the play. There, Leontes also perceived his wife as artificial—not a statue but a mask of false virtue. "We are mocked with art," he says in praise of the statue. At the onset of his paranoia, by contrast, art's mockery panicked him.

In the first half of the play, we recall, Leontes undertakes to control artifice by force. To order what Camillo would call "the infinite doings of the world" (1.2.253), the King invents a ruthless, simplistic plot. In this melodramatic triangle he casts Hermione as the lascivious wife, and Polixenes as the treacherous friend. In so doing he usurps their actual lives, and eventually the critical voices of his counselors (among them the ill-fated Antigonus), absorbing them one after another into his "play." The trial scene dramatizes the ascendancy of Leontes' "mad" art: his own distraught mind *is* the trial, and all other viewpoints surrender to his. Unlike Paulina's art, Leontes' isolates men and spreads death.

Death is one experience which we cannot glibly conventionalize. It takes the actual and ostensible deaths of Mamillius and Hermione to underscore the evil nature of the King's play. Whereas magic frees wishes and volition, Leontes belatedly learns that tyrannical creation immobilizes the wills of others. In effect, a failure of the will to live kills Mamillius. Like the political interlopers in the history plays, the King comes to understand that forcible manipulation of the natural order can destroy it. He pays for his insight with the loss of his family.

As bodied forth by the statue, Paulina's creation is redemptive. Where Leontes suspects that "sometimes Nature will betray its folly" (1.2.151), Paulina cooperates with "great creating Nature" and the oracle. Using deceit as Hamlet does to elicit truthful feelings, to "transport" the purged Leontes, she stages a reconciliation. Her art serves not to accomplish what nature cannot—to restore a Hermione who has never been lost—but to open self-conscious minds: to renew deadened spirits. As Sebastian laments in *Twelfth Night*, "In Nature there's no blemish but the mind" (3.4.351).

As in ritual magic, the action of the play recreates the participants and their relation to powers beyond man. The dialectical structure of the play gives rise to many opposites which are at last—literally and symbolically—wedded together. Art and nature, the spheres of man and the divine, merge. (This is the drift of the intricate debate between Polixenes and Perdita in the festival scene.) Sicilia and Bohemia, realms of sophistication and pastoralism respectively, reunite, as do the powers of kings and of the oracle. Wonder joins things ordinarily dissevered, as the experience itself makes vivid. Of the reunion of Leontes and Camillo, a witness reports:

> there was speech in their dumbness, language in their very gesture; they look'd as they had heard of a world ransom'd, or one destroyed. A notable passion of wonder appeared in them; but the wisest beholder . . . could not say if the importance were joy or sorrow. . . .
>
> [5.2.13–18]

The mingling of joy and sorrow applies also to the structure of the play. It begins as tragedy and moves toward comedy: in the end it is neither one nor the other.

During the play individuals undergo re-creation as well. Hermione plays dead, and is "resurrected" with what her husband deems "magic in thy majesty" (5.3.39). Although unaware of it herself, Perdita also undergoes a form of playing dead. As she returns from Bohemia, the "bastard" infant has become a goddess-like queen. Leontes at last espies a resurrection of Mamillius in Florizel. To the Prince and the as yet unrecognized Perdita he confesses:

> I lost a couple that 'twixt heaven and earth
> Might thus have stood begetting wonder as
> You, gracious couple, do.
>
> [5.1.132–34]

And of course the King himself plays dead to the world, enduring a deathlike penance. More truly than he knows he prophesies that "tears shed . . . Shall be my recreation" (3.2.236). Before the statue he exclaims, "Would I were dead" (5.3.61). Moments later the statue awakens, and his renewal is complete.

The play's ritual culminates at this moment, as Paulina conjures the statue to life. As the beholders gaze all action halts; time itself momentarily relents. But the scene is not simply a random miracle. Rather, it *reenacts* the earlier scene in which the King fell from grace: it is an exorcism. Generated by the fusion of knowing and wishing, magic enables Paulina to urge Leontes that "It is required/You do awake your faith" (94). After sixteen years of penitence, of learning charity of imagination, he may once again yield to the awesome powers of belief. And in one sense nothing has changed. Hermione is still the peerless queen; her likeness "Excels whatever yet you looked upon" (16). Leontes may assume the same idealizing viewpoint that precipitated waste and loss at the beginning. What has changed is his inner relationship to that viewpoint.

Whereas initially Leontes sought to subdue unruly life, now he has acquired a capacity for wonder. He retains his belief in absolutes (his own evil stings him as sharply now as it presumably did after the trial), but he no longer tyrannizes reality. Exactly reversing his earlier orientation, speaking of his wish to believe that the statue lives, he cries:

> No settled senses of the world can match
> The pleasure of that madness.

> [72–73]

His present "madness" is not madness at all insofar as it draws him into a community of experience, a deeper consensus. As before, he contemplates the mingling of artifice and nature in his beloved. But now this mingling signifies promise rather than peril.

In short, the King has learned to play. Instead of reviling conjectured impersonation, the disguised adultery, he trusts "Each one [to] demand and answer to his part/Perform'd" in life (154). Reconciled to the appropriate role for a king, he accepts himself as a player, in a role shaped partly by nature. As a deviser of "plays," he now makes, rather than sunders, a marriage—as the betrothal of Paulina and Camillo bears out. Love, not malice, moves him.

Our response to the play resembles in some respects the response of the onstage audience in Paulina's chapel. For the statue only exists as an *action* of minds: the characters' and our own. Trying to conceive the image as an artifact, we share a similar amazement when it lives. "If this be magic," Leontes vows, "let it be an art/Lawful as eating" (110–11). Life is "lively mocked" by art, as Paulina says (19), but in an unexpectedly corporeal manner.

Insofar as there is no actual work of art or a Julio Romano involved, the beholders' wishful awe innocently transcends the supposed reality and suits the "living" reality perfectly. And this is the ambiguity which affords the play its magical dimension: in disastrous and redemptive ways art *is* life and life art. The play's definitive experience is of landing on the preposterous seacoast of

Bohemia and being eaten by a real bear. Our situation is akin to Leontes' relation to "th' infinite doings of the world." We too win "nothing" by trying to deny wonder. We too need a new openness to creation.

As the play astonishes us it contrives to make us sense a resolution just beyond our reach. As spectators we watch Paulina watch her onstage audience try to watch themselves ("we are mocked with art") watch an imagined artifact dissolve to nothing as the Queen "becomes" real. As in perspective painting, we are teased with an illusion of infinity. Analogously, the play as a whole deploys a series of creators who generate its action through such human agencies as Paulina, yet who are progressively remote from us. These creators decoy us to look beyond the onstage realm for a resolution to its wonders. Beyond Paulina there is the unlikely but imaginable anachronism Julio Romano; "Time," who foists upon us a glib "tale" to rationalize his larger tale, the play proper; and in the metaphysical distance the likely but inconceivable oracle, whose voice, Cleomenes reports, "so surpris'd my sense / That I was nothing" (3.1.10). These putative creators of the play lead toward the godlike position of Shakespeare himself. The closer our minds draw to that generative source, however, the more it eludes us. Even when we see through this illusionism, we cannot grasp the hidden springs of the play.

Besides merging art and nature, Shakespeare also weds truth and mockery. At once the play invites seriousness and ridicule. Paulina is not only a sort of priestess, "remarrying" the royal couple in her chapel with a "spell," but also a comical shrew. The play itself is a ceremony of deep feeling and yet no less "an old tale" which, "Were it but told you, should be hooted at" (5.3.116). Hence the tenuous allegory we discern at work. Perdita, for example, is a focal point of allegorical meanings. In the festival scene she presides goddesslike on behalf of "great creating nature." Perfectly blending play and reality, will and wishes, she brings integrity to life in the play. In Florizel's words, "all your acts are queens" (4.4.146). He speaks more wisely than he knows—with magical clairvoyance—since Perdita is truly a queen, however reluctantly she "plays" one.

The oracle makes Perdita's role redemptive. At her recovery Camillo and Leontes looked "as they had heard of a world ransom'd or one destroyed" (5.2.14). And this in turn suggests her role as a *figura* of Christ.[23] We might think of her as an incarnation of Proserpine also. It is tempting to consider Hermione's return to the world a "resurrection." At the same time, in the figure of Time, allegory becomes concrete—in fact, parodic.

In parody the mind holds in view two perspectives at once. A parodic action rejects or criticizes what it represents, yet simultaneously it implies an ideal. Like irony, that is, parody may subsume complex attitudes. In addition it is a negative strategy: it identifies what is *not* true and *not* ideal. The crucial point is one which warrants some emphasis: *in parody self-consciousness makes the conventionalizing process a means of transcendence.* (By disqualifying customary forms of love, the Sonnets thereby invoke absolute love.) Because it can only *imply* an ideal, parody creates an ambiguity both liberating and treacherously expedient. It may direct us toward an inexpressible order or toward a horrible void.

Whereas in Dante allegory articulates a divine reality, in Shakespeare allegorical elements body forth no single absolute scheme. Instead they tease us with parodic richness. The women of the late romances have an allegorical dimension which the plays' self-awareness always threatens to take away. The personage Time in *The Winter's Tale* is not only the abstract process of time, but also a garrulous muddle-headed old man—a figure of the playwright which allows the playwright himself (and us) some critical merriment. He claims to be master of his "tale." Yet his promise to "try all" (4.1.1) comes to nought in his apology for leaving "the growth untried/Of that wide gap" of time between the third and fourth acts of his tale (6). Like allegory itself, he promises sense; in practice he dispels it, imploring "Let me pass" (9). With that glib, wry plea he virtually turns invisible before our eyes, and new mystery comes to life.

Much the same thing could be said of Autolycus, the creator of ballads, who crookedly stages a parodic version of the good Samaritan's adventure to gull the clown.[24] Beaneath his succession of disguises he is, like Time, nobody: a mystery. By swapping clothes with the fleeing Prince, he does make possible the restoration which ends the play. But more important, he allows Shakespeare to parody his own function as creator.

Inevitably the dramatist must manipulate us to direct our conception of his art. As Leontes' behavior shows, however, manipulation is easily perverted to tyranny. Parody enables manipulation to be functionally selfless, and to release us. In Autolycus and Time and Paulina's caricatured shrewishness Shakespeare good-naturedly acknowledges the defects of art and the creator's role. To the extent that he cannot truly intercede for us with divine forces, and does indulge our yearning for magic, Shakespeare is partly a charlatan like Autolycus. To the extent that he parodies or negates his own role within the play in order to set us free from manipulation, he is in effect lending us his costume to escape a confining world, just as Autolycus assists the young lovers.

In *The Winter's Tale* Shakespeare turns parody into a means of affirmation by exploiting its kinship with allegory (in which an image at hand also imitates something on another plane, although unmediated by self-consciousness). This use of parody strives toward magical transcendence. The act itself, not the parodic content, comes to be an expression of faith. His art directs us toward its deficiency, its failures of truth, that we may intuit an absolute truth. Speaking of the Sonnets, we termed this process negative creation. Since it cannot (and must not) *prove* its truth, the play moves in a sustained equilibrium of negation and belief.

This equilibrium underlies the playful portrayal of Julio Romano. Reportedly the Italian master would "beguile nature of her custom" (according to Vasari's *Lives of the Painters*, he fashioned statues that breathed, and buildings equal to those in heaven, until Jupiter jealously carried him off.)[25] On the anachronistic and hyperbolic face of it, Shakespeare seems to be jesting about the artist's pretensions. For Julio Romano's art would magically live, exempt from mortality:

> had he himself eternity and could put breath into his work,
> he would beguile nature of her custom, so perfectly is he her
> ape. [5.2.105–8]

Paradoxically, Shakespeare himself vindicates all that Julio Romano pretends to be. Insofar as we let custom rule our conception of life, he does beguile nature by bringing us to wonder. So too, the play can be given an "eternity" of performances, and he *can* "put breath into his work" through the actors' speeches. All told, he both denies and affirms this surrogate artist.

One way of construing Shakespeare's relation to the play is to see him doing as his characters do: playing dead. Unlike Jonson and some of his contemporaries, he avoids any didactic or self-aggrandizing role as dramatist. Rather, he seeks to free his play: to make it not a glorious artifact, but living art, an art

Which does mend nature, change it rather; but
The art itself is nature.

[4.495–97]

Art acts upon, yet is part of, nature. It follows that the creator and what he creates are indistinguishable, like Yeats's dancer and the dance. What's more, the dance or the play *is* nature. In ritual magic the performer may be said to lose himself in the rite. Through negative creation Shakespeare does something analogous, declining to impose a conventional or self-serving order on the play. His career as an actor makes this process peculiarly concrete. An actor-playwright would be in a natural position to appreciate his play as a ceremonial *action* (as opposed to an aesthetic artifact) in which the creator "loses" himself by becoming one of the characters he has engendered. In every performance of the play he would be able to watch his imagination come to life in the theater, even as he shares in its immediate realization. The play would be directing his behavior.[26]

But how do we, the audience, participate in such a ceremony? In the Sonnets the poet-lover's voice is the poem. Saying it over, we act the poet; his vision becomes ours. And since by his vows he seeks to lose himself, the poem issues in enacted love: a rite which transcends the parties to it.

As spectators to drama we cannot in a direct way become the play we go to watch (or in Elizabethan parlance, to hear). Normally we abide by the role of onlooker, regarding our position as a relatively passive one. The players present; we take in. In the late romances, however, Shakespeare contrived to make our participation as complete as it is in the Sonnets. Staging her play-within-a-play Paulina praises both her audiences for their wonder (5.3.21), and we have examined how that condition comes about. But it is action which fulfills the play; the reunion of "dissevered" individuals.

"If this be magic," Leontes vows, "let it be an art/Lawful as eating" (110). Insofar as it exists only in his own mind, the miraculous transformation is partly his own creation. And we are similarly implicated. For we imagine into being the statue and, no less, the play itself. Only by our cooperation can the events and materials of theater generate the imaginative transaction a play is. Shakespeare and a company of actors provide the conditions for *The Winter's Tale*. But the play itself is an event in space and time.

It comes into being only as we act to interpret and, as epilogues usually insist, to affirm it. Potentially (to some extent inescapably) every play is many plays. Always the dramatist risks being misconstrued or mocked; his art may spawn prolific falsity. And therefore Shakespeare seeks to turn self-consciousness into wonder, to orient us. The metaphor the play suggests for our participation is marriage. The union of characters onstage is not merely physical, but an imaginative and emotional union also: a new and deeper consensus capable of restoring meanings, of healing the divisive "madness" of the play's opening. And this union has a counterpart in the marriage of minds which joins all who create the play itself—Shakespeare, the actors, and we ourselves. Our imaginative engagement *is* the play.

As in the Sonnets, this living art is an experience. In its capacity to give life to otherwise unrealized emotions—to buried wishes—such art might be said to resurrect us. We are meant to feel renewed. To be sure, we have only a moment of revelation before the King commands "hastily lead away" (155). As our critical detachment begins to return we may realize that we have seen no final resolution. There has been no time for the testing of new love. Leontes' invention of a marriage between Paulina and Camillo is, after all, both hasty and peremptory. For that matter, he and Hermione vanish offstage before either speaks an intimate word to the other. At the last, then, we may sense that the wishes and love elicited in this moment of grace are part of us, yet beyond our manipulation, like "the infinite doings of the world." Magic is finally belief. In Paulina's words, "It is requir'd/You do awake your faith" (5.3.95). And faith, as we discover in our involvement in the play, is an imaginative act, a movement of the self. In this perspective the exiting players do not merely leave us behind to ponder. On the contrary, we are included in Leontes' parting wish to pass

> from hence, where we may leisurely
> Each one demand, and answer to his part
> Perform'd in this wide gap of time, since first
> We were dissever'd: hastily lead away.
>
> [5.3.152–55]

We have lives to resume outside the theater, and experiences of the play ("this wide gap of time") to share. In another, deeper sense the words call upon us each to share "his part/Perform'd" since we were "dissever'd" by our loss of childhood and innocence. While it is the last speech of the play, we are aroused to take part in its promise of community.

Envoi

"Comedy is not, obviously enough, the same thing as ritual," says C. L. Barber, adding that

> in a self-conscious culture, the heritage of cult is kept alive by art which makes it relevant as a mode of perception and expression. The artist gives the ritual pattern aesthetic actuality by discovering expressions of it in the fragmentary . . . gestures of daily life. He fulfills these gestures by making them moments in the complete action which is the art form.[27]

This is an apt formulation, I think, because it tactfully equivocates. Ritual is a *pattern* yet also, embodied in art *form*, an *action*. It is vestigial yet somehow dynamic. Barber holds that the saturnalian or holiday pattern "releases" and in turn "clarifies" in spectators and characters alike feelings of community and harmony with nature. Drama "must control magic by reunderstanding it as imagination." But in practice he is not so categorical. Discerning wonder and skepticism together in one speech, he can conclude that "Neither awareness cancels out the other." At the close of *A Midsummer Night's Dream*, he concedes, "imagination . . . has reached to something, a creative tendency and process. What is this process . . . ? It is what happens in the play. . . . To name it requires many words in motion"—all the words of the play. This "creative process," in short, is irreducible; it is the "motion" or action of the play. Which is to say, though he treats ritual as a "pattern" or an analogy to drama, Barber manages not to deny its dynamic effects. All told, this is a useful, even judicious inconsistency.

By comparison, John Holloway promises polemical certainty. Each of the plays is "not a statement or insight or special kind of informativeness—not these things essentially, although it may be all of them incidentally—but . . . *a momentous energizing experience*.[28] He goes on to explore the roles of scapegoat and ritual sacrifice in ways that reasonably produce the sort of "informative-ness" he presumably takes to be incidental. The point is, we cannot unblinkingly hold in mind "an experience peculiarly com-prehensive and demanding, an experience unified, ordered and imposed." Nor is experience constant from play to play. Still, this emphasis on the kinetic is salutary. We have seen that only as we enact them do certain of the Sonnets reveal their deepest coher-ence as praise. Only by entering into the "play" of *The Winter's Tale*, guided to see that our imagination of it *is* the play, can we fully appreciate the transcendence figured by Hermione's "resur-rection." Only thus can art, losing its artifice, live for us. As James Calderwood says of *A Midsummer Night's Dream:*

> The dramatic experience in which playwright, actors, and audience all participate . . . becomes a kind of secular ritual of communion, with the play itself the focal illusion whose existence and significance are created by a collective act and whose value lies partly in the fact that it enables a sharing of inner experience otherwise inaccessible.[29]

From the beginning, in certain sonnets, Shakespeare sought to give substance to a magical conception of creation. In the late romances he fulfilled this conception in drama as well. In Part Two I hope to suggest some of the modes and meanings of creation he explored in the long middle course of his career. To that end we will be looking at not only the structures of individual plays, but also the behavior of their characters.

The Sonnets begin to dramatize the poet's inner struggle with incompatible feelings and modes of creation. Ideally, it would seem, art enables the poet to shape an ecstatic, absolute love. Yet repeatedly he discovers extra-rational thinking to be ephemeral and unstable; it threatens to falsify his beloved, denying faults and the poet's own anguish. We begin to perceive inchoate dramatic roles in the poems, and rather than selfless wonder we encounter ironic self-awareness.

In the plays reason and magic struggle as consumingly as they do in the Sonnets. But the plays tend to objectify the figure of the creator, placing him in larger perspectives than the Sonnets allow. The upshot is an increasingly comprehensive examination of the meanings of the creative act. Shakespeare sees not just the poet-lover but all men as creators. The late romances carry out a vision which the Sonnets adumbrate: they present life *as* art, and human endeavor as a sum of creative actions. Leontes' invention (or reinvention) of reality issues in madness and death; Paulina's fosters spiritual rebirth and love. Their actions show us men realizing themselves and the world from the forms of "great creating nature." The plays ahead of us subject that central idea to a great many angles of scrutiny—ethical, psychological, political, and so on.

What needs to be kept in mind is that for Shakespeare creation was, as we have begun to perceive, radically a part of life: a disposition of the self. Given the *beaux-arts* mentality we have inherited, and our investment as critics in the apparatus of good sense, we may find it difficult to fix this expanded concept of creation in mind—*The Winter's Tale* is in part a celebration of that difficulty. I do not mean (or need) to claim that we should forego all of our more conventional notions about Shakespeare's art. There is no point in denying that he was a practical worker in the theater who created for himself the prosperous career commemorated in Stratford. On the contrary, I am convinced we understand Shakespeare best when we perceive, as he must have, that creation is not hierophantic and remote, but a miracle behind the mask of the everyday.

Part Two

What, then, is the right way of
living?
Life must be lived as
play. . . . —Plato, *Laws*

Are you a god? Would you
create me new? —*Comedy of
Errors*

Introduction

The chapters that follow have a twofold purpose. They trace some developments in dramatic form which preceded the "magical" structure exemplified in Part One by *The Winter's Tale*. But a complementary aim is to examine how a few plays objectify the meanings of creation in their characters' experience. Shakespeare commonly uses "create" to signify the generation of identity, as in *Lear*, when Goneril "makes" Edmund her husband: "I create thee here / My lord, and master" (5.3.78). But this is only the most transparent of examples. Repeatedly the plays dramatize their characters' creative faculties, and the complex moral consequences of "conceiving" the world.

The protagonist of the Sonnets is overtly a poet; in the verses before us his every breath creates. By his vows he strives to make love in a rite which transcends the parties to it. When magic falters in the Sonnets, however, the poet begins to resemble a dramatic character. He becomes supremely conscious of role-playing (Sonnet 138) and the personal limits of love. Even the mild worries of Sonnet 23 express the problematical relationship between identity and creation:

> As an unperfect actor on the stage
> Who with his fear is put beside his part . . .
> So I, for fear of trust, forget to say
> The perfect ceremony of love's rite. . . .

The plays themselves abound in characters for whom creation is explicitly art. There are Peter Quince's rude mechanicals, Hamlet the author-director of "The Mousetrap," and *Pericles'* Marina, who

> sings like one immortal, and she dances
> As goddesslike to her admired lays;

> Deep clerks she dumbs; and with her needle composes
> Nature's own shape of bud, bird, branch, or berry,
> That even her art sisters the natural roses.
>
> [5.pro.3–7]

When the courtiers in *Love's Labour's Lost* turn at last to love-making, they become sonneteers and blunder into aesthetic problems such as Sonnet 18 poses about the truth of art (4.3.25–280).

Everyone knows that many characters in the plays are tacitly artist figures, as Coleridge long ago concluded of Prospero, and Hazlitt of Iago. This is not to equate Shakespeare and Iago, say, in a romantic simplification of the writer's relation to his work. Rather, Iago is "an ominous caricature of the playwright's own methods," even as Paulina's recreation of Hermione by means of her "statue" might be said to caricature benign art.[1] The most ubiquitous and thoroughly scrutinized of these artists-by-analogy is perhaps the player-king, whose many avatars dramatize in the larger spheres of history and culture individual efforts to order life.[2]

But kings are uncommonly potent; their creative actions are by definition exceptional. To give our inquiry the proper scope it would be well to recall Ulysses' stipulation in *Troilus and Cressida* that

> no man is lord of anything—
> Though in and of him there be much consisting—
> Till he communicate his parts to others.
> Nor doth he of himself know them for aught
> Till he behold them formed in th' applause
> Where th' are extended. . . .
>
> [3.3.115–20]

This is an extreme position, as the canny Ulysses himself admits in order to preempt Achilles' reservations about it. The passage envisions all the world a stage, and behavior living art. Each man, Ulysses reasons, is an actor-dramatist, his identity *formed* in the interplay of his own and others' wills. Alone a man can neither know nor be himself. To exist he must "communicate his parts to others" as an actor bodies forth his role. Identity then is an interpretive act. And consensus is essential. For it is "applause"— in effect, love—that completes the creative process and confers existence.

Ulysses makes autonomy a supra-personal phenomenon. A man

is most himself when "formed" by forces beyond him. This notion appears in many different guises in Shakespeare. In Sonnet 112 the poet vows

> You are my all the world, and I must strive
> To know my shames and praises from your tongue;
> None else to me, nor I to none alive,
> That my steeled sense or changes right or wrong.

Despite some cryptic phrases these lines suggest that the poet comes to himself only through his beloved.[3]

On another level Ulysses' view implies a conservative, even authoritarian doctrine of commonweal wherein the social bond takes precedence over self-assertion. In a world where consensus has turned treacherous (*King Lear* and *Hamlet* come to mind) this vision of commonweal has tragic significance. As he sunders his kingdom into thirds Lear attempts to command "applause" from his daughters and counselors:

> Which of you shall we say doth love us most,
> That we our largest bounty may extend. . . .
>
> [1.1.53–54]

Deceived by the responses, he relinquishes his role as king. Before long he has begun to lose his sense of self. On the stormy heath, no longer "lord of anything," he rages against the corruption of the social bond and personal love: against false justice and his malicious daughters. His madness measures his dependence upon the forming powers of love. Without the possibility of applause (to use Ulysses' term) man is but the mad, naked "unaccommodated" animal ("the thing itself") Lear discovers isolated in the storm (3.4.100–108).

There is a mode of identity in Shakespeare which is opposite the one sketched so far. I am thinking of characters such as Prospero and Marina and the women of *The Winter's Tale*, who are "formed" not by consensus but by a mysterious inward (or transcendent) power. Though Bohemia conceives her a shepherdess, for example, Perdita instinctively behaves like a queen. Despite attempts to cast her as a whore in the brothel at Mytilene, Marina preserves her talismanic virginity and redeems depraved customers by the way. By mastering his exile and his art, Prospero withstands and apparently recreates the corrupted social order of Milan. Similarly Paulina transforms Leontes' aggressive delusion into penitent wonder. At root these figures have a magical potency; they are priestly. Creation for them is the exercise of spiritual influence, disciplined and informed by grace.[4] They bring new meanings into being, essentially by shaping the perceptions of others, as Paulina guides us to behold Hermione's Galatea-like rebirth from art.

Equally self-creating, albeit no models of virtue, are Shakespeare's fools. Anarchists of imagination, so Protean as to be virtually selfless, fools are exempt from social bonds even as their riddling discourse exceeds the laws of logic. Among those bearing a family resemblance to the fool are Falstaff, who proliferates roles for himself as fecklessly as he does foes in buckram,[5] and Autolycus, who exists on the vagabond outskirts of society as a trickster, a succession of disguises. Whether priestly or anarchic, then, these figures resist being "formed in the applause." Rather, they form the applause through their enigmatic potency, or manage to elude it.

These modes of identity are of course not dogmatic categories, but two opposed tendencies: a frame through which to look at a complex subject. In the plays and in individual characters these modes often conflict. In *The Winter's Tale* we saw them at least momentarily reconciled. For Hermione's return to life is theatrical in exactly the sense Ulysses proposes. She is conjured into being and confirmed in her "new" idealized nature by the beholders. At the same time it is clear that like Paulina, she has surrendered none of her integrity.

The following chapter explores the relation between creation and identity in an early play, *Love's Labour's Lost*, whose themes foreshadow later and more complex developments of Shakespeare's imagination.

IV. The Fierce Endeavor of Your Wit:
Living Art in *Love's Labour's Lost*

Like the poet of the Sonnets, the King of Navarre dreams of creating—in his own words—"living art." He opens *Love's Labour's Lost* with a spoken fiat, conjuring up a giddy hallucination of immortality:

> Let fame, that all hunt after in their lives,
> Live regist'red upon our brazen tombs,
> And then grace us in the disgrace of death;
> When, spite of cormorant devouring Time,
> Th' endeavor of this present breath may buy
> That honour which shall bate his scythe's keen edge,
> And make us heirs of all eternity.
> Therefore, brave conquerors—for so you are
> That war against your own affections
> And the huge army of the world's desires—
> Our late edict shall strongly stand in force:
> Navarre shall be the wonder of the world;
> Our court shall be a little Academe,
> Still and contemplative in living art.
>
> [1.1.1–14]

This sudden decree dictates a repudiation of life in order to transform it into immortal "living art." Ostensibly the scholars will withdraw from the world and the vicissitudes of emotion, into a daily regimen as rigid and imperative as the rhetorical structure of the edict itself. Mind will reign over all existence, determined to abolish all change and threats to its control by cultivating "still and contemplative" isolation. The courtiers will re-create themselves as "heirs of all eternity," destroying their old mortal selves in a "war against your own affections" and "the world's desires."

Despite its violent metaphors, the decree is in fact a rallying cry to self-intoxication.

As in magical thinking, the King makes a wish and the words embodying it appear to be as substantial as forces in the natural world. As a command, his edict enjoins the courtiers to live out the words of an oath originally willed by Navarre himself. That is, he manipulates his fellows as he would his "immortal" self. As his own sworn oath, and as an invocation to oaths, his edict serves not merely as a legal tool to engineer a future of "study," but also as the primary means of mobilizing the will to wishes.

Navarre behaves as if through "study" the courtiers can transmute themselves into the voice of "fame," which will somehow literally "live regist'red" in graven words. And as long as experience can be confined within the imagination, figurative and actual immortality can be kept indistinguishable. Consequently he diminishes the reality of the things he most fears by invoking them in his speech as arbitrary tropes which he can manage at will. Time he manipulates his fellows as he would his "immortal" self. As his clichéd icon, a "keen edge[d]" scythe. He exploits the ambiguous substantiality of metaphor, befuddling himself and his onstage audience. In the void of imagination he pits the perfunctory role of "brave conquerors" against the fantastic conception "the huge army of the world's desires," pronouncing a battle without conflict or loss, for an ordained, impossible victory. And so against the genteel projection of death as a "disgrace" he counterpoises "Th' endeavor of this present breath," the power of the spirit and "study," and the magical power of wishes too. For "this present breath" is also the edict itself, with its willful incantation "Let fame . . . live," and its repeated vow that

> Navarre shall be the wonder of the world;
> Our court shall be a little academe,
> Still and contemplative in living art.
>
> [12–14]

Insofar as men must create and choose their conceptions of the world, knowing is the experience of "living art." When men create unwisely, however, trying to "cast" themselves as the voice of eternal fame, for example, all their experience becomes artificial life, a host of disembodied and grotesque illusions.

To take such slender characters as Navarre and his courtiers too soberly would be unfair to the play. Yet through them Shakespeare does play out ideas and attitudes which are—however comic and fragile—by no means gratuitous. The play carries its debates even to the concluding song. And the fear of death which abets the King's opening speech is answered at the close by Marcade's untimely entry.[1]

The Sonnets provide one context in which to appreciate the comic wrong-headedness of the edict. Addressing his muse in Sonnet 100, the poet echoes the King's terms:

Give my love fame faster than Time wastes life;
So thou prevent'st his scythe and crooked knife.

Navarre's version of this desire for immortalizing art amuses us. Not love but vanity moves him. Like a species of love sonnet, only self-directed, the fame he conceives would celebrate him and his court to the audience of infinite posterity (the boast that "Navarre shall be the wonder of the world" exalts the King no less than his kingdom). Whereas the poet practises self-effacing negation to elicit magic, the courtiers would command it, yearning not to wonder, but rather to be wondered at.

Sympathize as we may with Navarre's anxiety about common life and death, his solution is unworkable. Far from transcendent, his imagination is merely aloof. As spectators we share a "common" imagination in watching the play. He must speak to us, although of course he cannot know that. Our common understanding will be mirrored onstage by the viewpoint of the ladies, who will also see the humor in the courtiers' self-obsession. The King's determination to live by force of will tyrannizes him and, as Costard reveals, his domain. Without a capacity for awe, his "living art" must deaden with familiarity what comes within its grasp. In the decree, for example, he makes death as banal as he does wonder—a matter of "disgrace," of social appearances. Made "common," death reflects the self-isolating and self-inflating character of the immortality breath "may buy."

The King's language details his wrong-willing. While he treats words as if they have static meanings, mastered absolutely, their implications often qualify or confute his intention. Fame, he says, may "grace" men. In his use "grace" has its root sense "to praise," but also suggests the superficiality of ornamentation and flattery: and appropriately, since here it designates not praise of God or being, but of self. Love has virtually no place in the speech at all. What Navarre and his followers desire is power, the sort of knowledge that first brought death and "dis-grace" to Eve and Adam. With fame to "grace" or flatter them they cheerfully aspire to be godlike.

The impiety of this wish has important disguises. Outwardly Ferdinand's sophistication belies any deep commitment to such grave business. Though the word of a king is in fact law, an air of lighthearted play obscures the issues of responsibility. Moreover, the edict is "graced" by logic. The formula "Let fame . . . " resembles the premise of a Euclidean proof. And logical connectives do follow in the eighth line's emphatic "therefore" and "for so you are." Yet at bottom the speech is a command, founded less on reason than on wishes. In the King's use, as we noticed, metaphors have a peculiarly corporeal quality. What's more, he defines his endeavor to suit himself. Neither love nor God, but fame he proclaims to be "that which all hunt after in their lives." By making all men appear accomplices to his own ambition, he makes his own aggrandizement look more justifiable and, ironically, more common. He initiates one of the fundamental situations of comedy, one man selfishly trying to legislate what is natural for all.

Insidiously, Ferdinand's solipsism tends to justify itself. By categorically devaluing common death and life, he nullifies the human community which makes opening oneself to time and fellowship supportable. As a result he must increasingly depend on his invented self, alienated from his own emotional resources. So that death looms the more fearful and, in a vicious circle, spurious immortality appears the more necessary. The King's solution, in short, is part of the problem.

It is a measure of Ferdinand's folly that he fails to realize himself even for us, let alone for all posterity. The more he labors to secure his identity indefeasibly, the more his words inadvertently efface him. We cannot finally ascertain where the King is in his speech. Given its ambiguous sophistication and motives, his rhetoric dissipates his own character. Peremptory definitions and contradictions undermine his ability to mean. Himself prolix, he nonetheless fancies his "living art" will be "still and contemplative." With implausible modesty he calls "the wonder of the world" a "little Academe" whose honor breath "may buy."

The boundless life the decree would dictate is paradoxically a dead form and a form of death. Seeking to be "mortified" (28), the courtiers undertake to play dead to the world and their mortal, desiring selves. Their vagueness as characters signifies not some deficiency in Shakespeare's art, but the comic consequences of their oath. In the pursuit of "things hid and barr'd . . . from common sense" (57) they obscure themselves.

Granted its different context, the King's wish for "study's godlike recompense" (58) resembles the "inordinate thirst for knowledge" through which "Prospero, like Adam, fell from his kingdom. . . ."[2] Prospero, we remember, was forced into exile, where he learned true knowledge and benign magic. Only thereafter, in a conclusion *The Tempest* merely points toward, could he renounce "rough magic" and return to life among men. At the close of *Love's Labour's Lost* the King exits to a "forlorn and naked hermitage" (5.2.796) for a penance which has a similar function to Prospero's exile. Afterward he too will perhaps return to life with "living art" behind him. The point is, both plays show us efforts to devise a reconciliation between knowing or art, and life among men. In neither play is the search actually concluded.

The Edict Objectified

The King's immediate opposite, the worldly Costard, first offends against the edict. As a clown, with no pretense to occult knowledge or authority, let alone to a coherent identity, he has been caught pursuing the "simplicity" of renegade and exuberant desire (1.1.213).

Shakespeare objectifies the King's posture in his law-enforcer, Dull, who acts out the will of the royal lawmaker in the physical world. Demanding to be shown "the duke's own person," he treats the agent of authority, the duke, as one divorced from his corporeal self—as the King in fact is. Dull goes on to muddle his explanation with a malapropism and the stuttering truncation of Armado's name. His "lawless" use of words points up his royal master's own abuse of them in the name of order and honor.

By parlaying the multiplistic sound-sense relations of words into double talk, Costard destroys his own confession of desire in the utterance, before the law-enforcers can literally pronounce him guilty. Since Navarre has made words the medium of all human action, Costard can stymie him by flaunting the customary rules of meaning. While the King tampers with those rules himself, he blithely assumes his subjects will respect them. Never acknowledging that men must agree to make words mean, he dictates oaths as if the ritual of swearing can magically ensure meaning. Unlike the courtiers, however, Costard resists such rules. To protect his supposedly guilty desires, he plays on the words "form" and "manner" until they, and the form and manner of his speech, turn to unmanageable chaos (1.1.204–10). Such deliberate obscurantism ironically comments on Navarre's glib manipulation of form and manner to perpetrate in his edict *his* improvident wishes. So too, as Ferdinand has done, Costard brashly hurls impertinent slogans about. Shouting "and God defend the right!" he invokes the defunct chivalric tradition of trial by combat. His cry burlesques a medieval style of magical thinking about justice.

As a creature of reckless wishes, Costard plays out an aspect of Navarre's nature. Like the Constable, he allows Shakespeare to give comic concreteness to Ferdinand's psychic energies. Together the clowns bring to visible conflict onstage a simple-minded will to order and a body of oppressed, antic desires. Still, the Constable and his charge pointedly lack one other attribute of the King's, his outsized, naive pride. Hence Armado's role.

Since the King has made words the medium of all action, Armado's accusation must be voiced for judgment to take place. His bombast flatters Ferdinand and himself as well, giving extravagant embodiment to the royal vanity. His letter begins with a preposterous fulfillment of the edict's wish for an immortality rivalling the gods'. The Spaniard inflates the sovereign as posthumous public fame might:

> "Great deputy, the welkin's viceregent, and sole dominator of Navarre, my soul's earth's God, and body's fost'ring patron—" [214–16] [3]

Striving to keep the complaint unarticulated and himself unjudged, Costard incidently exposes this impious gibberish by applying to it the criterion of exactness: "Not a word of Costard yet" (217). Self-preoccupied, pride readily confounds judgment.

The subsequent verbal skirmish is telling. When Ferdinand further declaims "So it is—'" and is once more interrupted, the aborted phrase sounds as if it means he fatuously vows the letter's flattery of him to be true (218). But these inept words which Armado puts in his patron's mouth, Costard instantly takes away. For quibbling on "so," he nullifies the word's integrity as a vow, and in a sentence which itself declares that "saying" a thing is so makes it "but so" or worth little:

It may be so; but if he say it is so, he is,
In telling true, but so.

[219-20]

When on a reflex Navarre turns to command "Peace!" Costard transforms the command into a harmless saw: "[Peace] be to me and every man that dares not fight." Forced to be more precise, Ferdinand cries "No words!" (223). In his desperation he reveals the despotism over language which his wishes depend on.[4]

Although patronizingly dubbed "this child of fancy," Armado merely recombines tatters of literary fashion in his letters. Witless euphuistic elaboration lends a superficial portentousness to every detail of the experience he reports. His pointlessly erudite rhetorical questions parody the King's and his own obsession with artificial control over life:

The time When? About the sixth hour; when beasts most graze, birds best peck, and men sit down to that nourishment which is called supper. So much for the time When. Now for the ground Which? which, I mean, I walked upon; it is ycleped thy park

and so on (224-370). Such a catechism trivializes what it would raise to importance. Its question-and-answer form suggests a mind divided against itself as well.

Armado behaves like an actor overcome by his heroic role, no longer able to tell life from play. Like Costard and clowns generally, he exists totally in the present, a changeless and in a way immortal "non-entity." Insofar as he exists by sheer mimicry of others, he resembles the parasitical rivals of whom the poet complains in Sonnet 78 ("every alien pen hath got my use"). While Costard has no concern for a social identity, by contrast, he has an integrity peculiar to fools. In his name-calling Armado "casts" Costard in one role after another—"that low-spirited swain, that base minnow," and so on—each time drawing from the Clown an incredulous "Me?" Only at the exact name "Costard" does the Clown claim himself, and then he does so with a significant comic outcry of feeling as well as confirmation: "Oh me!" (244).

In Shakespeare acceptance of the fool and the fool in oneself is usually a sign of wisdom. Not that Costard is a model citizen, however true to his feelings. Just as he hears yet ignores the law—"I do confess much of the hearing of it, but little of the marking of it" (266)—so he uses Jaquenetta while disregarding her as a person. Capriciously he redefines her as a "wench," "damsel," "virgin," "maid," and "a true girl." In effect, she is not an individual for him, merely an object of desire. While he celebrates the joys of the flesh, those joys seem to exclude love. Living out his impulses, acting out wishes, Costard cares little for communication with others. For his punishment, after all, he would rather "pray a month with mutton and porridge" than "fast a week with bran and water" (280–82). He mocks his own willingness to exploit words in a contrite "act" of prayer. But he also implicitly mocks the hypocrisy of the edict's deceptively pious prayer for glory. For used glibly, the sacramental words of a royal oath would be as insubstantial as a clown's prayer.

Berowne from Study to Love

Like the Princess, Berowne sees how untenable the edict is. Wary of self-preoccupation, he knows enough to inquire "the end of study" (55) and to warn that "necessity will make us all forsworn" (1.1.147). He is sufficiently aware of love's claims to twit the King:

> Study me how to please the eye indeed,
> By fixing it upon a fairer eye. . . .

[80–81]

At the same time he perceives how vacant Costard's promiscuity is. Like the Princess, he can play the fool yet is no fool. Unlike her, however, he has no alternative vision of life that might enable him to act on his insight. More than cynical about the decree, he is impotent to resist it. In a way he cannot live without it. His arguments against the oath move Navarre to reject him with mild parental scorn: "Well, sit you out. Go home, Berowne. Adieu" (110). Instantly and meekly Berowne capitulates. His decision comes as an unreasoned assertion, the product of unexamined feelings. He will stay,

confident I'll keep what I have swore,
And bide the penance of each three years' day.
Give me the paper, let me read the same,
And to the strictest decrees I'll write my name.
                                        [114–17]

From the sound of it, he feels compelled to beg to do what he knows to be unwise.

One source of Berowne's peculiar impotence lies in his relation to the King. By enacting the edict, Navarre's subjects assent to its creation of an "omnipotent" fantasy king. We see that Armado, Costard, and Dull give expression to aspects of the King's character. But the reverse is also true: as an apotheosis of himself the King would give form to his subjects' needs and wishes. Insofar as they live out his will in the edict, they participate in its re-creation of him as an avatar of the community. He incorporates them one and all. At the outset the action onstage derives entirely from his will. By regulating emotion and behavior, his dictates would shape all characters. As an actor-playwright might, he has "cast" his cohorts (and himself) as "brave conquerors—for so you are" in a struggle which becomes the play. And by acting out the edict's "plot," his subjects can live exempt from responsibility, passive yet secure. The more they invest him with authority, the less they need to labor toward autonomy themselves. The edict, that is, reflects the community's wish to have its order and being in the quasi-divine figure of the King (as in the ambiguity of the name "Navarre"). He would embody in the human sphere, and mediate, the forces which hold sway in the cosmos: a role parodied in Armado's epithets for him, "the welkin's viceregent" and "my soul's earth's God" (214–16). On one level, then, the play unfolds a myth about the transition of society from a magical orientation toward one based on personal autonomy and contractual social relationships. However, the myth is a tragicomic one inasmuch as death and perplexed responses to death finally arrest the transformation, casting doubt on its completion.[5]

Like a powerless son, Berowne wishes to be part of the King's paternal authority as well as to outgrow it. At first he tries to hide his irresolution in ambiguity. He would undermine the oath by playing at swearing to it, offering to recite it as an actor would his lines, without lasting commitment—"I can but say [the others'] protestation over" (33). He then wishfully tries to negate the oath's individual strictures by repeating each with the incantatory refrain "The which I hope well is not enrolled there" (37–46).

Held to the oath, he evades a confrontation as long as he can by playing the fool. He compounds word play and paradoxes to confound his auditors:

> If study's gain be thus, and this be so,
> Study knows that which yet it doth not know.
> Swear me to this, and I will ne'er say no.
>
> [67–69]

The repeated, indefinable demonstratives point to meanings which cannot be wholly grasped in the hearing. His riddling tantalizes us with a promise of revelations. Yet the oath he improvises is double talk meant to preempt the edict, and the King will have none of it. He goes on to bring out the solipsism of "study":

> Too much to know is to know nought but fame;
> And every godfather can give a name.
>
> [92–93]

"Fame" he seems to mean in the old sense of "rumor" or "report." Plodders after truth only know the names they prodigally scatter: names or conceptions which are no closer to the things they designate than rumor is. Fame is a body of dead artifacts. For his part, Berowne would not be a godfather but a lover, a true progenitor.

Although he seems to side with common sense, Berowne nevertheless waxes ecstatic about Neoplatonic courtly love as "the end of study." Woman he envisages as "a fairer eye" which orients the lover's mind in its benighted subjectivity: "that eye shall be his heed/And give him light that it was blinded by" (82–83). He imagines a relation with women as utterly absorbing and otherworldly as the scholars' relation to study. Like the King, Berowne yearns to be magically transformed, but by love.

When stricken, Berowne resembles the poet of the Sonnets, abjuring "painted rhetoric" and vowing his beloved "passes praise" (4.3.235–37). Love he construes as a creative force:

> From women's eyes this doctrine I derive . . .
> They are the books, the arts, the academes,
> That show, contain, and nourish, all the world,
> Else none at all in aught proves excellent.
>
> [4.3.346–50]

In Sonnet 112 the poet's voice could be Berowne's. "You are all my world," he vows, and concludes:

> You are so strongly in my purpose bred,
> That all the world besides methinks are dead.

If they referred to study, these lines could speak for the King at the opening of the play. Berowne, by comparison, locates the all-consuming power of the spirit in love rather than fame.

The Princess and the Limits of Play

With the arrival of the Princess and her ladies love triumphs. The courtiers behold; they succumb. As in a masque like *Proteus*, the potency of virtue appears self-sufficient, ordained, a function of the dramatic form. It is the nature of comedies that those who scorn love should fall lovesick. Yet the close of *Love's Labour's Lost* is, like the play's title, puzzling. And so the ladies' ascendency deserves a closer look.

Although the edict proposes to "war against . . . affections," Berowne's ecstatic speeches show us that transfiguring study has much in common with transfiguring love. Both mobilize the self in an intensely willed, revelatory experience. Love for Berowne is not a physical reflex as Costard argues it: "Such is the simplicity of man to hearken after the flesh" (1.1.212–13). Nor is it consensus or mutuality, as it is for the Princess. Rather, as the middle action of the play discloses, love for the courtiers is a self-intoxicating invention, an exuberant flight of imagination.

As strangers from a foreign land who cannot be admitted into the kingdom proper, the women have the force of repressed energies coming finally into consciousness. Negotiating on behalf of a dying royal father, with a king who declares himself dead to the world, the Princess shows herself able to initiate action. With her ladies she stirs her hosts to life as well. From this standpoint she prefigures the emblematic women of the late romances, especially *The Winter's Tale*.

Like the women of the romances, the Princess encourages social communion, responding to the courtiers' oath as a challenge. The men would isolate themselves, forbidding any woman to approach the court "on pain of losing her tongue" (1.1.123), whereas from the outset the Princess "Importunes personal conference" (2.1.32). In time she will direct the subversion of the suitors' Muscovite masque in an effort to purge their relations of manipulative artifice.

At the same time, and again like the heroines of the romances, the Princess evinces an indefinable potency. From the first she is in control of events; she presides over the action. Although she would foster communication, she is personally independent, even rather inaccessible. In her initial encounter with the King, for example, she uses some of the fool's strategies to perplex and direct her host:

King.   Fair Princess, welcome to the court of Navarre.
Princess.   "Fair" I give you back again; and "welcome" I have not
            yet. . . .
King.   You shall be welcome, madam, to my court.
Princess.   I will be welcome then; conduct me thither.
                                                    [90–95]

Their meeting is a contest of wills. Yet Shakespeare takes pains that her motives appear not shrewish and self-aggrandizing, but modest. Where the edict would subjugate love and time by sheer force of will, the Princess acts to keep values and motives ungraspable.

When the Princess is first introduced, the play provides us a telling insight into her nature. Boyet compliments her "dear grace," and she reminds him that praise is a relation and not an artifact: not dead conventions of flattery, but conventions as a "coming together" of eyes and minds. "Though but mean," she instructs him, her beauty

> Needs not the painted flourish of your praise.
> Beauty is bought by judgment of the eye,
> Not utt'red by base sale of chapmen's tongues.
>   [14–16]

Much as the courtiers would be knowing in order to "buy" honor (1.1.5), Boyet praises her beauty in order "to be counted wise." But beauty cannot be given expression by self-serving words ("utt'red by base sale"); it can be gained or realized only by judgment of the eye. One meaning of "bought" seems to be its old

sense of "redeemed" or "ransomed"—the eye's discernment redeems or liberates beauty. The word play sharpens the crucial
distinction in the passage, between false grasping and wordless
appreciation or praise.[6] We recall the importance of this contrast
in the Sonnets. In Sonnet 83 the poet begins, "I never saw that
you did painting need," and adds:

> For I impair not beauty, being mute,
> When others would give life, and bring a tomb.

"All pride," the Princess tells Boyet, "is willing pride" (2.1.36).
And she acts on this principle.

In their first repartee about the oath the Princess and her host
match wills. It is she who breaks off to begin serious business:

> But pardon me, I am too sudden bold;
> To teach a teacher ill beseemeth me.
>
> [106-7]

While she mocks the King's pretensions to immortalizing knowledge, she questions her own willfullness too. Her irony begs
reconsideration of both their roles. The point is developed in
subsequent sallies between Berowne and Katherine (113-27).
When Berowne tries to control the lady's response by a question
calling for a predictable answer ("Did I not dance with you in
Brabant once?"), she thwarts him by mimicking him. Her echo
asserts dancing to have been as much her initiative as his. When in
retaliation he chides her sharp wit and inadvertently her liveliness
("You must not be so quick"), she counters that he wants merely
to subdue her as he would a spirited mount. Forcing the joke,
justifying himself, he calls her wit "too hot." And again she parries
him, playing on words to set free wit and "leave the rider in the
mire." By now unseated, thrown into the mire of commonplaces,
Berowne is reduced to asking "What time o' day?" He has failed to
heed his own just warning that it requires not "might" but
"special grace" to master "affects" (1.1.150).

The ritual hunt in Act Four raises the problem of mastery in the
wider context of nature. Guided by the Forester, and herself a
symbol of governance, the Princess must enact the power of the
human order over wild or extra-rational life. However her dialogue
with the Forester exists largely that she may clearly abjure self-
aggrandizement. In terms which recall and criticize the edict, she
argues that the craving for

> Glory grows guilty of detested crimes,
> When, for fame's sake, for praise, an outward part,
> We bend to that the working of the heart;
> As I for praise alone now seek to spill
> The poor deer's blood that my heart means no ill.
>
> [4.1.31–35]

Praise and the heart she puts in dire opposition, although she allows neither extreme to dominate her. She refuses merely to follow her feelings or to please others. Rather she tries to accommodate the conflict by playing. Her voice scorns yet wistfully accepts the necessity to "play the murderer" (8) by joining the hunt. When Boyet teases her for resembling a shrewish wife who domineers her spouse "Only for praise," she eludes the charge by playfully contending that "any lady that subdues a lord" has earned her praise (36–40).

Because of her unusual insight, the Princess is the focus of conflicts which would otherwise go unheeded. Yet she has no positive role through which she can act to harmonize discord. For example, she deems the rider who has driven his horse "hard against" the "uprising" of a hill "a mounting mind" (1–5). Her puns recall the mind's arrogance in the edict (the rider she conjectures "was the king"). Her word play enables her to give some perspective to the antagonism between mind and "uprising" nature, even as these same forces are clashing at last in the love-smitten courtiers. Though she recognizes the contradictions in the souls about her, however, she holds aloof from action, ironical and observant. She cannot reconcile the mounting mind and nature, any more than she is able to achieve a truly "personal conference" with her host. The most profound communication, she knows, is the wordless "judgment of the eye." Yet she cannot give that spiritual action any palpable social expression. She inspires love, yet love fails to find a convincing tongue within the play.

Love Mad and Laboured

The courtiers react to Cupid's sting by redirecting their original labors at "living art." They become poets of love, incantatory and ecstatic. Rosaline has already portrayed Berowne as a sort of Orphic storyteller whose words have cast spells over young and old alike (2.1.69–76). Ironically Rosaline would ravish *her* listeners with praise of Berowne's "gracious words" in the same way she fancies those words have ravished *their* audience—a moment's infatuation which the Princess chastens ("such bedecking ornaments of praise").

Even "mad as Ajax" with passion, Berowne keeps his experience a matter of words. His aristocratic verse has collapsed into the discourse of fools: prose that wanders in circles of word associations. Vainly swearing he "will not love" despite his feelings, he has lost touch with himself. Now he is "coursing" or chasing himself. Halfway through this "mad" speech, however, he redefines himself as a lover, forswearing one absolute oath to engage another: "By heaven, I do love" (4.3.12). Immediately he begins inventing new hierarchies to replace those the edict had supplied. To reorder the self unruly passion has upset, he self-consciously plays at being the fool:

> she hath one of my sonnets already. The clown bore it, the fool sent it, the lady hath it—sweet clown, sweeter fool, sweetest lady! [14–16]

By labeling himself a fool, Berowne conventionalizes new experience which otherwise would confound him. Shakespeare's wise fools accept foolishness as a natural dimension of all lives. Having no factitious social selves to protect, and no pride, they need not and *cannot* "seem" as a rule. Berowne, on the other hand, uses the role of fool to resist wonder. When he later adopts the posture of demigod to spy on "wretched fools' secrets," he makes the name "fool" a scornful tag: a smug gesture which soon enough turns to mock him (4.3.74–76).

In their rhapsodies about love the courtiers parody the magical strategies of Shakespeare's own sonnets. For they grasp after self-dramatizing effects, with none of the "negative capability" we find in the Princess and in the Sonnets themselves. Ferdinand conjures in verse a routinely disdainful courtly beloved of such incomparable worth that "No thought can think, nor tongue of mortal tell" it. After imperiously legislating women away, suddenly he is abject and his beloved "triumphing in my woe" (31).

His fantasy culminates in a wish to drop his art among the leaves in hopes it will reach his beloved and speak for him.

How shall she know my griefs? I'll drop the paper.
Sweet leaves, shade folly. Who is he comes here?[7]

[38–39]

As in the edict, his impulse is to reinvent himself as a apotheosis
(the ideal king, the consummate lover) then to abandon that self
to be cherished by others, whether one beloved or all posterity, in
a sort of transcendence. What clinches the absurdity of the fantasy
is his effort to avoid wholehearted commitment. By "sweet leaves,
shade folly" he means to hide his passion from his fellows.

In his sonnet Longaville also makes love a verbal operation
(56–67). Reversing the terms of the edict to free himself from it,
he vows that being forsworn wins new "grace" which "cures all
disgrace" in him. Instead of vowing immortal meanings, he now
vows words "but breath, and breath a vapor is." Transfixed by his
wishes, he cannot appreciate the hilarious futility of an immortal
scholar trying to make all words meaningless by using meaningful
words. No more does he consider that if his sonnet is true, and his
love absolving, then he need not hide from Dumaine.

For us, such speech is pure spectacle, worthless yet dazzling.
Because we are demigods whose understanding in this play-within-
a-play exceeds even Berowne's, we can afford the courtiers some
sympathy and admiration as well as laughter. From our vantage
point of audience community, for the moment at least, the scene's
meaning appears conventionally secure. It flatters us as benevolent
omniscient judges. Confident of our existence, we laugh when
Dumaine wishes himself "the heaven's breath." Like the others, he
identifies with the divine "breath" or Word, and yet in another
sense he is already comically windy (97–116). As in the edict
("Th' endeavor of this present breath"), Dumaine's yearning to
"triumph" over the natural world is a will to lose himself in words.
And while he protests that for his beloved Jove "would deny
himself for Jove,/Turning mortal," the joke is that Dumaine more
desperately than ever denies himself in hopes of being transcendent.

Love induces a common will in the courtiers. Dumaine prayer-
fully implores "O that I had my wish" (88), and the others' echoes
of his cry climax in Berowne's "Amen . . . Is that not a good
word?" (90) As a result, the friends' subsequent hypocrisy toward
one another reminds us that the edict's "living art" has led to
tampering with language and deception. Each of the lovers impersonates one of the edict's "brave conquerors," and scourges the

others. Though Berowne has been more consciously a player than the others from the start, even he tries to preserve his righteous pose to the end. He bids the King "dismiss this audience" before he will confess (206). The command is absurdly wishful: the onstage spectators can be ordered away, but we remain. And we laugh at this last effort to deny the multiple perspectives of play.

During this scene the courtiers begin to learn that like language, identity is not static and absolute, but a dynamic relation between living personalities. When Berowne betrays his guilt by shredding the telltale, love-letter, Longaville rightly concludes: "It did move him to passion, and therefore let's hear it" (198). Acting on the discrepancy between Berowne's visible "passion" and his depiction of the letter as "a toy," Longaville exposes the truth.

Although they begin relating emotions to behavior, the scholars never fully unlearn their old prejudices in the play. Nevertheless, the question which must have prompted the edict in the first place—how shall a man live?—becomes vital once again. With a cry Berowne discovers the importance of consensus to meaning: "O let us embrace" (210). Henceforth the friends begin exploring new modes of conceiving love.

At first they attempt in a public forum what each had labored to accomplish in isolation, the magical perfection of their loves and beloveds. Their conjurations rapidly become a magnificently ridiculous contest. Responding to the King's taunts, Berowne celebrates his lady in increasingly dissociated, absurd terms ("O wood divine!"); he begs to take a new, impossible oath to verify his words (244–48). At last the old habits lead to monstrous and hilarious excess:

> O, if the streets were paved with thine eyes,
> Her feet were much too dainty for such tread.
>
> [274–75]

What saves them is the King's interjection: "But what of this? Are we not all in love?" (278). Reasserted, consensus brings them back to the pursuit of a new art of living to replace the edict's "living art."

The next endeavor, Berowne's justification of women and re-creation of the oath, does advance their search. His litany reenacts the edict, but with new and liberating meaning (285–361). As he has before (1.1.67–69), and as Costard and the ladies have done, Berowne plays the fool to undo tyrannical strictures. "Consider," he begins, "what you first did swear unto" (4.3.287). Whereupon he conjures a new vision, not of fame but of love. In his peroration he compounds paradoxes and riddling word play to keep the oath he is creating ungraspable:

> Then fools you were these women to forswear;
> Or, keeping what is sworn, you will prove fools.
> For wisdom's sake, a word that all men love;
> Or for Love's sake, a word that loves all men;
> Or for men's sake, the authors of these women;
> Or women's sake, by whom we men are men. . . .
>
> [351–56]

Redirecting energies the edict elicited, his incantation urges the lovers to embrace his resonant yet indefinable "doctrine" of love.[8] The edict's opening fiat he echoes in a plea for cooperation and openness:

> Let us once lose our oaths to find ourselves,
> Or else we lose ourselves to keep our oaths.
>
> [357–58]

This new oath commands not a war against desire and the self, but a search for self. It means what it does not because of rigid (if ultimately arbitrary) laws, but because his listeners *feel* assent to it. In this light the doctrine not only integrates the courtiers' selves, bringing mind and emotion together for a moment, but also joins them as a group.

Berowne's litany construes women as a creative force. They arouse the lover to surpass himself, mobilizing Eros to overcome the prison of self-obsession that fame would be. "Temp'red with Love's sighs," the poet's lines would "plant in tyrants mild humility"—which is of course what Berowne's poetry is even now doing to the King (343–45). For love "lives not immured in the brain," but brings into play all the resources of experience; it "gives to every power a double power" (323–28).

Like the lovers, we are meant to be charmed or "ravished" (344) by this glorious harangue. Yet Shakespeare gives us cause for reservations too. For though Berowne labors to exorcise the spell of fame and integrate women into his imagination, in the end his doctrine of love is still magical. To be sure, he has passed beyond the limits of the edict and the lovers' fatuous sonnets. In his use of irony and riddling word play he creates the possibility of wonder. Even in his sly use of religious precepts ("And who can sever love

from charity?'') the playfulness in his voice complicates his meaning, making his lyricism more than merely expedient or self-intoxicating. We may wish to respond to this speech as we do to the
more magical of Shakespeare's sonnets, feeling love the living
"word that loves all men." But we would have to keep in mind the
ambivalence toward magical thinking in the Sonnets as a whole.

In Berowne's doctrine women take the place of immortality as a
goal sought. They are not yet mortal, let alone sexual, and have no
claims to communication and mutality. Instead

> They are the ground, the books, the academes,
> From whence doth spring the true Promethean fire.
> [299–300]

Whether offered by fame or women, "true Promethean fire" is a
perilous blessing. Apart from the fate of Prometheus himself, the
yearning for godlike knowledge precipitated Adam's fall from
grace to abject self-consciousness. And so while the courtiers come
closer to life by seeking out the ladies at last, they do have a trick
of the old rage for glory yet.

No sooner does Berowne finish than the metaphor of conquest
reappears. The King rallies the courtiers to play "soldiers in a war
not "against your own affections" but for love. Longaville interrupts to advocate "plain-dealing" (336). The term suggests plain
talk, but also a business transaction—a meaning Berowne bluntly
elaborates:

> Light wenches may prove a plague to men forsworn;
> If so, our copper buys no better treasure.
> [381–82]

Turned practical, Berowne fears as "light wenches" the women he
has earlier idealized as celestial lights (1.1.77–87). Love he would
buy as the edict would "buy . . . honor" (5). Subsequently during
the masque the King negotiates with Rosaline about buying the
ladies' company (5.2.224–26). Trade and "treasure" suggest prostitution—and comically, inasmuch as the lovers lack both the
courage and the compliant women necessary for action. In fact
their desire to buy love betrays their continued craving for control
and emotional dissociation.

As in the Sonnets, Berowne's exaltation of women has a fearful
counterpoint. The poet dreads his beloved's "sensual faults";
Berowne worries that women may prove "light" or promiscuous.[9]
Having courted imaginative omnipotence, the courtiers turn to

mundane reality with a heightened fear of inconstancy. Hence they resort to the formal art of the masque to present and safeguard themselves.

Labours Lost as a Challenge to Play

Costumed as Muscovites, the lovers hide not only from the ladies, but from themselves too. The second sonnet of Sidney's *Astrophel and Stella* tellingly defines their strategy ("and now like slave-born *Muscovite*, / I call it praise to suffer Tyrannie"). Like the pageant of Worthies, which realizes in grotesque parody the consequences of the edict's bid for everlasting fame, demonstrating the sort of life supposedly immortal words confer upon the famous dead, the masque of Muscovites perpetuates the tyrannical yearning for glory. The Princess recognizes the suitors' arrogance: "They do it but in mockery merriment" (5.2.139). She would retaliate against the masks for preventing communication:

> Their several counsels they unbosom shall
> To loves mistook and so be mocked withal.
> [141–42]

Like Costard withstanding the edict, the ladies parry the Muscovites until the "shallow shows" are expended. They bring the posers closer to authentic feeling and expression: "The King was weeping-ripe for a good word" (274). As in the masque of *Proteus*, the ladies win by their self-conscious awareness of playing and its limits. As Rosaline indicates, the men have tried to use play for smug, self-defeating ends. They were "fools . . . disguised like Muscovites in shapeless gear" (303). Since "shape" is a synonym for "actor," "shapeless" implies that the masquers trapped themselves in their own "gear" (their costumes, but also the traditional word for the Vice's strategems). Once again they have been calculating in play. Only by losing the self can a man play convincingly. In the end Costard "proves the best Worthy" (557) because he gracefully declines to take himself seriously:

> It pleased them to think me worthy of Pompey the Great.
> For mine own part, I know not the degree of the Worthy, but
> I am to stand for him. [504–6]

Returning unmasked and chastened to seek "one word" (313), Navarre acknowledges meaning as consensus. Spurned by the Princess's wit, he begs her to "construe my speeches better, if you may" (341). Berowne in turn tries to achieve spontaneity, but his pledge to be natural bristles with histrionic vehemence (394–415). His surrender is imperious ("Cut me to pieces with thy wit") and rash. Promising to present himself hereafter only by "honest" art, shunning "speeches penned" and "taffeta phrases," he trips by renouncing ostentation with the ostentatious fillip "sans." Now, however, he does recognize his compulsion, and humbly asks for patience: "Yet I have a trick / Of the old rage. Bear with me, I am sick" (416–17). Relaxing his will, he finally allows women a natural voice: "Speak for yourselves. My wit is at an end" (430).

So the courtiers confess their deceptions, and begin to find out what is *not* true. In a conventional comedy insight and intimacy would follow. Instead the clowns' crude pageant takes the stage, then a message of death. The pageant permits the courtiers openly to exorcise vainglorious pretension akin to the edict's. For joined by the ladies, in a spirit of play, they confront and clarify their own preposterous dream when witnessing the rout of the "immortal" Worthies. They learn to applaud the likes of Costard, who accepts his foolish mortality and cannot be discomfited. Holofernes, pretense personified, they drive out of role, into dramatic oblivion. Armado survives their harrassment with Falstaffian vigor largely because he *is* the storm of antic bombast he pretends to be.

The pageant's demise coincides with the entrance of Marcade and death. From the beginning the characters have played out roles and conceptions of the world whose failure draws them closer to freedom of action. With the negation of the pageant's hapless "immortalizing" art, the playworld appears to approach autonomy. For while the souls onstage are banishing illusions in a spirit of mirth, they will shortly have to begin creating new roles for themselves. The intrusion of death challenges all order; it confirms life's awful indeterminacy.

Form Confounded as Living Art

The plot culminates, then, in a moment of potentiality, a glimpse of wonder. Marcade's "tale" of death forces yet frees the characters to conceive things anew. At this juncture we might expect the lyrical mode of the play to turn freely dramatic, with a more spontaneous interaction of voices. Yet sacrifice and penitential solitude prevail. Love finds no role within the play. In part the explanation lies in the demands and limits of Shakespeare's dramatic form at this period. To impose marriages would conventionalize and falsify the play. Dictating such a conclusion Shakespeare would be as tyrannical as the edict, taking life from the play. As it is, the ending ironically forms a sort of "living art" from the apparently confounded form of the whole play.

In terms which recall the play's title and themes, as if anticipating death's arrival, the Princess has championed the Worthies' pageant:

> That sport best pleases that doth least know how;
> Where zeal strives to content, and the contents
> Dies in the zeal of that which it presents.
> Their form confounded makes most form in mirth,
> When great things laboring perish in their birth.
>
> [5.2514-18]

The certain failure of enthusiastic ambition, she says, will evoke redeeming mirth. Indirectly she is reproving the "Muscovites" for their deceptive "sport," but her lines have yet a deeper significance.

Initially the Princess sought "personal conference." She seemed to value consensus. Love, however, she has believed inexpressible, a "judgment of the eye" rather than a social relationship. For her the truest communication is presumably beyond words, "the heart's still rhetoric" (2.1.229). In the passage above, as in her conception of love, there is a magical assumption that the will which "strives" to "know" or "content" others will have its grasp confounded. Like those who "inherit heaven's graces" in Sonnet 94, she holds herself aloof from worldly action and mutability. For those who behold, negation ("form confounded") can paradoxically be a creative act ("makes most form in mirth"). The Princess advocates the power of renunciation, of letting go. To the "judgment of the eye," worldly effort is ever an imperfect strife.

"All pride is willing pride," the Princess has chided, and this premise figures widely in the play. The edict would use self-sacrifice to win glory. Let the scholars give up their lives to study, and posterity will love them into immortality. At various times the friends wish themselves transformed into "the heaven's breath" or

Muscovites in order to win love. Consistently characters sacrifice themselves as if love or magic will grant them new identities and extraordinary fulfillment. At times the wish appears ridiculous, and yet the women are subject to self-sacrifice too.

Anticipating Marcade's revelation ("Dead, for my life!") the Princess reveals how much her father, the old king, has held sway in her thoughts. She responds strongly, with a hint of clairvoyance. Closely considered, the Princess's outcry also means "He is dead that I might live" or "He is dead because I live." This stroke of characterization has some of the complexity of later comedies. Anxiety about a new lover who must usurp her father's place in her heart—a recurring conflict in Shakespeare—would explain why the Princess decrees the penance which arrests the play. She behaves as if her father's death is a sacrifice for or because of her, and she must make an expiatory sacrifice of her own. Otherwise, were courtship undertaken, she would believe herself betraying her father. She acts, we might say, to disarm "dangerous" emotions, chastening both her lover and herself. Bereft of her childhood identity, now a "new-sad soul" (5.2.719), she can no longer "understand" the suitors (740), let alone contemplate a "world-without-end bargain" such as marriage (777).

The Princess embodies qualities we may associate with the heroines of the late romances, yet she lacks their uncanny power to reconcile and actualize values. Like Perdita or Paulina, say, she bespeaks what Berowne has called "special grace." But she cannot enact it. The ineffable "judgment of the eye" remains incommensurate with "common" sense and sensuality. The heart cannot freely speak; the lovers never do escape the confines of the park. Within the play there is no beneficent magic which can create harmony.

Yet magical thinking *does* shape the play's conclusion. For the edict is ironically fulfilled, but in a manner the conjuring scholars never imagined. From this standpoint, the oath-takers are chastened for their presumptions to powers beyond themselves.[10] In the end, as the edict specified, Navarre *is* touched by "wonder," and the King does embark upon an "austere insociable life" of meditation and study. And where the edict sought to manipulate posterity and thereby time itself, now a ghostly parent manages the will of his child—his genetic posterity—and the future.[11] For the Princess must become the ruler her father was, and the old king has attained a sort of immortality. Subject to a will she cannot argue against, the Princess moves with grieved reluctance to shut her "woeful self up in a mourning house" (796). But ultimately the old king's fate bears upon all those onstage. To become substantial, shadowy selves need the light of human community and self-expression. Yet the play envisions a year of solitary silence, and at best a "challenge" thereafter. Only Berowne is partially excepted.

From his first expedient oath-taking to his dubiously eloquent defense of "honest plain words" (741–64), Berowne combines imaginative vitality with the cynicism of a word-monger. And so Rosaline levies upon him a penance which has a desperate reconciliation as its goal. Hitherto he has brandished a cruel wit which he has been wont to "execute," like a despot, "on all estates /That lie within [his] mercy" (833–34). Rosaline would redirect

> the fierce endeavor of your wit
> To enforce the painèd impotent to smile

> [841–42]

Berowne must try to open his aloof and mocking wit to sympathy and grace. Like death in the edict, he has "disgraced" and degraded his victims. To live up to his penance he will have to transcend mockery and glib philosophy, and surpass even the bland consolation the King has offered the Princess (728–39). He would have to become a serious clown, a jesting priest, asserting community and meaning at the dire verge of life.

In its more complex way the play—which "doth not end like an old play" (862)—also seeks to pass beyond the "idle scorns" of a conventional comedy. As the characters reach a moment of potentiality, so the play's form disrupts the bounds of predictable comedy. To this extent the play moves toward wonder. Unlike *The Winter's Tale*, it is not overtly magical in its effects, yet magical thinking does influence its form. Shakespeare celebrates what love is not, depicting it obliquely. He repeatedly negates conventional conceptions in order to imply a truer love, a more authentic reality. But insofar as he proceeds by negation, mocking inadequacy, his wit is apt to resemble Berowne's. "To move wild laughter in the throat of death" is impossible (856). Yet the "fierce endeavor" of wit to engage life and death is in a sly sense what motivates the play's conclusion. Were Jack to get Jill, love's labors and the play itself would be trifles, expediently contrived to please its spectators' escapist fancies.

Still, the play *is* a play. Lest we become too moral or somber in our responses, the final song draws us toward wonder. Playing both the lyrical Apollo and Mercury, patron of crooks, Shakespeare beguiles us away from any complacent resolution to our feelings.[12] The awe which death has wrought turns into a song in praise of being. And the more we appreciate the song, the more we discover a lively deception, full of irony and mystery.

The play issues not in praise of fair ladies or glorious heroes (as the edict would), but in a ditty "compiled in praise of the owl and the cuckoo" (873). Though it purports to celebrate spring and winter, seasons of birth and death, love and loss, the song's icons are the ignominious cuckoo, with its oddly ominous "word of fear," and the owl, whose traditionally morbid voice is touted as "a merry note."

Unlike the play, the song announces itself as natural and even "common," as concrete and therefore trustworthy as the names of the flowers it lists. Neither its art nor its subjects betray any pretension. Yet it is a mocking song. Piping about the cuckold, whose clutching at love by locking up his wife traditionally confounds him, the song warns of the frailty of the human order. The laws of wedlock are not immutable. Winter in turn baffles our apprehension with prospects of food and a communal fire made cherishable by the cold. The refrain gives homely yet sympathetic life to the epithetical Joan that Berowne abused (4.3.178).

What does the song have to tell us about creation? Implicitly it mocks the aristocrats' wishful grasping. Power is transitory; acceptance—the readiness—is all. Sensuous and irreducible in all its ironies, the song mocks efforts to manipulate life. At the same time it gives the lie to polite pastoralism, mocking as well as praising "common" life, so that acceptance appears as a demanding activity, not an easy consolation.

In the song creation is selfless, then, not a triumph of wit or art, but a merging of human and natural energies. The flowers "do paint" the meadows, just as their names recreate them for us in the mind's eye.[13] Shepherds pipe, and maidens bleach their own versions of "lady-smocks all silver-white." Like the whipster of false love Berowne might have been, the cuckoo "mocks married men," a comic satirist. As an avatar of the poet-king as moralist and edict-maker, the parson prattles on unheeded amid the hubbub of winter colds. And the "staring owl," all-seeing and immobile, alert in the darkness which frames mortal life, gives out an Orphic note.

The created world itself creates. To recall the distinction Ulysses makes, men are "formed" not inwardly and autonomously, but by forces beyond themselves. In truth, in *Love's Labour's Lost* virtually none of the characters are able to play out wise personal action *within* the playworld. That challenge is pointedly deferred.

And yet the play does begin a search for new creative forms, both in the characters and in the dramatic structure. With Marcade's epiphany, the Muscovites' and Worthies' demise opens up the artificial world of the park and the play itself, as if Shakespeare is determined to show us he knows much that he cannot yet express in the theater. And the conclusion's art reveals not only limitations in Shakespeare's craft, but possible resources too. For he has begun to make parody (in the pageant and song) and manipulated perspectives (in the radical shift in viewpoint which Marcade introduces) means of transcending mere artifice.[14] So, too, the characters at last nearly cease to be types. The Princess finally acts in a manner that asks us for deeper psychological insight. Coming as the play itself is opening up, the inklings of complex motivation in her complement the expansive mysteries of the final song. We are left to sustain in the song's ironical equilibrium all the discords and possibilities raised before us, brought to wonder. Knowing the whole of Shakespeare's career, we can appreciate both the limited scope of that wonder and the greater developments which it foretells.

V. A Rite to Bay the Bear: Creation and Community in *A Midsummer Night's Dream*

Love's Labour's Lost celebrates no marriages. "That's too long," sighs Berowne, "for a play." In the end Shakespeare leaves the conflicts of the play suspended in the lyrical debate of Spring and Winter. The following two chapters examine *A Midsummer Night's Dream* and *Romeo and Juliet*, contemporary plays which do give love dramatic form and time to develop. But while both plays include marriages, one issues in a magical blessing, the other in fatal catastrophe. Rather than speculate about dates and the influence of one play upon the other, I wish to look at them as divergent resolutions of the arrested action of *Love Labour's Lost:* opposing visions which lead, respectively, through the great comedies and tragedies to the tragicomic art of the late romances.

Let me briefly sketch the unrealized conclusion toward which *Love's Labour's Lost* moves. Marriage would join the courtiers and the ladies, but their two kingdoms also. In the marriage of Jaquenetta and Armado it would bring together within Navarre common and noble estates. A union might also integrate spirit and flesh, magical thinking and "common" sense. Hopefully, as in the first group of the Sonnets, the conception of children would reconcile the courtiers' initial dread of love and death.

While the play shows us characters groping toward such a conclusion, the question underlying the edict—How shall a man live?—goes unanswered. With his plays on "labour" and "living art" Shakespeare emphasizes that such a union must be created. And the courtiers do improvise one approach to life after another: a vatic edict, sonnets, a masque, courtly palaver. But at length, as they begin to escape from artifice, "the scene begins to cloud" and death suspends their efforts. Ironically the play's "living art" turns out to be the song which teases and consoles and beguiles us.

A Rite to Bay the Bear

Why do love's labours go unfulfilled? Within the play the answer seems to be anxiety. From the edict to the closing penances, we meet dread in many comic guises. Death and love both threaten men with loss of self, and that threat may encourage magical thinking, a will to conjure imaginative omnipotence or immortalizing love. As we saw in the Sonnets, however, transcendent love may lead the poet toward self-intoxication and, in Sonnet 35, self-corruption. In *Love's Labours Lost* there is no form—no form of behavior, and no dramatic form—which can reconcile belief in "the heart's still rhetoric" (2.1.229) and the need for "personal conference." There is no language, no "living art," which can be both wondrously ineffable and consensually precise. Love remains either an inexpressible "judgment of the eye" or a debased, promiscuous sport. The play's "living art" may allow us a moment of awe, but it can make no marriages; the ritual efficacy of *The Winter's Tale* lies far in the future. In *A Midsummer Night's Dream*, where "Jack shall have Jill" and "nought shall go ill," Shakespeare's command of ritual make a decisive advance.

Love, Reason, and the Lurking Bear

A Midsummer Night's Dream reformulates the problematical relation between reason and magical thinking. The play grants each mode of experience its proper sphere, city and wilderness. Almost at the outset the lovers pass out of Athens into the wilds of imagination, where Oberon's magic reigns. They return with a new openness, and a muddled but profound sense of wonder. As Hippolyta concludes, "'Tis strange, my Theseus, that these lovers speak of" (5.1.1). Here is part of the reasonable Duke's well-known reply:

> I never may believe
> These antique fables, nor these fairy toys.
> Lovers and madmen have such seething brains,
> Such shaping fantasies, that apprehend
> More than cool reason ever comprehends.
> The lunatic, the lover, and the poet,
> Are of imagination all compact. . . .
> The poet's eye, in a fine frenzy rolling,

98

Doth glance from heaven to earth, from earth to
    heaven;
And as imagination bodies forth
The forms of things unknown, the poet's pen
Turns them to shapes, and gives to airy nothing
A local habitation and a name.
Such tricks hath strong imagination
That if it would but apprehend some joy,
It comprehends some bringer of that joy;
Or in the night, imagining some fear,
How easy is a bush suppos'd a bear?

                             [5.1.2–22]

Secure in his palace, ignorant of the fairy world, Theseus gently belittles those who have experienced a midsummer night's dream. And because our "shaping fantasies" are rapt in the play's illusion even now, his criticism of the lunatic, the lover and the poet might include us.

We are likely to feel uneasy in such visionary company as Theseus describes. Though our sympathies go with Hippolyta, who can discern "something of great constancy" (26) in the lovers' strange reports, we are also apt to share the Duke's disquiet about the effects of "strong imagination" (18). After all, we have been party to the secrets of the nighttime wood: the royal marital squabble, the tricky caprice of Puck, and the deranged scrambling of lovers "bedabbled with the dew and torn with briers" in a landscape "black as Acheron" (3.2.443 and 357).

Since "the story of the night" (5.1.23) *is* actually a poet's fancy—namely Shakespeare's—the Duke's skepticism is as marvelously justified as it is naive. And although we muse at his passionate dismissal of passion, we also wish to be reassured by his argument. Unlike him, however, we cannot order all our feelings into place by belittling imagination, proclaiming the truth of reason as if by decree.

Our need for reassurance has much to do with love. At the start we could share with the characters a reasonable belief that we knew what love was. But in the meantime love has become as evanescent and perplexing as the "mad spirit" Puck (3.2.4). We have watched Titania dote on the braying Bottom, and seen the quartet of lovers assault one another all for love. So love appears increasingly mysterious to us as its consummation approaches in the play.[1]

For all his previous impatience, Theseus holds aloof from love as its fulfillment nears. Though he complains of "the anguish of a torturing hour"—the hours before bedtime—it is not the pressure of ardor which discomforts him (5.1.37). He upholds cool reason, a viewpoint which separates him from his betrothed and the other lovers. He behaves as if trying to suppress a threat associated with imagination. In the lunatic, lover and poet, he concludes, exceptional joy interchanges with fear. For "in the night . . . how easy is a bush supposed a bear." Implicitly he views emotions as insubstantial: illusions born of "airy nothing." Moreover, he construes joy as the opposite not of melancholy, but of fear: fear of misinterpreting a bush as well as fear of being devoured.

As a bugbear is to irrational experience, so the bear is to the forest. Creatures that meet a bear, says Helena, "run away for fear" (2.2.94—95). Like the celebrated bear who welcomes Antigonus to the stormy, implausible seacoast of Bohemia in *The Winter's Tale*, the animal objectifies the violent anxiety which may prey on those who go unprepared (and perhaps, like Antigonus, unwillingly) into new, unknown territory. And there is a bear hunted out in the play.

When the royal couple set out to celebrate the May rite on their wedding morning, Theseus promises that "my love shall hear the music of my hounds"—hunting animals descended from those Hippolyta remembers baying a bear "in a wood of Crete" (4.1.100—123). The hounds and their hunt would be the May rite. Described as music, they are mysterious, existing for us only as distant sounds, a "musical confusion of hounds and echo in conjunction," as vividly ephemeral as Prospero's masque of Ceres. And like art, the hounds carry human governance, the Duke's will, into the wild domain of nature. The hunt Hippolyta portrays in paradoxical terms: "I never heard / So musical a discord, such sweet thunder."[2]

As it draws us into the wilds of imagination, the play uses its art to keep bugbears at bay. Shakespeare seeks to guide our aroused emotions toward insight and wonder, so that the antics of such a "mad sprite" as Puck may baffle but not alarm us. Within the play the May and wedding rites, and the mechanicals' playlet too, function as art does. For marriage not only accomplishes a positive good, a union which ideally liberates individuals from themselves, but also serves to allay the fears which shadow intimacy. Men cannot lightly suffer acute alienation, but neither can the self be casually breached by others.[3] In his first conversation with Hippolyta, Theseus reminds us that love is a benevolent ordering of

difficult, even destructive emotions. "I wooed thee with my
sword," he recalls, "and won thy love doing thee injuries"
(1.1.16–17). Metaphorically, then, to bay the bear is to disarm the
malevolence which prowls the heart as well as the overtly alien
wood. Through the music of his hounds Theseus would assure his
beloved of his gentle power—"such sweet thunder"—in the territory of passion. Through the Duke's speech Shakespeare would in
turn assure us of the order within the apparent disorder of his
play.

Tyrannical and Puckish Creation

The onset of disquietude and disorder comes early in the play.
Egeus interrupts the festive beginning, "Full of vexation . . . with
complaint / Against my child" (1.1.22–23). In response to the
threat of losing his daughter, he becomes irrational himself, trans-
forming the law into an obsessional reflex. Behaving as if the
lawful city is wholly disconnected from the wilderness, he makes
no allowance for contingency, and sees no irrationality within
Athens or himself. As a result he is particularly vulnerable to
anxiety, and becomes a source of consternation to others.

To Egeus, Hermia is, in the Duke's words

> but as a form in wax
> By him imprinted and within his power
> To leave the figure or disfigure it.
>
> [49–51]

As a father, that is, Egeus is a creator, and a despotic one at that.
Demanding total control over his "creation," resolved to have
either Hermia's independence or her life abolished, Egeus pre-
sumes to a godlike role. And insofar as he mechanically honors the
old man's complaint, the Duke ignores the motives of father and
daughter, their hopes and fears. Instead he prefers to subdue their
conflict by fiat, recasting it as a few legalistic options which
Hermia must weigh. His metaphor of forms in wax depicts creation as static: not a searching-out process, but a forcible and
paradigmatic "imprinting" of an artifact. It is a familiar situation
in Shakespeare: without sympathy, reason and law grow deranged

as madness. Like Navarre's edict, the Duke's pronouncement disrupts the order it aims for.

In fact, dreamlike dissociation marks the interview. Voices intercept one another with grotesque serenity. Egeus enters wishing the Duke nuptial joy; in the same breath he calls death down upon his own daughter. The juxtaposition of benevolence and cruelty calls into question the meaning of both. Dissociation—the disruption of cause and effect—is endemic in New Comedy. The apparently gratuitous malignity of Egeus, for example, has direct antecedents in the *senex*.[4] In Shakespeare, however, dissociation is not incidental or just a literary convention, but a means of expressing insights about the workings of personality and creation.

In Egeus's behavior dissociation dramatizes one of the play's basic themes: how may men create harmony between city and wilderness, lawful reason and wondrous imagination? It is meaningful, for instance, that Egeus declares rather than lives out his wrath; he seems estranged from his own feelings. As if conducting a pageant he bids the rival lovers each stand forth, personae in the story of his grievance. Indicting Lysander, he gropes redundantly for proof of his own outrage, conjuring it into existence: trying, one would think, to convince himself.

> Thou, thou, Lysander, thou hast given her rhymes,
> And interchanged love tokens with my child.
> Thou hast by moonlight at her window sung,
> With feigning voice, verses of feigning love,
> And stol'n the impression of her fantasy
> With bracelets of thy hair, rings, gauds, conceits,
> Knacks, trifles, nosegays, sweetmeats, messengers
> Of strong prevailment in unhardened youth.
> With cunning hast thou filched my daughter's heart,
> Turned her obedience, which is due to me,
> To stubborn harshness.
>
> [28-38]

There is a comic dislocation in this grand presentment. He portrays his adversary as a rival poet, a verbal magician whose verses have irresistibly bewitched Hermia and turned her abject obedience into rebellion. Yet Lysander is mild if not vapid. Intimidated, he indulges in fatalism, committing himself to a fate he dare not fight against. "So quick bright things come to confusion," he sighs (149). Inadvertently love appears not worth a struggle. He imagines all "sympathy in choice"—the freedom to love as the heart desires—at the mercy of abstract "jaws of darkness" which "do devour it up" (141 and 148).

Rather than uncanny, Lysander's verse is callow stuff. Ironically it is Hermia whose "good persuasion" spurs him to action (150–56). And when they do flee the law, it proves to be Lysander's failure to persuade Hermia to let him lie by her side which makes possible Puck's mischief. At the extreme, addled by Puck and the potion, Lysander actually becomes interchangeable with Demetrius, each prattling in the other's inept heroic idiom, his long-forestalled anger released yet absurdly misdirected at his harmless rival (3.2.401–30).

Egeus's true nemesis would be Puck. Where the old man would be an absolute creator, Puck mocks such willfulness. Like the Olympian trickster Mercury and Prospero's Ariel, he exists to effect a governing will. Exempt from physical laws, Puck is an expression of power, promising his master instant gratification of wishes. At the same time his chicanery reminds us of the inconstancy of wishes and the ungraspable mystery of the spirit. For Puck is reputed a "shrewd and knavish sprite" (2.1.33). Accused of creating mayhem, he assures his lord that he merely "mistook" his task (3.2.347). Yet even as he blames the lovers' mix-up on chance he confesses that "their jangling I esteem a sport" (353). His epilogue, with its promise of sense and recompense, turns on a telltale equivocation: "as I am an honest Puck." The murk he produces to mask his antics in the wood only localizes the epistemological haze he generates everywhere in the play (355–59).

From Madness to Recreation

The basic action of the play is a pursuit of the heart's desire—for most of the characters, a pursuit of love. What precipitates the plot is Egeus's irrational attempt to manipulate his daughter's affection. Thereafter the lovers flee from the rigidly conventional law of the city into the magical sphere of the fairies.[5] In the wood the miscarrying passions of Oberon and Titania entangle the lovers in mad transformations. Later, roused by the May rite of baying the bear, the adventurers waken from a "death-counterfeiting sleep," wonderstruck. For a moment we see them as newcomers to the world, unable to tell what is real. Only by mutual questioning—consensus—can they corroborate themselves and love anew (4.1.142–96). As they stand recreated before him, Theseus rescinds his earlier judgment, pledging that "these couples shall eternally be knit" (178).

So far our attention has been on the city; it is time we looked at love and the fairy realm. As Egeus's behavior illustrates, Shakespeare uses dissociation to dramatize irrationality. In the Sonnets we have observed that dissociation is fundamental to magical thinking. By disrupting conventional awareness the poet seeks to "lose" himself in the "perfect ceremony of love's rite" (Sonnet 23). If he succeeds, the effect is one of transcendence; should he fail, madness threatens. We should not be surprised to find dissociation at the heart of the fairy kingdom, where magic rules.

Shakespeare contrives to make us view the fairy wood complexly. On a stage like the Globe's the play presents a sly joke to its audience inasmuch as we are apt to realize that the insular city and the wood are physically the same place. The crucial distinction—and ultimately the play itself—is in our minds. From time to time we are similarly aware of the disconnection between the actual persons the fairies seem to be, and the power of imagination they signify: "the humor keeps *recognizing* that the person is a personification, that the magic is imagination."[6] The result is that we laugh, convinced we comprehend what we see, yet puzzled too. Like the awakened Hermia, we seem to

> see these things with parted eye,
> When every thing seems double.
>
> [4.1.186–87]

Within the play disconnections bedevil the lovers from the beginning. Their meek, conventional demeanor obscures mixed feelings about love which only surface in the wood, away from the city and the law. Lysander's half-hearted plea for "one bed . . . and one troth" provokes Hermia to a display of belligerently proper chastity (2.2.41–61). With affection thus distorted, language becomes an agent as insubordinate as Puck. The words "lie" and "troth" breed puns on deceit and truth. Swearing that "lying so, Hermia, I do not lie," Lysander confutes himself. Word play exposes lying to mean not simply innocent sleep at his beloved's side, but also love-making and, as in Sonnet 138, prevarication.[7] Once we begin to hear quibbles it is difficult for words to regain their innocent simplicity.

Hermia's apology, with its mincing couplet and unwitting quibble on his name, also undermines rather than secures truth:

> beshrew my manners and my pride
> If Hermia meant to say Lysander lied.
>
> [54–55]

Were "say" emphasized, the lines would suggest she disapproves not of thinking ill, but of admitting it openly. Since she speaks of herself in the third person, her phrase inadvertently presents her as alienated from herself. It implies that her actual feelings are as unknown to her as the wood is.

At one time or another each of the lovers is discordantly decorous, moved like automata by the "laws" of courtly romance—laws the more ridiculous for being, in Shakespeare's day, sentimental trifles. In the face of the Duke's ultimatum Lysander grows vociferously meek, appealing to books about love for guidance (1.1.132–34). He improvises his postures from cultural debris, preferring the sententious ("The course of true love never did run smooth") and the sublimely tragic ("So quick bright things come to confusion"). When Hermia's hypocritical self-denial forces him to lie apart from her, he cultivates a self-effacing role. Yet he does desire. For touched by the love-juice he acts out a passion for Helena which also retaliates against Hermia's rejection of him. Such tangled motives are expressed in the bungled escape from Athens. Lysander quickly loses sight of his goal, lamenting, "I have quite forgot our way" (2.2.36).

In *Love's Labour's Lost*, we remember, fantasies of renunciation serve to preempt painful anxiety, substituting consoling visions of glory or love. The courtiers wish to play dead to themselves and be transfigured. The ladies' penances would purge them of that "madness." Rosaline in fact would dispatch Berowne to attend the truly moribund, "the painèd impotent," in order to sharpen his appreciation of actual death and life.

In the fairy wood, we find, Helena yearns at one point for the suicidal transcendence customary to unrequited love. She vows to follow Demetrius

> and make a heaven of hell,
> To die upon the hand I love so well.
>
> [2.1.243–44]

Hermia has used self-denying chastity to keep Lysander and unsettling desire at a distance. When she wakes to find Lysander gone, she instantly swears to have either death or love, virtually becoming the self-immolating tragic type Helena has acted (2.2.156). In both instances the dread of rejection inspires a histrionic fantasy of self-destruction and apotheosis.

The point is not that these characters are robust psychological creations, but that Shakespeare recognizes how profoundly love alters the lover's sense of worth and potency. Oberon's explanation of the love-juice describes the paradoxical powers and vulnerability that love imparts. The philter, Oberon recounts, originated when the chaste moon "quenched" an arrow Cupid had aimed at a "fair vestal." The thwarted arrow struck a white flower, turning it "purple with love's wound" (2.1.155–68). By frustrating Cupid's sweet aggression, the chaste moon may be said to cause the night's madness. The force of love is a reaction, both to an intensely admired but unapproachable beloved, and to the lover's own "quenched" impotence. Such a passion is perhaps inescapably ambivalent. Certainly the lovers' abrupt changes of heart and lunatic fervor suggest a need to resolve ambivalence.

Pursuing Helena, bewitched, Lysander can at last reveal to Hermia what timid propriety has earlier suppressed, that "the hate I bare thee made me leave thee so" (3.2.190). His anger brings him a step closer to authentic emotions. Yet the lovers feel hostile as well toward any rival whose success might expose the lover's impotence and in turn self-contempt. Hence Hermia's fury when Helena innocently calls her "low" and "little" (290–327). And hence the urge to brawl which overwhelms the ordinarily meek Demetrius and Lysander: an urge which expresses not only jealousy but self-disgust too. Since they sound and act alike, in attacking each other they are in effect attacking themselves.[8]

For the courtiers of Navarre the wish to play dead to the world would be ironically borne out in their penances. In the fairy wood, however, the lovers' fantasies of self-effacement are ironically fulfilled before our eyes. Puck, who has made the mortals delirious, induces a "death-counterfeiting sleep" from which they arise renewed (3.2.364). The theatrical term "counterfeit" identifies their purgative sleep as a play-death. From the outset the sleepers had been untrue to their own feelings. When they come to their senses in the midst of the May rite, they reply "amazedly" to the Duke, with a new openness and simplicity.

Until they awake to wonder, then, the mortals comically vacillate between equally deranged extremes. One of the play's principal jokes is that highly conventionalized sense resembles fairy delirium. City and wilderness do interact. The threats the bear symbolizes are not merely "out there" but in the heart also. It could be added that the Duke's celebrated skepticism about imagination is humorous not simply because fairies do exist, but also because they are parodic reflections of the Athenian mortals. The fairy rulers mirror Hippolyta and the Duke; the play's ceremonial close affirms the unions of both royal couples.

In spite of his praise of reason, Theseus is capricious in action. One moment he is nearly as coercive and legalistic as Egeus (1.1.117–21), the next he exudes hymeneal benevolence. What moves him toward a creative role remains mysterious. As for the lovers, they awake into a creative role only by the grace of magical intervention. We should turn our attention next to the spirits who appear to generate that magic.

Love and Creation as a Fairy Quarrel

At first glance the fairy rulers might appear to be the most fully creative figures in the play. They impart order and fertility to the pastoral world. Quarrelling, they are "the parents and original" of nature's "distemperature" (2.1.81–117). As a "king of shadows"— with "shadows" a synonym for "actors"—Oberon functions as an interior dramatist, a player-king whose love-juice plot becomes the play's central plot. In an echo of Egeus, Oberon and Titania vie to form the changeling.

Though they seem capable of marvelous freedom, Shakespeare hedges the fairy monarchs' creativity with comic limits. The play's wit domesticates supernatural forces, even as it locates magic in ordinary experience. In the dispute over the changeling, for example, Oberon and Titania play out distortions of self-effacement much as the mortal lovers do. To Oberon's assertion "am I not thy lord?" Titania retorts: "Then I must be thy lady" (63–66). The ambiguity of her "must be" (suggesting coercion or conjecture) undermines her apparent assent. As a result her submissive respect for her husband and king is complicated by scornful passive resistance to him. Significantly, however, Oberon himself resorts to quizzical indirection when he counters her criticism of his flirtatious disguise as Corin (64–73). He prefers to accuse her of infatuation with Theseus, rather than challenge her immediate behavior. In all likelihood we are meant to believe his grievances are partly "the forgeries of jealousy," as Titania charges (81). For in spite of his majesty, Oberon dares not bluntly seize the changeling. After pleading "I do but beg a little changeling boy,/To be my henchman" (120–21), he schemes with Puck to humiliate the Queen. It is fitting that Titania believes him to have courted Phillida in the guise of a mild shepherd rather than in the terrific form a Zeus might assume.

For her part, Titania does apparently seek a male whom she can lead "through the glimmering night" as she supposedly did Theseus and surely would do with the changeling (77). What matters is not the literal truth of the spouses' accusations, but that each decries in the other behavior which exposes his own weaknesses. Titania objects to Oberon's secret yearning for a strong woman, a "warrior love" like Hippolyta, who can be mother as well as wife to him. He in turn protests her manipulation of men: for example, her seduction of Theseus.

Neither king nor queen can directly voice the dreads and desires which glimmer fitfully in their dispute. Consistently the royal feelings are displaced: in the "distemperature" of nature, and in plots to form the changeling. "Jealous" Oberon, as Puck calls him, would "have the child/Knight of his train, to trace the forests wild" (24–25). Despite his domineering ways, Oberon fancies he can create a knight free to live out an idealized romance in the wilderness. The wish is partly a repudiation of Titania's equally possessive desire to domesticate the boy, feminizing him with flowers; and it is partly compensation for her rejection of Oberon, whose "bed and company" she has forsworn (62). Titania would dominate the child and, more insidiously, dominate her husband by using the child to thwart him. Husband and wife, that is, wish to supplant one another by imposing vicarious roles on the unformed child. Titania's is a vision of a relation through which she could become a powerful and adored wife-mother while escaping an overpowering husband. Oberon's is a complementary vision of eternal male adolescence: freedom from personal, sexual love; the pursuit of wishful glory.[9] Both strategies answer to anxieties about dominance and inhibition.

The quarrel over the changeling sheds light on Egeus. We might usefully regard his tyrannical anger as a means of countering a dread of abandonment aroused by the prospect of losing his child. Like Oberon, he takes obedience to be love, and independence to be rejection. And like the fairy rulers, he tries to use "his" child for vicarious ends, as if by forcing her submission to a husband demonstrably subservient to him (as Demetrius is), he could secure himself in their relation permanently. Love-making in such an artificial marriage would express not the lovers so much as the old man who "created" them.[10]

Bottom in Paradise and Parody

Before the fairy monarchs become "new in amity" and the lovers awaken wonderstruck, there is only one character who serenely lives out his heart's desires: the foolish and uninhibited Bottom. Harboring no secret passions, Bottom wholeheartedly embraces the role which love-juice and the ass's head thrust on him. Titania's wooing of him is a vision of the child as Oedipal conqueror, tended by an all-gratifying mother-wife. As a parodic version of Oberon, he orders fairy messengers on errands, enjoying appetite and scratching with regal assurance. Yet thanks to Titania's bedazzlement, he fulfills the wishes obscured in her struggle for the changeling.

All told, the episode is an ambivalent one, eliciting sympathy as well as derision. To Mustardseed's "What's your will?" Bottom replies: "Nothing, good mounsieur, but to help Cavalery Cobweb to scratch" (4.1.24). His commands and desires are simple; he has no unaccommodated emotions to haunt him. Because the play shows willfullness to be benighted or, in Egeus, brutal, Bottom's innocent "nothing" delights us. Not dominance but scratching satisfies him; he adapts.

The truth and beauty of Bottom's dream come of our recognition of it as an infantile paradise enclosed by the dangerous universe. As ridiculous as it is cherishable, the dream enacts a release from the stresses of self-consciousness. It truly "hath no bottom," inasmuch as the transformed weaver loses himself in his new condition, desiring nothing beyond a natural scratch and "a handful or two of dried peas" (40). Although his humility is the peculiar humility of fools, and omits effective love no less than arrogance, he is unmistakably happy. The discord between Oberon and Titania, on the other hand, has loosed a "progeny of evils" upon the countryside. The ills include disturbances within nature, but also the loss of man's ritual link to nature. In place of the festive forms which endow rustic life with coherence—"the nine men's morris is filled up with mud" (2.1.98)—men now encounter theatrical sham:

> The spring, the summer,
> The childing autumn, angry winter, change
> Their wonted liveries; and the mazed world,
> By their increases, now knows not which is which.
> [111–14]

Bottom's dream presents one ironic remedy for such disorder. As an ass he is at once an impersonator and yet wholly authentic. Become an animal, he is a "naturalized" personality, reintegrated by magic into nature.[11] Deception can have no meaning for him. Unconscious of himself, oblivious to time and hence to death, he revels in a sort of immortality. And, as we must keep in mind, he is simultaneously ridiculous.

Like the play, Bottom's "dream" exists in a paradoxical relation to us. With its affectionate pastoralism and jokes about Bottom's animal ignominy, the interlude summons a complex response from us. We are closest to its truth when least able to evaluate it. Moreover, that relation is played out repeatedly in the play. Once parted from his ass's head, for example, Bottom yearns to perform his dream as a ballad "in the latter end of a play, before the Duke" (4.1.220–21). Restored to himself, that is, he would be something of a commercial artist, putting his experience to use. Yet his dream is more profound than a performer can say, let alone take credit for. And as it turns out, he relinquishes it. To his comrades he promises "I will tell you everything" (4.2.28), the promise which concludes nearly all Shakespearean drama. But when questioned by Quince, Bottom renounces explanations. He commits himself and his fellows to getting on with the play—both "Pyramus" and the play proper. Determined to have "no more words," he sets about living out the immediate scenario (45).

Wedding and Play

As an occasion for pageantry and high emotion, weddings ought to be good theater. Yet Shakespeare declines to mount any such ceremony onstage. One reason is that an effort to solemnize love's meaning might fail to convince us. For the lovers' triumph is not wholly of their own creation: it depends on the benign manipulation of Theseus and a "king of shadows"—on Oberon and ultimately Shakespeare himself. True, the lovers do awake from their trancelike conventionality, as Navarre's courtiers eventually may do. But nowhere do we see them actually living out the authentic love they discover. At the close of the play they come together to view a playlet, ostensibly a tragedy. Yet their communion lies not in shared tragic emotions, but in a gentle, mocking repudiation of the playlet's bad art. Intimacy never finds a voice or expressive forms: decorum orders the scene. And so to bed. In the epilogue Puck teasingly warns us that this harmony may dissolve like a dream. Given so much ambiguity, the bold consecration of love in a nuptial rite would be sentimental, in Berowne's phrase, "like an old play," an expedient contrivance.

Although the play's characters do bring love to consummation, their creative powers are sorely restricted. We are guided to appreciate their re-creation in the wood, and momentarily thereafter they acknowledge their past myopia—Demetrius likens it to an illness from which he has recuperated (4.1.176–79). Still, they marry without ever understanding the "power" which has changed them. Because Shakespeare has separated forest and city, magic and sense, the lovers need not actively strive to accommodate conflicting modes of experience. They return from the fairy realm with safely distant piety toward the supernatural. In the last analysis, that is, Shakespeare has exercised an overtly providential control over his characters' destiny. To maximize the illusion of freedom within the play, however, he produces a characteristically oblique conclusion. Like the poet in Sonnet 116, who invokes what love is *not* in order to make a "marriage of true minds," he affirms love by negations. The chief negation is the playlet "Pyramus" which, since it puts two lovers asunder, is the opposite of a wedding.

In many ways the playlet recapitulates the play. Lost in night, monitored by an inept moon, and at the mercy of their own conventionality, two lovers act out the self-destruction which has threatened the lovers in their audience. Their demise expresses the fragility of the order men create and swear one another to. As Puck breezily concludes of the love-juice mishap: "Then fate o'errules, that, one man holding troth, / A million fail, confounding oath on oath" (3.2.92). When Bottom surrenders to the nonsense of his dream, he identifies himself with it, and thereby preempts the threat of fate. His adventure ends with him asleep in a beloved's arms. When Pyramus and Thisbe try to use sterile literary forms to control fate and rout nonsense, on the other hand, the result is a merry cacophony of annihilation, with Pyramus howling, "Now die, die, die, die, die" (5.1.297).

The playlet allows its audiences some distancing laughter at magical thinking. Unlike the Athenians, we have witnessed not only the power of magic, but also its elusiveness. At once Puck is an agent of limitless wish fulfillment *and* mischief. His caprice concretizes the ungovernable nature of magic, and the dissociation inherent in it. In the Sonnets, to repeat, conjuring proceeds by negating customary sense. It leads the poet away from direct personal action, toward a visionary ardor. In Navarre and his courtiers the failure of magical thinking has comic consequences: belatedly they come to learn how fully they have lost touch with themselves in their quest for glory.

The interaction of Oberon and Titania reveals a similar barrier to the direct presentation of self. Their quarrel is not a series of spontaneous creative actions, but an exchange of delicate recriminations, formal as a dance, controlled as a performance. Titania hurries away warning "We shall chide downright if I longer stay" (2.1.145). The fairy messengers and Puck himself dramatize the gap between what the monarchs will and what actually ensues. What the royal mind proposes, Puck disposes. Curiously, Puck's presence enables Oberon to wax lyrical about "young Cupid" (2.1.148–74), yet the speech amounts to a soliloquy. At no point does the King communicate his affection immediately to Titania.

A related instance of displacement, worth noting, is Theseus's promise that "my love shall hear the music of my hounds" (4.1.103). It is as affectionate a gesture as we ever see him make, and yet it remains arrested feeling, merely potential. Though the hounds suggest a liberating hunt, an encounter of the human and fairy spheres, neither the fabulous animals nor their musical voices ever materialize. They exist beyond the stage, in imagination alone. Like Puck, they enhance their master's faculties. And inasmuch as they function as intermediaries, they mark the gap between city and wilderness even as their hunt would link the two.

The playlet construes the lovers' plight in magical terms. "Wall" reifies the dissociation we have been reviewing. Specifically he bodies forth the inhibition and parental malice which divides the lovers. Shaped by their inner strivings, the wall becomes animate, variously an accomplice or cursed foe. Hence the joke when "Wall" disappears with the lovers:

Thus have I, Wall, my part discharged so;
And, being done, thus wall away doth go.

[5.1.204]

Because it displaces actual obstacles to the protagonists' happiness, the wall makes those obstacles mysterious and unchallengeable. The tendency to impute magic vitality to emotionally charged objects (or as Romeo and Juliet will poignantly show, to words) may deflect energy away from problem solving. At the same time, urged to a kiss, Thisbe discovers that "I kiss the wall's hole, not your lips at all" (202). Her distress sums up the fortunes of love elsewhere in the play. Her affection is displaced and open to bawdy ridicule; it comes to nothing even as it is dramatically being created.

"Wall" clarifies a crucial distinction for us. Magical thinking is as efficacious or destructive as the feelings it releases. The silly, self-intoxicating conjurations of Pyramus and Thisbe match the silly self-destruction they blunder into. Their roles are inept, but not simply inept. Rather, they allow Shakespeare to dramatize the manner in which rigid habits of thought may usurp life. Pyramus and Thisbe live out bad art as the quartet of lovers tried to do. It makes mad puppets of them as the love-juice did the four adventurers in the wood. The lovers undergo a play-death from which they awaken restored; similarly the playlet's lovers can arise from death and, as actors, announce a happy ending and "a Bergomask dance" (355).

From one standpoint the playlet's end enacts the demise of bad art and the rebirth of the personality. Like the pageant of Worthies, "Pyramus" fails meaningfully. We exorcise false postures and beliefs by virtually mocking the life out of the playlet's characters. Shakespeare conducts a comical sacrifice. By clarifying the experience of the play proper (as the play in turn illuminates our lives), the demise of "Pyramus" releases its audiences from sterile conventions. It signals a fresh beginning for the onlookers, a new ability to play.

The mechanicals are ignorant of the sacrificial aspect of their performance. In fact their dramaturgy burlesques the compulsion to self-disablement which has haunted Athenians and fairies alike. They would tame their art by reminding spectators that its horrors are illusory. They would hold anxiety at bay by falsifying dramatic truth with simplistic reason. The problem, however, is not that onlookers actually believe or disbelieve in the reality of plays, but that they are ever tempted to deny the "dangerous" wilds of imagination and passion within themselves. By conventionalizing drama as it does life, an audience falsely tames awareness; large areas of experience then become unknown and frightening.

As a result the humor in the failure of "Pyramus" is complex. The mechanicals' confusion of conventions brings wonder-ful paradoxes into being: "merry tears" and (with word play appropriately relating martyrdom and eroticism to comedy) "the passion of loud laughter" (70).[12] "Pyramus" works as the play does to open and integrate the mind of the beholder. Garbled though it appears, Quince's prologue makes meanings which exceed his command and our expectations. Unwittingly he acknowledges that the vain cultivation of technique marks the start of the performer's downfall: "To show our simple skill,/That is the true beginning of our end" (110–11). Given the irrationality which subverts "Pyramus" and trips through the play-world with Puck, Quince hits upon a truth when he announces that "all for your delight,/We are not here" (114–15). "Consider then," he intones, "we come but in despite" (112). To live "in despite" is to be beyond volition: in effect, to be touched by wonder.

Both "Pyramus" and the play itself "come but in despite." They succeed as comedy by negation. Deliberately they offer us "failed" art, and present what love is not. Shakespeare emphasizes the limits of art that we may be free to transcend them. He has Puck off-handedly disparage "this weak and idle theme" in his epilogue. When Theseus refers to "this palpable-gross play," meaning "Pyramus," we may think of the play itself also. Bottom yearns to produce a ballad about his "bottomless" dream, but cannot. Shakespeare knows the ephemeral character of dreams, yet he knows too that without some ballad, however homely or foolish, men must be silent and isolated. Hence his self-mockery. Dream as he may, the artist at last creates things flawed and not quite alive to liberate our awareness.[13] As in Berowne's penance, the jest's prosperity is for the hearer to realize. In this sense art is a labor of love which requires selflessness and sacrifice—not a portentous immolation, but an ironic perspective.

This is the meaning of the joke Shakespeare gives to Theseus, that if the playlet's author "had played Pyramus and hanged himself in Thisbe's garter, it would have been a fine tragedy" (347–49). Although the play may be a wonderful "dream" in the eye of the beholder, the artist expends himself on "shadows," "antique fables," and "fairy toys." Because he cannot articulate his ideal play, he courts waste and rejection. Were he to hang himself, his own palpable-gross body would substantiate his sacrifice and make good his claims on our emotions.[14]

On another level the joke is perhaps less mordant. As the prospect of hanging implies, the artist's effacement is not simply virtuous. Because his work challenges the city's laws in order to keep them vital, and exposes us to the wilds of imagination, he is a suspect man. While the Duke concedes that "this palpable-gross play hath well beguiled/The heavy gait of night," art has temporarily put the spectators out of touch with nature. They fear to "out-sleep the coming morn" (354). Lest we retaliate against him for our own fears of outsleeping the morn, Shakespeare offers us the putative author of "Pyramus" as a scapegoat.[15]

By virtue of his role, the dramatist is susceptible to dreams of glory akin to those which tempt Quince's crew. "If our sport had gone forward," Snug laments on the morning of the wedding, "we had all been made men" (4.2.17). The Duke, they believe, must lavishly reward such valuable servants. Yet artists resemble kings themselves since they may hold many a mind in thrall. And in the play the playmaker-king of shadows, Oberon, certainly suffers no ill. Thanks to his magical resources, he satisfies his wishes by sacrificing some pride to pity, but nothing worse (4.1.44). Nevertheless, Shakespeare is not Oberon any more than he is simply the to-be-hanged author of "Pyramus." While the play does celebrate the creative promise of imagination, giving the fairies the last word, there is a balancing effort to exorcise the delusions creativity affords, and to reestablish the creators' fellowship with men. For Shakespeare the artist, the play at once affirms art and the hope of absolution from art.

The Play as Prayer and Hunt

In *Love's Labour's Lost* characters dream of magical potency and love. Yet such goals appear unattainable or merely fantastic, and the pursuit of them proves amusingly futile. Visionary zeal itself garners much ridicule. In the present play creation is no longer the eccentric ambition of a few headstrong mortals, but part of nature. As the Duke's court retires, the lord of night comes forward with a magical blessing which briefly integrates the mortal and natural orders. Yet no sentimentality panders to our insecurity. The catalogue of evils banished in Oberon's rite itself recalls the frailty of the human lot. Creation, however, remains apart from men.

Oberon and the hypothetical author of "Pyramus" remind us that although love and magic do achieve expression in this play, they are tied to special figures—ultimately to Shakespeare himself. Among ordinary mortals creation seems to be unapproachable or to require a drastic selflessness. The changeling's mother has to die giving birth to him; Egeus must fall silent that his daughter may come into her own; the lovers marry knowing nothing of the forces which have shaped them; Bottom can make nothing of his dream. In the ardent conjurations of Romeo and Juliet we will witness a more direct exploration of this problem: a calamitous venture to bring love and magic into personal experience.

As Puck's last wily tag warns, we cannot be sure that the fairy king will rule and love steadfastly ever after, any more than we can trust Theseus to do so—no matter how tantalizing the wish that

> If we shadows have offended,
> Think but this, and all is mended. . . .

If thinking could make things so, we would be creators equal to Oberon. But "this," the epilogue, turns on Puck's equivocation "as I am an honest Puck." And in that doubt chaos lurks. As the Duke's fabulous hounds chase the dangerous bear without capturing it, so the performance extends our experience but does not do away with irrationality.[16] We must manage to balance the opposite meanings contained in Quince's promise that by the actors' show "you shall know all, that you are like to know" (5.1.117). By humorously prompting us to accept more meanings than logic usually permits, the play frees our awareness to range into the wilds of imagination, to hear on the edge of earshot the sweet thunder and musical discord of wonder. Only by such an outward movement do the solipsistic city-dwellers attain the possibility of freedom and community. Only thereafter may they come to creation. By sharing in that imaginative movement, that waking dream, we participate in the community and creation it projects.

VI. Till Strange Love Grow Bold:
Playing Dead and the Creation of the World in *Romeo and Juliet*

A Midsummer Night's Dream carries out the movement toward love and personal creation arrested at the end of *Love's Labour's Lost*. Its characters rejoice in weddings; they awaken to a new openness which at least promises that they will more actively shape their own destinies thereafter. Nevertheless, this happy outcome makes only a limited solution to the problems evident in the earlier play. In the context of *Romeo and Juliet* those limits stand poignantly revealed. This is not to deny the charm or the dramatic coherence of Shakespeare's "story of the night," but only to place it in the larger frame of his ongoing imaginative effort.

In dreams we touch areas of ourselves ordinarily beyond us. The dream would help integrate the personality, circumventing inhibition to illuminate feelings and difficulties which have found no resolution in waking life. *A Midsummer Night's Dream* contrives to reconcile reason and extra-rational experience by assigning them separate yet compatible functions. Depicted as city and wood, kingdoms of daylight and darkness, the two spheres draw into closer harmony during the play yet never wholly interact. The sensible mortals remain unconscious of the fairy magic which surrounds and transforms them. Shakespeare, that is, keeps unruly emotion and magical thinking safely removed—indeed inhibited.

One result is that the city-dwellers partake of a dubious innocence. They *cannot* abuse magical awareness as Navarre and his courtiers do. Despite the play's disturbing undertone, its causality is providential. True, the lovers and the fairy rulers evince more involved motivation than first meets the eye, but it goes undeveloped. Oberon plays out his revenge on Titania, whereupon his pride fortuitously turns to pity and a resolve to remedy all errors.

The tumultuous forces latent in the play remain in abeyance, and as a result its conflicts threaten to appear merely contrived.[1]

If the performance has been successful, we are able to leave it with a renewed appreciation of imagination and the larger forces—call them fairy spirits, destiny, or even grace—which shape life. Still, we recognize that it is a "dream," a privileged interlude of awareness, which enlivens us. We are not urged, as in *The Winter's Tale*, to believe that art *is* life, and that reason and imagination are somehow wondrously cognate. The play prefigures such a belief, yet Shakespeare perhaps had not as yet developed the dramatic means or vision to enact it. Instead Puck emphasizes the tenuousness of magic and art and dreams themselves. Afterward we will go outside the arena of the performance, into the real world. We may be delighted at our adventure. Yet as Saint Augustine did, we may also thank God we are not responsible for our dreams.

In *Romeo and Juliet* no reassuring barrier partitions reason and the irrational. On the contrary, even in the public life of Verona they merge fatally. What's more, no benevolent, nearly omnipotent kings exist to enforce happiness. We sympathize with the lovers partly because they *do* attempt to create a realm where passionate imagination can be supreme, and love untouched by malice. Yet they shun the world in order to create, conjuring immortal love like the poet of the Sonnets: striving to light the vast dark heavens with their poetry.

In this play creation has a psychological dimension both more explicit and more realistic than we have met in the early comedies. As the title verifies, the lovers are individualized. The play connects its characters' creative failures with distortions of love and truth in social relations, and projects those relations into the past as well. An "ancient grudge" underlies Verona's present disorders. For Juliet, Shakespeare sketches a damaging childhood, and shows that damage to be beyond her awareness and therefore beyond remedy. Her love must counteract paralyzing pressures on her.

In the absence of a good-hearted king of shadows, the lovers must be responsible for themselves. Mere innocence cannot preserve them as it carried Bottom and the Athenian youths to grace. If creation must serve love in the world as well as in the mind, innocence calls for an active role and self-knowledge. Juliet's play-death in the tomb, by contrast, brings her not to a wondrous renewal, but to self-destruction. For playing implies an awareness of the limits of one's role, and hence a sort of freedom.[2] The lovers need to play in that strenuous and vital way, and for all their splendid poetic energy they cannot.

Miscreation and the Public Voices

We might begin as we did in *A Midsummer Night's Dream*, by listening to the voice of order and rational authority in the play. For like Theseus, Prince Escalus faces an outburst of irrationality which conditions our responses to all that follows. And just as the Duke's judgment backfires, scaring the lovers into the wood and confusion, so the Prince's strategy for suppressing the feud also proves ineffective. Granted, he is an eloquent, forceful presence. Why then is his determination frustrated?

The example of Theseus provides us a clue. For like his counterpart, the Prince spurns investigation of the problem at hand, attempting to legislate a solution. Onstage he is a belated intruder upon the feud. That he should believe the mayhem "bred of an airy word" bespeaks an aloofness from his subjects and their inner lives (1.1.87). Moreover the phrase is crucially ambiguous. On one hand, it suggests the Prince disblieves in hidden, irrational motives for the strife (as Theseus denies the fairies). On the other, it makes an unwitting statement of magical belief, a belief which recurs often in the play: that words have mysterious causal powers.

That the ambiguity escapes the Prince is telling. He appears sublimely confident about the meanings of things, relying on "an airy word" of his own, "the sentence of your movèd Prince," to impose peace (86). For support he appeals not to the law specifically, but to his own emotions. In this he anticipates old Capulet, who justifies his ultimatum to Juliet by declaiming "It makes me mad" (3.5.176–96). It reinforces the parallel that the old man terms his decision to wed her to Paris a "decree" (138). Like Lear and Othello and, not least, old Capulet, the Prince tries to control others by brandishing his anger as a threat.[3] Only when his orotund "names" for the miscreants embarrassingly fail does he involve himself (1.1.79–83). And even then he too readily dismisses the crisis with a decree. Rather than facilitate communication between the factions, he invites only the "masters" separately to hear his "farther pleasure in this case" (99). Given his self-dramatizing, peremptory tactics, it is not unreasonable to feel that the Prince's solution contributes to the problem.

But then, what is the problem? Clearly the feud is its most striking symptom. But symptom of what? The answer seems to lie in the characters' misunderstanding or, more exactly, miscreation of their world. For one thing, the feud is virtually a fiction. Verona has forgotten the actual source of the "ancient grudge" which grips the city. In part, then, the cause of the feud is the *idea* of the feud. The play dramatizes a community tormented by its own destructive imagination. The feud conventionalizes violent impulses and comes to dominate awareness, as in the reflex fury that seizes Tybalt at the sight of "foes." Joining the opening fray, mistaking or ignoring Benvolio's motives, Tybalt lays about him with clichés:

> What, drawn and talk of peace? I hate the word
> As I hate hell, all Montagues, and thee.
>
> [68–69]

Were those onstage free to re-construe the feud mentality, this mechanically heroic posturing would be funny—I am reminded of the puppetlike Demetrius and Lysander in their quarrel, and of Costard crowing "and God defend the right!"

The feud expresses conflicts generated within a remorselessly competitive, male-dominated society. Verona makes personal worth a function of social opinion. The characters intensely feel themselves formed in the applause of others (in Ulysses' phrase), and they dread ridicule and rejection. In their clashes the men assault one another with scorn as well as swords. When Mercutio believes Romeo to be placating Tybalt, he sets off the fatal quarrel crying: "O calm, dishonorable, vile submission!" (3.1.74). Again and again the threat of humiliation seems to dictate individuals' behavior.

The servants are the first to invent (or reinvent) the feud in the play. They exist in a social limbo, taken for granted by their masters, denied individuality: merely used. As servants, their identities have become conventionalized. Old Capulet, for example, carelessly dispatches an illiterate retainer with party invitations he cannot read. Like the lovers, but in an ugly way, the servants are powerless yet understandably desperate to transcend their condition. In their hearts, we gather, servitude galls them, for they direct all their jokes, boasts, and insults at "weak slaves." In one perspective, as Gregory uncomprehendingly puts it, "the quarrel is between our masters and us their men" (20). However much they despise their servitude, however, they deflect their anger toward one another rather than protest to their masters. In the street the clashing factions virtually mirror one another: each assults in its opposite the servility it apparently fears and resents in itself.

The lovers try to forestall persecution as they would the intruding sun in their lyrical aubade (3.5.1–25): by making in words a world equal to their wishes. Romeo's vow, "Let's talk; it is not day," locates their dubious freedom in speech. It makes a troubling irony that the brawling servants similarly use language to "free" themselves. Although they dare rebel only in their verbal liberties, they "make" hate as Romeo and Juliet do love. Their malice spawns as their puns do, changing their will to serve—which is a form of love—into aggression the way Sampson's simple minded word play turns love into rape by quibbling on "maids" and "maidenheads" (1.1.15–26). In this scene certain words function as a code, disguising rancor to satisfy hypocritical decorum. They mimic their masters in a vicious parody of manners, parroting "sir" at one another.

On another level, the servants treat words as deeds, as if insults such as "sir" and "better"—airy words—are blows to be returned. This concentration of emotion upon words is not liberating, as in the Sonnets, but defensive. For the speaker seizes on words to subdue a threat or intensify his sense of power. The attitude is a common one in Verona, encompassing even the Prince's remark about violence "bred of an airy word." Romeo himself fatally attacks Tybalt to make him "take the 'villain' back / That late thou gavest me" (3.1.122–23). After Tybalt's death he fantasizes that Juliet cries his name as if the name, like a bullet, "did murder her" (3.3.102–5).[4]

Like Navarre's will to be immortalized by the words of his edict, the magical investment of words in this play leads not to wonder but to estrangement. Navarre's vision of glory, we recall, made him an enemy to play, obsessed with control (the edict would have the court "still and contemplative," and would confiscate the tongues of women). At Capulet's party Tybalt acts out a sinister version of such insecurity. In an echo of the servants' quarrel he abuses Romeo:

> Dares the slave
> Come hither, covered with an antic face,
> To fleer and scorn at our solemnity?
>
> [1.5.53–55]

For Navarre and the courtiers the dread of mockery is inconvenient but mild. Tybalt denounces play as if he fears that festivity disguises some impending betrayal. Anxiety about "masked" motives apparently prompts his impulse to subdue doubts by rude force.[5] As so often in Shakespeare, rhymed couplets signal a spuriously simplified response:

Now, by the stock and honor of my kin,
To strike him dead I hold it not a sin.

[56–57]

In effect, Tybalt reacts to uncertainty with an unspoken ultimatum: be gone or be dead. In this respect his behavior unexpectedly resembles the Prince's and old Capulet's, for under stress
they too rely upon ultimatums to assure their control. Insofar as
his attitude implies contempt for the wealth of inner experience
which cannot be literalized, including the sentiments resonant in
the lovers' playful meeting, it calls to mind old Capulet's conde-
scension toward Juliet's feelings. Attributing her grief at Romeo's
banishment solely to Tybalt's death, the old man tries to dis-
qualify her emotion by construing it as art and linking it to acting:
"Thou counterfeit'st a bark, a sea, a wind" (3.5.130–37). Troubling, impalpable feeling, he insinuates, is illusory. He puts his own
energy into contracting social arrangements—what he calls "our
decree" (139). He disparages artfulness even as he spins out a
tedious, stale comparison ("the bark thy body is . . . "). No more
than Tybalt does he realize that we see what we look for—what we
will—so that life *is* play, and art inescapable.

We can understand this denial of play as a will to reduce the
world to a condition of instrumentality, a servitude which relieves
anxiety and flatters the "user" or master with a conviction of his
own power. When Tybalt attacks Romeo's mask, his "antic face,"
he acts out a craving for security and glory. Worse, his presumption to "save" the party would destroy the social forms he claims
to esteem. He would abolish an important means of dispelling
anxiety, festive play.

Lady Capulet presents a feminine counterpart to the role Tybalt
takes. Advertising Paris to Juliet as "this precious book of love,"
she maintains that through him her daughter can make her fortune:

That book in many's eyes doth share the glory,
That in gold clasps locks in the golden story;
So you shall share in all that he doth possess,
By having him making yourself no less.

[1.5.92–95]

As her ornamental praise should lead us to suspect, the woman
takes a calculating, competitive stance toward love. Her advice,
however, is oddly ambivalent. While she appears to advocate

active, even mercenary self-creation, Juliet's role would entail submission to her husband's destiny: she would take a part in the "golden story" of Paris's life, sharing his glory, rising as an inferior to become "no less" than him. Though she objectifies Paris, depicting him as a book, an artifact to be handled, Lady Capulet indirectly calls for a parasitical passivity in Juliet. Since the parents in fact have "wrought/So worthy a gentleman to be her bride" (3.5.146), Juliet has only to surrender to expediency. In Paris's words Juliet must allow herself to be "made" a mother (1.2.12).

The divided role which Lady Capulet recommends to Juliet is already evident in her own actions. In her marriage to Capulet she is variously assertive and passive. Ambivalence stirs in nearly every word she utters. At her first entrance she ignores the brawl before her. "A crutch, a crutch!" she cries at her husband. "Why call you for a sword?" (1.1.74) Is she being protective toward her husband? or is she subtly deriding his impotence, perhaps in the same breath?

We are meant to feel, I think, that Lady Capulet resents her own "made" marriage. Certainly the Capulets' edgy domesticity ironically sharpens our identification with the lovers. In the tempestuous squabble over the ultimatum to Juliet, Lady Capulet's fury shifts unstably between her daughter and husband. Toward Juliet she seems jealous. When the child refuses a marriage of convenience, her mother appears to see in her a rebellious fidelity to feeling which she herself may have compromised in her alliance with Capulet. The threat of recognition would account for her fierce wish to destroy its embodiment, Juliet: "I would the fool were married to her grave!" (3.5.140). When the old man waxes dictatorial a moment later, she cannot resist identifying with the bullied wife-to-be and reproaching him: "Fie, fie! what, are you mad?" (157). Angry herself, she would deny him anger. Like the quarrelsome servants, she behaves as if she resents yet cannot openly repudiate her "master" Capulet.

Left alone with her daughter, unable to resolve her divided emotions, Lady Capulet resorts to silence. Given Juliet's needs at this juncture, silence is tantamount to punishment. Yet Lady Capulet cannot help but negate herself also. "Talk not to me," she warns, "for I'll not speak a word" (203). And this is the end to which "use" comes everywhere in the play: to self-disablement and the ruin of language. By the morning of her wedding Juliet has made herself "dead" and all the names which the Nurse masters cannot wake her. The failure of those names confirms the failure of public language in Juliet's life as the miscarriage of the Friar's message does in Romeo's. In the hysteria following her discovery of Juliet, the Nurse's grieving noise has more authority than the self-pitying histrionics the parents and Paris present.

Nowhere in Verona do we hear voices capable of reasoning toward consensus. Even old Capulet's judicious peacemaking at the party soon gives way to peremptory, competitive temper. "Am I the master here?" he challenges Tybalt. "Go to, go to! / You are a saucy boy" (1.5.75 and 81). With communication so circumscribed, estrangement is likely to follow. From the first mention of Romeo ("O where is Romeo?") to the stumbling futility of the Friar's closing message, dissociation dogs the action. Whether bred of an airy word or of some ill-remembered injury, the feud bodies forth that derangement of causality. At the crisis in the feud disconnection is startlingly concrete, for Tybalt stabs the playful Mercutio "through" Romeo, using him as a blind. In another perverse touch Shakespeare has the "saucy boy" Tybalt try to deflect that rankling indignity onto Romeo, calling him "wretched boy" (3.1.127).

The public voices we hear repeatedly deny the claims of emotion. In their street clash the servants act out desperately misdirected feeling; Tybalt is scarcely less compulsive. At times the elder Capulets bristle with unexamined motives and passion. Paris, that "precious book of love," usually sounds priggish and secondhand. Though Coleridge called Mercutio "a perfect gentleman," his sexual energy seems directed toward "geese" or prostitutes. Love he treats alternately as a conquest tantamount to rape, or as an act of submission, a humiliating loss of control. Bantering with Romeo, Mercutio justifies scathing bawdy jokes as "art" and scorns "nature." But his banter cannot disguise an ugly hostility toward sexual intimacy: "this driveling love is like a great natural that runs lolling up and down to hide his bauble in a hole" (2.4.92–98).

In each of these instances individuals might be said to play dead to vulnerable parts of themselves in order to create public postures—illusions—of security and personal power. I choose the phrase "play dead" deliberately. For we are looking, I think, at a pattern of behavior which pervades the play. In a poignant, even breathtaking way the lovers also play dead, but in order to project an ecstatic world whose sun and stars are love incarnate. In Juliet's enactment of the Friar's scheme, the concept becomes one of the play's central metaphors.[6]

Conjuring Love and Jeopardy

Our introduction to Verona prepares us to see the lovers not only separated from the public milieu, but in opposition to it. Their affection seems counterpoised against the malice around them. Audiences have long consoled themselves by monumentalizing Romeo and Juliet, even as contrite but ignorant Verona would apotheosize them as gold statues. The play, however, refuses simply to idealize the pair. In voices such as Mercutio's and the Nurse's we hear limited albeit salutary criticisms of their headlong rapture. The Juliet who is her beloved's sun is no less the Nurse's "slug-a-bed" (4.5.2). Desire, Mercutio jests in his Queen Mab inventions, *can* be Puckishly deranging.

To see the lovers in human rather than statue form, and to skirt complacent sentimentality, we need to understand how intimately *related* they are to the troubled society Shakespeare imagined around them. It is true yet insufficient to point out that against the deadening formality of that society, "the mutuality of the lovers stands out, the one organic relation amid an overplus of stylized expressions and attitudes. The naturalness of their diction is artfully gained . . . through a running critique of artificiality."[7] "Organic" in this apology carries a burden of undeclared, wishful sentiment. And while there *is* "a running critique of artificiality" in this play (as in virtually all of the plays we have examined), it embraces the lovers as well. Though their language is heartfelt and uncalculating, not its "naturalness" but its magical urgency hurries them toward exaltation and death. Before approaching the patterns of fantasy and role that link the lovers to the world they defy, let me first place in perspective their risky conjuration of love itself.

In the balcony scene, still under the spell of their meeting at the party, the lovers fervently renounce the names by which Verona corroborates and, unhappily, holds them. Defying Mercutio's heartless yet sensible mockery of love as a conjuration (2.1.6–21), Romeo steps out from hiding to "name" Juliet the sun, and her eyes stars. Like Paris and old Capulet, who has lyrically called his daughter "the hopeful lady of my earth" (1.2.15), Romeo casts her in a role derived from courtly love lore. Joyfully he squanders himself and his beloved in the remnants of a dead tradition which those about him unthinkingly exploit or merely scorn. Unlike his rivals, he delights in relinquishing his beloved to ennoble her, trying to place her beyond worldly reach.[8] He transmutes her:

> Arise, fair sun, and kill the envious moon,
> Who is already sick and pale with grief
> That thou her maid art far more fair than she.
>
> [2.2.4–6]

And again:

> Two of the fairest stars in all the heaven,
> Having some business, do entreat her eyes
> To twinkle in their spheres till they return.
> What if her eyes were there, they in her head?
> The brightness of her cheek would shame those stars
> As daylight doth a lamp.
>
> [15–20]

On the face of it, he is only playing out far-fetched metaphors. We may recall the ingenious oxymorons of his first long speech in the play (1.1.169–80). But that early speech concludes on a note of possible self-awareness: "Dost thou not laugh?" Praising Juliet, by contrast, he commits himself wholeheartedly to his visions, as if somehow they may preempt or fulfill reality.

Like the poet of the Sonnets, Romeo would lose himself in his beloved. Though he would recreate Juliet with a poet's imaginative omnipotence, he wishes himself no more than a glove upon her hand or a pet bird, owing all meaning to her. Endowing her with great worth, he would dispel his own identity. The place, Juliet warns, is "death, considering who thou art" (2.2.64). But Romeo is nothing daunted. Of her dangerous kinsmen he vows:

> My life were better ended by their hate
> Than death prorogued, wanting of thy love.
>
> [77–78]

In the Sonnets the poet conjures by means of negations. He repudiates all the world and the apparatus of customary sense. In so doing he courts dangers. Disavowing his will to act in the world, perhaps blinding himself to his beloved's "sins" (Sonnets 35 and 95), he risks "mad" chaos. For Romeo and Juliet the risks are magnified. As he bribes the apothecary Romeo openly defies "this loathsome world" and "the world's law" (5.1.81 and 72), yet his world is both more hostile and more intractable than the poet's. Enmeshed in ongoing events, required to act, the lovers cannot master their prolific and contrary feelings. Nor can they fully understand them. Romeo's "mad" tantrum on the floor of the

Friar's cell corresponds to Juliet's terror of madness as she drinks the Friar's potion; the lovers have no inner serenity which can shelter them from a hostile society. What makes the play tragic, then, is its ability to arouse our wishful sympathy with their denial of the world, even as it exposes that denial as a possible transgression against themselves.

The lovers rely on imagination to defeat social constraint by turning affection into living art. Each behaves as if, with the godlike yet immaterial power of a dramatist creating a character, he can restore in the solitary vastness of imagination a beloved who has "died" to the world.[9] If they pursued this fantasy heedlessly, they would be no more than victims—martyrs to love. But Shakespeare contrives to make their course dramatic. They fear, as Juliet says, a contract "too rash, too unadvised, too sudden" (2.2.118). And in their path ominous signs emerge, even at the outset.

As always when we are meant to question a character's efficacy, speech belies its user. Romeo's incantation in the garden, for example, disregards his cautionary "but soft!" Grandly he dismisses virgins as "fools," although both he and Juliet are open to this scorn. The "envious moon" he wishes killed momentarily becomes "yon blessed moon" and the object of a casual vow.

Juliet also confutes herself. When she wonders who "stumblest" on her counsel, her verb presages the Friar's tedious warnings about haste and his fatal stumbling over graves (5.3.122). Torn between reason and wishes, she is too prescient to believe in facile vows, yet unable to resist them. "Do not swear at all," she commands (2.2.112), only to pledge herself: "My bounty is as boundless as the sea" and so on (133). At one moment she disclaims "names" as capricious, and at the next would "tear the cave where Echo lies . . . /With repetition of 'My Romeo,' " just as Romeo "would tear the word" if he had his name written (161 and 57). She makes a small, touching play of her misgivings:

> Dost thou love me? I know thou wilt say ay,
> And I will take thy word; yet, if thou swear'st,
> Thou may'st prove false. . . .
>
> [90–92]

If "I" or "ay" will take or abscond with Romeo's "word" or oath, then unwittingly she warns against her own unsteady relation to language. When Juliet does give in to incantation, invoking the "boundless" depths of her feeling, "some noise within" silences her. She cannot or will not hear the noise as words, although it is probable the Nurse is calling her name and Juliet feels compelled to respond in any event.

Now there are numerous intentional quibbles in the play. Unintended meanings—meanings which in fact undercut intentions—suggest language gone out of control. Often the lovers tend to conceive language concretely, as if words have inherent vitality. To the Friar Romeo wails that "calling death 'banished'/Thou cut'st my head off with a golden ax" (3.3.21–22), as if his dilemma originates not in human motives which can and must be confronted, but in the dreaded word "banished" itself. In their dialogue the word recurs repeatedly until we recognize its peculiar emptiness as a sound, while Romeo becomes "mad" in his obsession with it. Like his beloved, who puns feverishly to dispel the meaning and potency of the "ay" she dreads to hear when she thinks Romeo dead (3.2.45–51), Romeo would destroy words. Believing the word "banished" can "mangle" him, he commands the Friar to "talk no more." The lovers, that is, are bound by an unarticulated ultimatum of their own. As Romeo decrees, "Thou canst not speak of that thou dost not feel (3.3.64). It may be that the Friar is incapable of imaginative sympathy; the point is, Romeo will tolerate no efforts at such identification. The dictum forbids the "use" of language for problem solving or exploration. (The lovers never forthrightly talk with potentially hostile public figures, including their parents, although I suspect Shakespeare gives old Capulet conciliatory speeches at the party to raise the possibility of such communication for us.) In their convictions Romeo and Juliet resist the creation of consensus much as Verona does.

Love Personal and Maddening

In the Sonnets, conjured love transcends personality when efficacious, and humanizes the lover when it fails. We feel pathos when Romeo's afflatus falters and he is reduced to a childish maxim about lovers parting like schoolboys going to school "with heavy looks" (2.2.157), or when he undertakes so vapid an oath that Juliet must halt it (107–9). It dismays yet relieves us to see his invention flag, human as the flesh it abjures. For the lovers become most real to us in the limits of their creation. With this paradox in mind, we may turn to the scene of Juliet's play-death in hopes of further illuminating the fantasy itself and, in turn, the character it expresses.

As Juliet prepares to evade her father's coercion by playing at death with the Friar's potion, she tries to control the frightening unreality of her act by identifying it with the theater, where unreality is natural (4.3.14—58). For the first time we see her truly alone. Stifling her desire to seek comfort from her mother and Nurse, she reminds herself of the play-within-a-play the Friar has devised for her, and the "dismal scene" she "needs must act alone" in it. Her soliloquy, however, reveals not the decisive personality a rebellious secret marriage demands, but an irresolute soul whose terror threatens to "freeze up the heat of life" and action. And Juliet's ability to "act" remains dubious. Crying "Thus do I drink to thee," she takes the potion and "dies." The gesture is grossly ambiguous. It might be regarded sentimentally as a triumphant "act," a glorious toast to her beloved. Yet the moment has a more sobering significance as the culmination of her long meditation. Her imagination has generated phantoms so real to her—"mangled Tybalt" vengefully about to kill Romeo—that she takes the potion and "dies" partly to escape a spasm of violent anxiety.

Early in her speech, abandoning thoughts of her equally inadequate mothers, Juliet looks inward. At that point, nightmarish hallucinations rapidly transform her strategic play-death into a mad scene whose cause is no longer the Friar, but estranged emotions in herself.

> Shall I not then be stifled in the vault,
> To whose foul mouth no healthsome air breathes in,
> And there die strangled ere my Romeo comes?
> Or, if I live, is it not very like
> The horrible conceit of death and night,
> Together with the terror of the place—
> As in a vault, an ancient receptacle
> Where for this many hundred years the bones
> Of all my buried ancestors are packed;
> Where bloody Tybalt, yet but green in earth,
> Lies festering in his shroud; where, as they say,
> At some hours in the night spirits resort—
> Alack, alack, it is not like that I,

So early waking—what with loathsome smells,
And shrieks like mandrakes torn out of the earth,
That living mortals, hearing them, run mad—
O, if I wake, shall I not be distraught,
Environèd with all these hideous fears,
And madly play with my forefather's joints,
And pluck the mangled Tybalt from his shroud,
And, in this rage, with some great kinsman's bone
As with a club dash out my desp'rate brains?

[4.3.30–54]

Isolated, and afraid of waking up isolated in the tomb, she fears not death but imminent madness: a "rage" in which she will dash out her own brains. Among her terrors is a fear of herself. Magical thinking and playing dead, we know, are equivocal. In a charmed wood outside of Athens lovers come to a joyous re-creation. Magic, we are to believe, releases affection that was buried in them all along. Why then should a gentle creature like Juliet discover herself on the threshold of madness? To respond to that question we must draw upon the childhood Shakespeare has provided her.

The Nurse's account of Juliet's weaning and the earthquake accompanying it depicts metaphorically the formation of the child's character. Forced by the bitter wormwood toward sudden independence, Juliet "could have run and waddled all about" (1.3.38). Predictably, however, she "fell upon her face," as the Nurse's husband put it, becoming the subject of a queasy joke about "falling backward" into the role of a sexual plaything for a future husband (42–43). Without comprehending, "the pretty wretch left crying and said, 'Ay,'" as if to accept the submissive role proposed for her in the jest. Though the Nurse shows her more fondness than her mother, the Nurse nonetheless approves of the harsh joke and the child's abnegation. Juliet's "ay" signifies her will to please, and the vow meaning "forever," but also the sign of self-identification, "I." The ambiguity of the word heralds the ambiguity of her personality. Hence her puns on "ay" later, when she fears Romeo dead.[10] We may remember then the day of her weaning and the quake in the earth and herself.

The Nurse's tale recapitulates a childhood in which surrogate or actual parents impose a freedom which has the force of a rejection. The child's first eager adventure ends in a fall which arouses panicky assent to whatever new dependency adults offer. Thereafter the child may deny her own will to fulfill the "ideal" role conferred on her, looking to others—to "authorities"—for the source of her own character.[11] In these circumstances love is apt to be threatful, as we sense it to be among the Capulets, for rejection is tantamount to negation or death. It is no coincidence that Shakespeare has both of Juliet's parents wish her dead when she declines to obey their ultimatum. Lady Capulet would have her "married to her grave," and her father bids her "hang, beg, starve, die in the streets" (3.5.140 and 193).

Naming his daughter "yet a stranger in the world" (1.2.9), old Capulet inadvertently discloses Juliet's lifelong alienation in her family. We are likely to notice, too, when Lady Capulet uses Juliet's surrogate mother, the Nurse, to summon her own daughter, and all the Nurse's names for Juliet elicit only a puzzled "How now? Who calls?" The response indicates the remoteness of mother from daughter (1.3.2–5). At the close of the party scene an unrecognized voice calls to Juliet from the depths of the house. The Nurse alone heeds it, ominously yet innocently remarking that "the strangers all are gone" (1.5.142). Juliet's surreptitious marriage only confirms her divorce from the social milieu around her.

Insofar as she cannot reconcile the demands of her marriage and those of conventional life, with its quarrels and vicious formality, Juliet is one of Shakespeare's most divided souls. To live up to Romeo's wishful, erotic incarnation of her, she must be the "fair sun" and "kill the envious moon," spurning her childhood self, ascendant. Yet, instantly cowed by her father's wrath, she watches in silence as the adults negotiate her fate (3.5.160–96). The Nurse argues in vain with the old man, while Juliet tacitly accepts his definition of her as "green-sickness carrion," "young baggage," and "disobedient wretch." Instead of indignation or even rage, Juliet's response to this abuse is panic. "O, sweet my mother," she pleads, "cast me not away!" Rejection, not death, horrifies her. Delay the marriage, she begs,

> Or, if you do not, make the bridal bed
> In that dim monument where Tybalt lies.   [201–2]

Her wish insists on her powerlessness, as if to deny every rebellious urge, guiltily seeking forgiveness or even punishment. At the same time we might hear a childlike, if by no means idle, threat: if you force me into an unwanted match, you will be killing me. If we know the outcome of the story, as even Shakespeare's audiences did, we may hear the threat still more explicitly: force me, and you will force me to take my own life. In this perspective she retaliates against her parents in kind, trying to stir them to guilt. Thwarted, she utters a sort of ultimatum to herself. Either her "ghostly" father must make her a "remedy," or "myself have power to die" (242–43). Her will has power only against herself. Toward her parents her will is veiled. Her paralysis, *even now*, is a form of play-death. In this context and with grim irony, the Friar's scenario permits her to carry out openly a long-standing, deeply motivated will to play dead.

Juliet's fantasy about the tomb objectifies her dilemma. As the family's monument to its social identity, the tomb harbors the remains of a heritage time has left anonymous and decayed.[12] The family's resources take form in Juliet's mind as a vainglorious dungeon and "some great kinsman's bone," an instrument for her self-destruction. Her "mad" scene develops around her horror of waking up to, and within, a family already "dead"—loveless and repugnant—to her. She dreads to find herself alone with the guilt of her incomplete rebellion against her parents and lineage. Her father pretends she has made him suffer:

> Day, night, hour, tide, time, work, play,
> Alone, in company, still my care hath been
> to have her match'd. . . .
>
> [3.5.177–79]

She neither discerns nor suspects this subtle martyrdom of his. On the contrary, her fantasy reveals how unworthy she feels. She envisions herself mad and childishly at "play with her forefathers' joints," then plunged into a "rage" of self-punishment. Dashing out her brain, the wits which have accomplished her marriage, the child in her would punish her rebellious self-assertion. It measures her alienation that what is basically a wish to disable her "dangerous" independence should manifest itself as an hallucinatory self-execution.

Grasping Love and Hate

Juliet's "madness" brings into focus the tragic paradox that the imaginative energy which releases the lovers' affection also releases distorted, destructive feelings. The extraordinary poetry which realizes their wishes also shows them to be estranged from themselves. Lady Montague introduces her son with a question which echoes in the pandemonium of names the mob cries in the streets after his death: "O, where is Romeo?" (1.1.114). More aptly than he knows, her husband regrets that his son "makes himself an artificial night" (138).[13] And parrying Benvolio's efforts to make light (in both senses) of his romantic moods, Romeo himself wittily—yet glibly—retorts, "I have lost myself" (195).

Like Juliet, Romeo behaves as if rejection means annihilation. Banishment—drastic social rejection—he equates with death. To the Friar he vows that the word "banished" is "the stroke that murders me" (3.3.22). Collapsing on the floor in a counterpart to Juliet's "mad" scene "with his own tears made drunk" (83), he concentrates more on self-obliteration than on love. No more than Juliet does he allow himself to rebel openly against the family and community that have frustrated love; nor does he consider appealing to their trust and affection. Instead he dramatizes his paralysis and painful self-contempt.

From the start the lovers experience the exaltation and anxiety of a love which covertly defies personal and social taboos. Juliet interprets their first meeting with thrilling dread: "I must love a loathèd enemy" (1.5.139). In the balcony scene love gains intensity from its rebellious violation of customary barriers ("stony limits cannot hold love out") and a threatened loss of self ("the place [is] death, considering who thou art"). And at first the lovers seem to transcend the implications of their defiance by loving with generous gestures of relinquishment. As events overtake them, however, their behavior becomes more rigid. Even in the balcony scene they seize on a marriage pledge and vain oaths in an effort to bind love. As the play hurtles toward a crisis, the lovers cling to the Friar and subterfuges, unable to risk all by giving love a public voice. Insidiously their ecstasy comes to seem a regression toward childhood modes of feeling as well. Before her irate father Juliet becomes a tongue-tied child. Romeo gives in to a tantrum on his "ghostly" father's floor.

Once source of the lovers' tragic limitations, then, is their denial of inward turmoil. Conjuring love beneath Juliet's balcony, for example, Romeo concentrates all his energies on praise. Though he commands an end to virginity (2.2.7–9), he sublimates sexuality and eventually dispels sexual identity. Juliet he renders celestial and remote. He wishes to be a glove upon her hand, or a tame bird which "much cherishing," she realizes, "should kill" (183–84). Yet having disposed himself to be wholly shaped by a woman, he becomes understandably apprehensive about this potential loss of self. His murder of Tybalt is in part a violently masculine reaction to a fear that "sweet Juliet /Thy beauty hath made me effeminate" (3.1.110–11). His subsequent collapse in the Friar's cell stems not only from the threat of banishment, but also from the danger to his identity.

Lying on the Friar's floor, Romeo wonders if his beloved hates him:

> Doth she not think me an old murderer,
> Now I have stain'd the childhood of our joy
> With blood remov'd but little from her own?
>
> [3.3.94–96]

Guilt has stricken him: guilt at the single public assertion of will he has risked. Caught between intolerable violent self-assertion and intolerable imaginative selflessness, he panics. His name he imagines murdering Juliet (104). To be absolutely loving—a tame bird—he has suppressed all natural ambivalence toward Juliet. The result is that his anger surfaces as a dissociated fear of harming her which he tries to deny or expiate by turning suicidally against himself.

Juliet's hallucination complements Romeo's guilty urge to suicide. She envisions Tybalt rising from the dead to slay Romeo (4.3.55–58), a retaliation which she has every reason to abhor and yet also to wish for. She stops the vision of revenge by bringing about her own "death" with the potion. Her anguish goes unresolved. One fantasy solution to the lovers' ambivalence is Romeo's poignant dream that Juliet has made him an emperor with a magical kiss:

> I dreamt my lady came and found me dead—
> Strange dream that gives a dead man leave to think!—
> And breath'd such life with kisses in my lips
> That I reviv'd, and was an emperor.
>
> [5.1.6–9]

It is a tribute to love, but no less a glimpse of his wish for enormous power: and power won not through any struggle with others or, in turn, with his own inhibition, but rather won through a kiss.

The Personal Basis of Miscreation

It is a tragic paradox, I have argued, that the lovers' pursuit of ecstasy creates not only affection, but "madness" as well. A corollary of the paradox is this: the qualities which most intimately link Romeo and Juliet to those around them—specifically, the tendency to play dead, and to grasp at life—are qualities which lead not to community, but to alienation and distress. While we have already scrutinized many of Verona's "public" voices, we need to illuminate further two momentous figures who are close to the heart of that paradox of alienation: the Friar and old Capulet.

Like his "children," The Friar tries to reconcile the claims of daylight and darkness by subterfuge. As a self-appointed mediator, he gathers "baleful" yet "precious-juiced" plants in murky twilight, looking to paradox for his power: "Virtue itself turns vice, being misapplied,/And vice sometime's by action dignified" (2.3.21–22).[14] His fatuous couplets and the fluidity of his viewpoint make his authority unreliable. Life, he holds, is a war between "grace and rude will" (28). He scorns will even as he willfully tampers with the arcane and equivocal properties of the plants he gathers. His strategems and indirection belie the complete trust in grace which he professes. As a result he facilitates the lovers' paralysis. He leads them to a dangerous marriage with a hopeful conjuration rather than a reasoned commitment:

> So smile the heavens upon this holy act
> That afterhours with sorrow chide us not!
>
> [2.6.1–2]

Despite his advice to "be homely in thy drift," he encourages them to obscure truth by using equivocations as they use the Nurse and himself. Romeo tries to put neutral words between himself and Tybalt, but his conciliatory evasion only affronts his rival (3.1.60–73). Confronted by her father, Juliet riddles so elusively that she weakens her own resolve even as she provokes him to tyrannical vehemence. By their mild duplicity the Friar and his "children" generate alienation.

The Friar shares with his counterpart, old Capulet, a striking will to play dead. Like the children, both "fathers" react to crises with an impulse to sacrifice themselves and thereby preempt an open conflict. In the end, claiming his "short date of breath" is not so long as his "tedious" confession to the Prince, the Friar excuses himself from accountability (5.3.228–68). If "ought in this," he offers,

> Miscarried by my fault, let my old life
> Be sacrific'd, some hour before his time,
> Unto the rigour of severest law.
>
> [265–68]

Apart from the pity sought in the speech, we should notice that a man who announces himself dead or nearly dead cannot be meaningfully punished.

At Juliet's supposed death, her father similarly plays the martyr. By "making" Death his heir he tries to preempt it:

> Death is my son-in-law, Death is my heir;
> My daughter he hath wedded; I will die,
> And leave him all; life, living, all is Death's.
>
> [4.5.38–40]

He asserts control by "willing" Juliet to Death just as he had tried to will her to Paris. In the throes of his despair, moreover, the old man is as compulsively suicidal as the lovers, although needless to say, he only plays at an apocalyptic death.

For all his self-pity, old Capulet presumably grieves out of love; there is bitter irony in his ambiguous howls: "O child! my soul, and not my child!" (62). The equation of his soul and child resembles the hazily romantic epithet for Juliet he has used earlier, "the hopeful lady of my earth" (1.2.15). In the earlier phrase he sounds more like a lover than a father: but not a sensual lover so much as a courtly, worshipful admirer. Given the word play on "earth," the epithet seems to invest Juliet (perhaps as a mother to his heirs) with immortalizing powers. Throughout the play his own sexuality suffers at his wife's jibes. He will "play the housewife" the night before Juliet's wedding, and as he shuffles about the house the Nurse calls him a "cotquean," and his wife mocks his inability to stay up chasing women (4.4.6–12). He can no longer be "a mouse hunt" or womanizer directly, in the flesh (11). However, Shakespeare hints that the old man has concentrated much emotion on his daughter. For some time he vacillates about committing her to Paris. At last, like many another father in Shakespeare, he casts a compliant suitor as his son, as if to maintain his influence with her. At the news of her first death, he wails to Paris,

> O son, the night before thy wedding day
> Hath Death lain with thy wife.

[4.5.35–36]

Wilfully he sacrifices her as he loves her, in an act of imagination. His awe fixes on the violation of the daughter he must surrender, and on the horrible intimacy of sexuality and death.

Now the Friar also stages a wedding for Juliet. He too appears touched by the love she inspires. Before the ceremony he warns Romeo that "violent delights have violent ends" (2.6.9). When his "daughter" enters, however, he celebrates her as a lover who

> may bestride the gossamer
> That idles in the wanton summer air
> And yet not fall, so light is vanity.

[18–20]

His praise echoes Romeo's balcony-scene comparison of Juliet to a wondrous angel.

> a winged messenger of heaven
> Unto the white-upturn'd wond'ring eyes
> Of mortals that fall back to gaze on him,
> When he bestrides the lazy-pacing clouds
> And sails upon the bosom of the air.

[2.2.28–32]

With his delight masked in vague paternalism, like old Capulet's, the Friar at once dismisses and covets the quickened imaginings of love. It is not too much, I think, to espy in his cynical refusal to leave the lovers alone together "till Holy Church incorporate two in one" an element of unwitting jealousy. Like old Capulet, that is, he seems to take satisfaction and comfort in managing love.

In Verona social artifice suppresses passion and affectionate play. The fantasy of playing dead is at once a cause of, and a solution to, that suppression. The fantasy encourages playing dead to oneself or others as a means of escaping conflicts and gaining potency. The lovers give up all worldly power for tragically insufficient visionary ardor. They would live in an imaginative union. Both the Friar and old Capulet act out versions of this fantasy, for both deny themselves direct expression of affection and power.

Like the Friar, who dreams of staging a rebirth for Juliet with himself the vital life-giver, old Capulet equates marriage and death, yet promises resurrection. "An you be mine," he says ambiguously to Juliet,

> I'll give you to my friend:
> An you be not, hang, beg, starve, die in the streets.
> [3.5.192–93]

That is, if Juliet will play dead to her rebellious feelings, her father will give her love and, implicitly, life. The alternative is annihilation. As in the Friar's benign plan, any such resurrection entails a secret and perilous wish to be godlike.[15]

Still, the fantasy need not take a cruel form. It promises to fulfill childhood yearnings, and to answer to childhood terrors, as in Romeo's dream "that I revived and was an emperor." We feel exhilaration as well as foreboding when Romeo summons Juliet out of the stasis of childhood with an exhortation to "arise, fair sun." There is a certain grandeur to their immortal longings which is akin, if not equal, to that of Cleopatra and her Antony.

But we incline most sympathetically toward the lovers because their imaginative striving reaches outward, to unite them, at least for a brief time. They afford each other, and in turn us, moments of tenderness and generosity which contrast with the darker shapes of fantasy in Verona. In her vision of herself trapped in the tomb, Juliet gathers her beloved cousin Tybalt out of death, into her arms. The resurrection by gold statues which Verona fancies at the conclusion has no such simplicity. When old Capulet vows to create an exemplary Romeo "as rich" as Montague's "Juliet," he may well be perpetuating the sort of competitive motives which produced the play's opening brawl. As the Prince's perfunctory conclusion suggests, life rigidly grasped is dubiously transfigured:

> For never was a story of more woe
> Than this of Juliet and her Romeo.

No matter how solemnly intoned, this neat hyperbole cannot be adequate to the life it would capture.

In the Prince's summary couplet as in the opening chorus, we hear voices reciting empty, pat explanations. Those who "go hence, to have more talk of these sad things" are shadows, in a way as unreal as the statues they would console themselves with. By contrast, we cannot simplify our response to the actions we have witnessed. For us the play lives *because* it reifies those great forces—call them fate or destiny—from which conventional thought insulates men, but also *because* those forces appear irreducible. Unquestionably there is a pervasive magical dimension to the lovers' fate. Many a curse casually uttered is borne out in the carnage in the tomb. There is Mercutio's "plague a both your houses" (3.1.103), and the curses of the Capulets. Juliet's mother has wished her "married to her grave" (3.5.140), and wished to poison Romeo (87—91). And as in *A Midsummer Night's Dream* the apparatus of destiny is potentially unconvincing.[16] But as in the playlet "Pyramus," so in the personal fantasies and distortions of will we have just been tracing: we are made to feel a need for human freedom, a need for will and wisdom. Fate or grace appears finally ineffable. Perhaps *Romeo and Juliet* would be a greater play if its characters had more resources and autonomy—certainly that is the direction in which Shakespearean tragedy developed. What matters for us is the play's ability to dramatize an endeavor to bring creation into accord with grace *and* rude will.

VII. Fortune Shows Herself More Kind:
Making Fortunes by Play in
The Merchant of Venice

As Shakespeare's art develops, his characters appear increasingly autonomous. In a *Comedy of Errors* or a *Titus Andronicus* the principals remain types, shaped by their Roman models. A Prince Hal or Hamlet, by comparison, may seem to be motivated from within. More than a creature of the plot, such a figure appears to be shaping the play's action and his own role from moment to moment. In the plays we have examined we have seen that illusion of personal creation taking form. And yet while these early plays are often about becoming autonomous, they tend to imply that goal without directly dramatizing it. Just as the characters begin to discover themselves, the scene closes or tragic misfortune intervenes. Like their counterparts in Navarre, for example, the Athenian lovers prepare themselves for greater creative freedom by mocking puppetlike styles of behavior in a play-within-the-play. But the epilogue abruptly follows, leaving the lovers' new lives an uncertain promise.

What does it mean that Shakespeare invokes autonomy as a problem? Any answer must take into account the equivocal attitude toward autonomy in Elizabethan drama. For even in Marlowe, notwithstanding his individualistic heroes, "the language of the *dramatis personae* is not yet in any consistent fashion determined by their characters; this is to be found for the first time in Shakespeare."[1] For that matter, Shakespeare himself is by no means strictly consistent. Witness in *Antony and Cleopatra* the discrepancy between Enobarbus's usual bluntness and his fabulous praise of Cleopatra upon her barge, which serves the needs of the play at that point (2.2.195–209) but not the characterization of the Lieutenant. Which is to say that our expectations of autonomy must acknowledge the limitations of a highly stylized dramatic art.

From this standpoint the problematical freedom of Shake-speare's characters might seem to be primarily a function of the dramaturgy he inherited. Narrowly propounded, such a view so simplifies our problem that it fairly disappears:

> Shakespeare's characters rarely give the impression that they are independent beings who, once set in motion, are free to work out their own destiny. On the contrary, they are tightly controlled by the author. . . . The characters are not "natu-ral" at all, but a product of their creator's imaginative art.[2]

As a reaction against naive Romantic dotage on character, this pass-age has its core of truth. But we cannot rest with such comfortable distinctions. For one thing, Shakespeare expressly dramatizes the re-sources and deficiencies of his art. His control of his creation is a per-sistent, self-conscious theme: and itself a problem for him. Hence his labors to open up his art to life. When *Love's Labour's Lost* approaches a pat comic resolution, he dispatches Marcade with a message which disrupts the play's form and renews our sense of contingency.

What's more, autonomy is a convention we tenaciously believe in. Watching drama we tend to assume that the characters, how-ever stylized, are "independent beings"—even as we assume that we ourselves are. Shakespeare repeatedly exposes this habit of belief, complicating our relation to the characters, not to destroy our illusion of their independence, but to elicit a wider awareness. In *The Famous Victories of Henry the Fifth* the Prince is a mechanically contrite type of the prodigal son. Shakespeare's Hal, who "can drink with any tinker in his own language," seems able to shape the action and his own role in part *because* he discloses himself as a sort of actor-dramatist who "intends" to "imitate the sun" until "he pleases again to be himself" and thus "be more wond'red at. . . ." Moving his characters toward an implied greater freedom, putting in perspective the puppetlike roles they have outgrown, Shakespeare guides us to see that self-realization is not a state but a process of becoming aware of, and thereby transcend-ing, the roles which communicate an identity. We have seen this process dramatized as an expanding capacity to play.

In the theater to play is to impersonate, to acquire a persona by artifice. In Shakespeare's use, however, the concept becomes in-creasingly complex. For the courtiers of Navarre, say, play at first only amounts to self-aggrandizing escapism. Thanks to the ladies' piquant tutelage and, presumably, the self-knowledge the lovers' penances call for, play comes to seem a potential means to love and community.

Romeo and Juliet are most nearly independent beings as they explore imaginative forms to express their new love. Soon, however, their behavior becomes compulsive ("mad" the Friar calls Romeo), and they fix on death itself trying to control destiny. Where initially they play dead to Verona and to disordered feelings in themselves, eventually the metaphor turns grimly literal in Juliet's feigned death and the lovers' suicides. One aspect of their tragedy, then, is their inability to sustain their freedom in play. Hence the irony that after suppressing imaginative freedom, Verona may finally cast the lovers and their "tale of woe" in self-consoling, falsely apodictic forms of gold. Unlike *The Winter's Tale*, where men learn to conceive life as play, there is no Paulina who can artfully dissolve the boundary between art and nature, truth and dreams, and thereby "resurrect" the statues.

In *A Midsummer Night's Dream* capriciously benign fairies re-create through madness and wonder the lost souls who flee the city's judgment. The lovers eventually find themselves in a position to appreciate the ineptness of the mechanicals' histrionic postures, yet their own capacity to play at life goes untested. The world or nature plays, as it were, but it remains beyond the mortals' reach.

Despite its fairy-tale ambience *The Merchant of Venice* tries to realize play in individual experience. Moreover, its lovers do manage to bring magical love into the social sphere. It is a troubled triumph, as many an audience has reported, but a revealing one also. For the action concerns making and unmaking fortunes— both in the sense of riches and personal destinies. From one perspective at least, its characters may be seen going about the business of acquiring identity. Although magical thinking influences the outcome, Shakespeare makes magic a function of personal behavior. As in *Romeo and Juliet*, that is, play is an expression of human will.

Fortune and Identity

"Fortune" signifies wealth and luck (or grace). But the word also embraces the ideas of destiny and a secure position in life. To make one's fortune is in one sense to achieve an identity, especially a social identity. At the heart of *The Merchant of Venice* are two trial scenes. In the first Bassanio, whose "state was nothing," wins prosperity and new identities for himself and Portia. In the second trial the wealthy Shylock loses the identity he has determined to prove at all costs. Obsessed, blinded by animosity, he loses not only money, but "his stones, his daughter, and his ducats," his health and even the most basic sign of his being, his Jewishness.[3]

From the outset the play dramatizes the contingent nature of identity. Antonio enters beset by such a strange depression that he has "much ado to know myself" (1.1.7). He is, he muses, not himself. In his alienation he cannot comprehend the mood or "whereof it is born" (4). His puzzlement prefigures the riddling song Portia introduces at Bassanio's casket trial:

Tell me where is fancy bred,
Or in the heart, or in the head?
How begot, how nourished?

[3.2.63–65]

Like fancy, Antonio's sadness originates beyond the pale of customary experience. If the imminent loss of his beloved friend Bassanio moves him, he cannot reach to the source of those emotions, let alone reason about them. He cannot help himself. Since the ocean usually suggests an area of indeterminacy in Shakespeare, associated with what we would term unconscious experience, Salerio's counsel is unwittingly apt. "Your mind," he declares, "is tossing on the ocean" (1.1.8).

As representative Christians, Antonio's friends shape our attitude toward the play's apparent heroes. Yet they are shallow, even meretricious. Instead of drawing Antonio out, they try to define his problem, imposing ill-suited explanations. Salerio snobbishly portrays the merchant's ships condescending to "the petty traffickers" (12). For he is convinced Antonio dreads to lose his prosperity:

Should I go to church
And see the holy edifice of stone
And not bethink me straight of dangerous rocks,
Which touching but my gentle vessel's side
Would scatter all her spices on the stream,
Enrobe the roaring waters with my silks—

> And in a word, but even now worth this,
> And now worth nothing?
>
> [29–36]

His sentiments smack of impiety. Under eternity all things are, as he fears, "now worth this, / And now worth nothing" (34). Yet he would clutch at worldly goods. Rather than worshipping, his soul blenches at "the holy edifice." Curiously, his friends seem to find this vanity unexceptional. Had Antonio not split up his cargoes for precaution, as he remarks, presumably he too might entertain such profane anxieties.

Salerio craves security. But one symptom of his craving especially concerns us. Though he tries to understand his friend by playing his role for a moment, imagining his feelings, in fact he cannot truly play. Instead, literally, he puts himself in the other man's place. The shipwreck fantasy is, after all, his own, as are the heightened emotions his scenario calls for. Antonio's actual state of mind is irrelevant:

> But tell not me. I know Antonio
> Is sad to think upon his merchandise.
>
> [39–40]

Insofar as he paints a melodramatic shipwreck, fancying himself the magnificent merchant-hero in crisis, he is in a way *using* Antonio. Not that Salerio is a villain, or complex. The point seems to be rather how ordinary these failures of sympathy are. The friends unthinkingly impose fictions on reality. When Antonio does deny he is worried or in love, they find their conventional imaginations exhausted and feebly conclude: "Then let us say you are sad / Because you are not merry" (47). Gratiano, when he enters, is nearly as intolerant of what he cannot reduce to sense. Despite his own verbose straining after wit, he churlishly insinuates that Antonio is posturing, playing the proverbially silent wiseman (86–99). Like Salerio, he is sensitive about status, resentful of anyone who might condescendingly say in effect: "I am Sir Oracle, / And when I ope my lips, let no dog bark" (93).

Then there is Bassanio to consider. He chides Gratiano, although he himself appears somewhat touchy about the friends' abrupt departure: "You grow exceedingly strange" (67). Yet Bassanio also is troubled about his identity. Aspiring to a social role beyond his means, he has "disabled mine estate" (123). He cannot live out the identity he wants.

Bassanio envisions himself an adventurer, a Jason in quest of the Golden Fleece. Like Salerio's shipwreck fantasy, this comparison is self-indulgent: pretentious and a little heartless too. What disturbs us most is his reduction of Portia to a hyperbolical artifact— the fleece—a tack the poet of the Sonnets would mock. Nevertheless, as Salario's rhapsody about endangered merchandise suggests, Venetians are preoccupied with assessing worth. Bassanio wishes not to be "abridg'd / From . . . a noble rate" (126), and his word "rate" itself combines the idea of calculation and quantity with that of style or manner or role.

In short, these are not wholly admirable heroes. But Bassanio differs from the others in one respect. Though by his own account he has been thriftless and rather thoughtless, he is flexible. He is willing to change. To repay his debts he would try the "childhood" course of risking a second arrow to find a first. And in that willingness to risk himself, as it happens, lies the clue to fortune.

Playing for Life and Love

What does it mean to "make" a fortune? For Salerio, ships laden with precious goods are "like signiors and rich burghers on the flood," to whom lesser vessels "cursy" and "do them reverence" (1.1.10,13). His imagination reduces the vast ocean to a city street in which the trappings of privilege are dominant. It is a sentimental, static picture. In a disaster the noble ships are passively overwhelmed without struggling. Dangerous rocks, he envisions,

> touching but my gentle vessel's side,
> Would scatter all her spices on the stream,
> Enrobe the roaring waters with my silks. . . .
>
> [31–33]

Bassanio, however, imagines the process as a personal, heroic contest. He is eager to risk himself to snatch fortune like the fabulous fleece. For him the quest is "playing" in the sense of wagering or a contest of wills. Certainly his visions are vainglorious. But we can appreciate his energy, his willingness to plead a "childhood proof" (144) in broaching his plan to Antonio.

There is another connection between fortune-seeking and play.

Salerio directly compares rich ships to spectacular pageant cars whose art awes lesser travelers (11). For Bassanio too the quest for fortune is implicitly a performance. He would play at being a Jason, and is borrowing to "furnish" himself for a noble role at Belmont. To be a suitor and "hold a rival place," he believes, he needs appropriate costume and props.[4] As it happens, Bassanio's actual "performance" in the casket scene is unlike anything Salerio—or Bassanio himself—might have fancied.

At Belmont, before the caskets, Bassanio must "make" a choice which will "make" Portia his wife and "make" him a position in life. His success in the casket trial brings about new identities for himself and Portia even as he brings into the world the image of her hidden in the lead casket. By liberating Portia, moreover, he makes possible the eventual release of Antonio in the courtroom, where Portia's "playing" may be said to recreate the meaning of the law. In quest of his own fortune, that is, Bassanio helps to shape the destinies of many: Antonio, Jessica, and Lorenzo among them. But many a commentator has scoffed at Bassanio as a mere fortune-hunter or as the pale beneficiary of an absurd romance plot.[5] In Empson's rather more sophisticated view,

> more than any other suitor he is an arriviste loved only for success and seeming; his one merit, and it is enough, is to recognize this truth with Christian humility. His speech before the caskets about the falsity of seeming is full of phrases from the Sonnets . . . and may even have a dim reference to the Dark Lady.[6]

How does such an unpromising hero succeed? His connection with the Sonnets offers us a hint, I think, but to take advantage of it we need first to ask why his rivals fail.

The riddle itself is pointed simple—a sardonic touch. For like Salerio, the rival suitors grasp at reality, and so intently that they miss the simple truth. Facing the promise and peril of choice, each manufactures static proverbs which flatter his vanity and minimize his personal commitment to the risks at hand. "A golden mind stoops not to shows of dross," concludes Morocco with a show of logic and an echo of Salerio's "overpeering" pomposity. "I'll then nor give nor hazard aught for lead" (2.7.20–21).

Aragon would also preempt risk by marshaling fatuous truths:

> "Who chooseth me shall get as much as he deserves."
> Well said too, for who shall go about

Cózening fortune, and be honorable
Without the stamp of merit?

[2.9.36–39]

In a distant echo of Bassanio's reference to Jason, who stole the
Golden Fleece, Aragon construes his suit as "cozening fortune."
Ironically he is willing to cheat fortune but only, as he scrupu-
lously protests, because he believes himself so worthy. Both rivals
lose sight of love, as if bewitched by the importance of their own
choices. And since their minds are by no means fully open, they
are quick to impose self-centered "solutions" on the riddle. Aragon commands: "I will assume desert. Give me a key for this"
(51).

Bassanio, by contrast, wholeheartedly risks himself. As an arri-
viste he cannot be passively haughty like the ships Salerio envisions "overpeering" ordinary craft. Though his success seems
partly gratuitous, he has no inherent status. In this respect—and
the point is important—he could be as close in spirit to the
outsider Shylock as to the Salerios of privileged Venice. What
distinguishes him from the Jew is his susceptibility in the casket
trial to wonder. If the play is not cynical, we must believe that the
business at Belmont changes Bassanio somewhat, and makes a
deeper soul of him. What convinces me we are meant to feel such a
change in him is the similarities between his approach to the
caskets and strategies we have encountered in the Sonnets.

Bassanio chooses because he is "moved" (3.2.106). At the
crucial moment he enacts his feelings with the incantation "Joy be
the consequence!" (107). Whereas his rivals arrogantly demand the
key as they conclude—as if they are in control—Bassanio surrenders himself. Ritual elements surround his choice: the music of
a riddling song, a "living" image, and an oracular scroll.[7] Each
paradoxically serves to structure or clarify the experience taking
place, while yet remaining enigmatic. The song, for example,
construes the situation in terms of "fancy"—the power of wishes,
will, and imagination. Yet we would be hard pressed to decipher
the verse. And so Bassanio's "argument" structures his own (and
our) responses to the casket mystery, but in negative terms. From
its opening demonstrative gesture ("So may the outward shows be
least themselves") to the instant of choice itself, his speech directs
attention to what is *not* true in the world. What the mind can
grasp is false; what defies expression alone has meaning. In the
Sonnets we referred to this strategy as "negative creation" inas-

much as it affirms a positive but indefinable truth by negative means.

Adjuring the "eloquence" of gold as "mere ornament," Bassanio argues for the worth of "meagre lead" (73–148). As Burckhardt shrewdly notes, "in the casket scene, the action turns on the *styles* of metals, conceived as modes of speech. . . ."[8] But he takes the opposite of golden obfuscation to be plainness. To that opposition I would add another, between grasping and negative creation.

As Bassanio exclaims of the image he has unlocked,

> look how far
> The substance of my praise doth wrong this shadow[9]
> In underprizing it, so far this shadow
> Doth limp behind the substance.
>
> [126–29]

He celebrates Portia's inestimable worth. As "substance" or actual words, his praise fails at truth. As profound *feeling*, however, his praise can be adequate to her, even though she would for his sake "exceed account" (157). "You have bereft me of all words," he cries. "Only my blood speaks to you in my veins" (176–77). He speaks as if praise is a force with autonomous vitality, a force which embraces an order of meaning which surpasses sense. Love, the truest communication, is comparable to the wealth of meanings in the buzzing of a crowd,

> Where every something being blent together
> Turns to a wild of nothing, save of joy
> Expressed and not expressed.
>
> [182–83]

Finding "fair Portia's counterfeit" inside the casket, Bassanio brings to light an image crafted by a superior, mysterious artist. "What demigod," he exults, "hath come so near creation?" (115). As I have suggested, his "realization" of the image corresponds to the initiation of Portia into life. In the past she has been "an unlessoned girl" (160), with "the will of a living daughter curbed by the will of a dead father" (1.2.21). Henceforth she will be a woman able to create in the courtroom a solution to Shylock's threat.

Until her suitor devises a means to open the right casket, Portia's image—an image of the fulfilled woman—cannot be entirely real to us. A creative "demigod" has originated the icon, but Bassanio must share in, or complete, the creative process. Analogously parents and nature have formed Portia herself, yet she and her lover must make what Sonnet 116 calls a "marriage of true minds" to be fulfilled. Thereafter she can enter Venice proper and herself create. Celebrating the image's "living" immediacy (3.2.115–29), Bassanio is "making" love. And it is this love which brings the woman herself into the life of the play.

The casket scenes suggest that if a man is to engage destiny, he *must* create a role for himself, a way of conceiving the world. Salerio's notion of passively magnificent nobility is, by implication, a foolish pipe dream. The rival suitors are active, yet they cling to formulas, flattering themselves that they can seize truth. Bassanio's play, by comparison, frees him from conventions. Only by choosing lead, affirming what is *not* true in customary appearances, do the lovers experience "a wild of nothing" in which a host of meanings are "blent together" into a "joy / Expressed and not expressed" (182–84). Theirs is a paradoxically active passivity, a creative negation.

In the casket trial magical thinking dispels inhibitions, releasing ordinarily inaccessible emotion. Overcoming the "ugly treason of mistrust" (2.3.28), Bassanio seems to be touched at the deepest levels of his personality. "Only my blood," he vows, "speaks to you in my veins" (177). Once released, love appears to be a supra-personal force, beyond rational control. As in the Sonnets, however, this ecstatic love also endangers the lovers even as it fulfills them.

Though the casket scroll urges the lovers to an immediate kiss, their ecstasy puts them beyond themselves. Hence their love is in a crucial way impersonal. When suddenly liberated emotions do coincide in two individuals, a joyful conviction of mutuality ensues. Yet the force of such a love comes partly from the lovers' momentary separation from mundane reality. The more disoriented they are, the more they focus on one another and on love itself. Bassanio confesses to confusion "whether what I see be true, / Until confirmed, signed, ratified by you" (147).

Antonio's message dramatizes the lovers' remoteness. In his impassioned despair over the note Bassanio seems to feel love is powerless to remedy an inimical world. He can create no role to carry love into Venice. Leaving behind him the glibly heroic posture of a Jason, he has sought a new identity for himself. But while love apparently does recreate him, he resumes a worldly identity for his return to Venice. In the courtroom his lack of any new power quickly manifests itself. Portia, on the other hand, carries the process of play beyond the casket scene. She alters the baleful fate in store for Antonio by disguising herself as an advocate, becoming "other" than herself. She concentrates not on the Jew, the actual obstacle to harmony, but on the spiritual basis of consensus: the law. To be "learned," as Shylock ironically deems her, is to see through conventions, and to play out that awareness in action.

The Two Merchants

Wonder brings new life to Bassanio and Portia in their "trial." Shylock's trial, which could have issued in "mercy and remorse more strange / Than is thy strange apparent cruelty" (4.1.20), instead virtually destroys him. Re-creation he sees as death. "You take my life," he cries, "When you do take the means whereby I live" (372). Shylock's trial has persistently baffled commentators because his ruin is so absolute. Some take him to be an incipiently tragic figure; others apologize on historical grounds for Christian hostility toward usury and misunderstood Jewry. The problem is twofold: the Jew's role earns enough sympathy from us to make his punishment disconcerting; the victorious Christians may strike us as snobbishly self-righteous if not downright cruel. If the trial depends on the lucky legalism of "Balthasar," the outcome is apt to seem ordained and anticlimatic.

Shylock, as Sigurd Burckhardt has demonstrated at length, has more personal and convincing speeches than the sententious, passive Antonio.[10] Where the Jew expresses his anguish directly and plainly, Antonio relies on weary grandiloquence:

> I am a tainted wether of the flock,
> Meetest for death. The weakest kind of fruit
> Drops earliest to the ground, and so let me.
>
> [114–16]

In addition, he perseveres at self-sacrifice so mechanically that we might wonder if some sense of humor ought to complicate our response. Both villain and hero act under the spell of prejudice. "I hate him," concludes the one, "for he is a Christian" (1.3.37). The other, making straight for martyrdom, assumes that all Jews are unappeasably vicious; Shylock is a Jew; therefore no effort to create a consensus with him will avail. "Let me have judgment, and the Jew his will," he beseeches his friends at the trial (4.1.83).

> You may as well do anything most hard
> As seek to soften that—than which what's harder?—
> His Jewish heart.
>
> [78–80]

There is a vagueness in these lines ("anything most hard"), yet a complacent intransigence too.

From Shylock's position Antonio's bigotry appears less tepidly genteel:

> You call me misbeliever, cutthroat dog,
> And spit upon my Jewish garberdine.
>
> [1.3.106–7]

Bigotry is of course the conventionalizing impulse writ large, and we have seen it amply mocked elsewhere in Shakespeare, not least of all in the Capulet-Montague feud. Though spat upon, Shylock is too fanatical and bloodthirsty for us to defend him. Antonio's hostility, however, often inspires excuses. Renaissance Christians, the argument goes, commonly associated usury with the Devil, and Shylock is frequently labelled a devil in the play. But to justify Antonio's hate as righteous scorn of a devil is to overlook the impropriety of a Christian doing business with the Devil in the first place. Moreover, Portia's constructive actions tacitly rebuke the "tainted wether's" uncompromising resignation. At the least that resignation might recall Salerio's sentimental fantasy of haughty vessels passively foundering at sea (1.1.25–35). At most, it might appear as smug and implacable as the prejudice which has earned him Shylock's enmity. I say "smug" because there is something irresponsible or indulgent about Antonio's attitude toward his feelings. To the Jew's complaint that "you called me dog" (1.3.123), he has replied:

> I am as like to call thee so again,
> To spit on thee again, to spurn thee to.
>
> [125]

It is worth remarking that he does not say "I *will* call thee so," but rather "I am *as like* to call thee so again"—as if his future aggression will be beyond his control, a matter of chance or fate.

To be sure, I have subjected Antonio to especially severe scrutiny. For the popular view of him, the reassuring view, takes at face value the sort of praise uttered by Solanio, who waxes fulsome about

> the good Antonio, the honest Antonio—O that I had a title good enough to keep his name company!— [3.1.11]

My point is certainly not that this paragon is actually a scoundrel, but that both merchants of Venice are in some measure flawed souls. If we heed the play closely, we discover that its satiric irony does not tamely stop at Shylock's door. In the outcome the near martyr has no more heroic stature than the would-be murderer. For Antonio's risk to be heroic, he would have to love life more convincingly. As a pale paradigm of virtue he might seem, comically, to relish death. As for Shylock, he has an opportunity to be heroic, even tragic, for he can choose to slay his foe and take the legal consequence. But he quickly subsides in confusion. He has played the role of absolute revenger, but irresolutely. When the law requires him to give up his own life in order to act out his hatred, he is cowed.

What then are we to make of the merchants' struggle? For us, the second trial becomes clearer in the context of the first. For the merchants' conflict enables Shakespeare to dramatize a society hostile to play and personal creation. The paired antagonists refuse to become fully creative figures, trying rather to enforce narrow, oppressive roles on themselves and one another. While Antonio does support his friend Bassanio generously, he has a destructive side to him as well. With his malice and miserliness, Shylock is more unabashedly destructive. Locked together in a fanatical stalemate, the two merchants produce only strife. They lose sight even of trade itself, the business of life. It is Portia who, thanks to Bassanio, at last dissolves the deadlock.

Bassanio as Insider and Alien

The play, I have been saying, is about the creation of identity: about "making it" or "finding onself." Let me look back briefly to the opening action. Depression and anxiety disturb the first characters onstage. Antonio has "much ado" to know himself.

Sympathizing, yet above all eager to have Antonio's problem out of the way, the officious Solanio and Salerio invent a portrait of him, projecting on it their own worries. Enter Bassanio. With his estate "as nothing," "disabled," he is a man in flux. Temporarily at any rate he is neither an insider nor an alien ("disabled" can mean legally excluded or disqualified from rights). Still, he does know the role he wishes to assume, a role which requires his acceptance by "gentle" Venice.

Salerio's tributes to the merchant elite (1.1.8–14) stress the aloofness of "made" men. By their bearing alone, he fantasizes, they awe the supposed inferiors they arrogantly "overpeer." To all appearances Venice is a competitive, rigidly stratified, male-dominated society. As the excluded Jews show, wealth and success do not guarantee access to the highest circles. And yet if a church brings to Salerio only a vision of shipwrecking rocks, the gentles are themselves scarcely exemplary Christians. Like their fatalistic attitudes toward the hazards of trade, their social pride seems to entail emotional rather than rational judgments. When Shylock first proposes his "merry sport"—ominous play indeed—Antonio is capriciously confident: "In this there can be no dismay" (1.3.175). Bassanio, however, takes a skeptical stance: "I like not fair terms and a villain's mind" (174). Yet Bassanio pays little heed to religious prejudice; he is willing to borrow from Jew and Gentile alike. By the close of the play he has joined those who despise and punish the Jew, yet his speeches remain free of religious argument. At the same time he comes more insistently than ever to "love" Antonio. What is the relation between this love and the animosity surrounding it?

Both Antonio and Shylock are merchants of Venice. Their opposition enables Shakespeare to dramatize two forms Bassanio's own fortune might take. Their antagonism indirectly expresses a conflict within Bassanio. Were he to feel rebuffed by elite Venice, he might well share the Jew's resentment, the jealousy and anger of "petty traffickers" demeaned by lordly burghers. Initially, however, Bassanio tries to draw upon both sides for help. He treats both merchants civilly, inviting them to dine together with him. Nevertheless, he can arrange no consensus between them, and the "feeding" of a social dinner becomes the grotesque threat of cannibalism in the bond of flesh.

Once Bassanio has found Portia and himself, he is suddenly free to perceive how perilously violent the two merchants' enmity truly is. There is psychological logic in the plot's timing. As it dissipates inhibitions, the wonderment in the casket scene reveals not only love but also unconfronted conflicts. Bassanio's response to his friend's message is illuminating. "Gentle lady," he confesses,

> When I did first impart my love to you,
> I freely told you all the wealth I had
> Ran in my veins—I was a gentleman;
> And then I told you true; and yet, dear lady,
> Rating myself at nothing, you shall see
> How much I was a braggart. When I told you
> My state was nothing, I should then have told you
> That I was worse than nothing; for indeed
> I have engaged myself to a dear friend,
> Engaged my friend to his mere enemy
> To feed my means. Here is a letter, lady,
> The paper is the body of my friend,
> And every word in it a gaping wound
> Issuing lifeblood.
>
> [3.2.254–68]

Shylock's intended murder arouses Bassanio not to a rage against the Jew, or even to an impassioned expression of love for his friend. Instead self-contempt overcomes him. His "nothingness"— his lack of an inherently justified identity—upsets him. He sees himself as a mere actor, a "braggart" feigning a worthy role. Then guilt captures his thoughts. To be nothing is to be innocent of ill will. Therefore he is "worse than nothing" since he has "engaged" his friend to his friend's enemy. Why has he done it? "To feed my means." His image echoes Shylock's. The pound of flesh, the usurer has vowed, "will feed my revenge" (3.1.46); he will go to dinner "in hate, to feed upon / The prodigal Christian" (2.5.14). This feeding would be cannibalism. It recalls the primitive belief that the cannibal assimilates his victim's powers by consuming his flesh.[11] Bassanio himself guiltily fears he has achieved his new life by the sacrifice of Antonio. The letter from Venice he views as his friend's mutilated corpse which, even as he embraces it, implicates him in the implied murder.

Bassanio's guilty love is understandable as a response to his transformation from one whose estate was "nothing" to a powerful insider. Hitherto Bassanio has allowed his patron to bestow a social life upon him—in effect, to "create" him. Generosity and passive gratitude have governed their relationship; Antonio has felt secure. Now, however, Bassanio shares in Portia's power; she and

Bassanio himself are potentially rivals to Antonio. In a highly competitive, male-dominated society, intensified affection may serve to stabilize friendships otherwise prey to rivalry and dissension.[12] The Venetian elite is such a status-conscious, stratified group. Through their love, a love insisted upon yet remarkably vague, Bassanio and Antonio appear to submerge the hostility their relative positions might provoke. To Bassanio his patron is "the dearest friend to me, the kindest man," and so on (3.2.294). This bland praise emphasizes a harmlessness which Antonio's hatred of the Jew complicates, to say the least. Moreover, Bassanio is affirming the innocence of his own feelings, although his guilty vision of Antonio's message is an assaulted, bleeding corpse calls attention to darker emotions in himself.

In the course of the play the hostility which might be expected among the Gentiles instead finds an outlet in their collective severity toward the one alien who does fight openly for his rights and, in an overt challenge to the group, is *proud* of his alien identity: Shylock. Furthermore, what nullifies Shylock is the loss of his Jewishness, the basis for his alien's pride. Bassanio impassively observes this defeat. Symbolically, the alien in himself is being subdued.

Play and the Two Judges

Shylock's submission puts an end to a form of play we have yet to analyze. On the face of it the usurer plays only in the narrow sense of feigning. He proposes a "merry" bond with vicious motives; he disguises and "feeds" his malice while dining with his enemies. While Bassanio and Portia willingly lose themselves in play for the sake of love, Shylock would *use* others and even himself for the sake of barren metal and barren hate. Where the lovers would open themselves to one another, Shylock would "lock up" his inner self as he does his house, his daughter, and his money (2.5.28–35). But there is a deeper distinction to be made as well.

In the Renaissance conception of usury, the usurer himself is inherently guilty of playing God:

Human beings are lent their bodies, or their existence, by "nature," or "God," or "the world." In recompense for this

loan, they offer a return to nature: the children they bring
forth. . . . Similarly, the usurer lends money, and the interest
he receives is an increase much like children. However, the
usurer's profit is a perversion of nature, for by rights money
is, as Aristotle said, "a barren thing" and it should not
"breed". . . . The usurer himself is a loathsome ape of nature
who parodies the action of God (which is one of the reasons
Shakespeare calls Shylock a devil).[13]

Lucifer's original transgression was of course to "impersonate"
God (the N. Towne Lucifer literally takes his place on the heavenly throne). This notion of play as a usurpation developed in the
theatrical role of the devilish Vice, who depended on disguise and
histrionics for his strategems or "gear," and whose intentional
deceit lent sinister connotations to the idea of role playing. Like
the Vice, the usurer is supposed to manipulate his victims to
ensnare them. Shylock's bond reifies his determination to have
Antonio not simply destroyed, but in abject bondage to him. He
explicitly compares the Christians' slaves, which he says they "use
in abject and slavish parts," to the pound of flesh the bond entitles
him to use (or abuse) as he sees fit. He would play divine judge
over life and death.

Like Lucifer, the usurer parodies the action of God. Though
Shylock is hardly the Devil, he does proceed to his revenge by a
devilish parody of Christian righteousness. Rather than hew to a
role purely his own, he mimics his adversaries. After detailing the
resemblance between Christian and Jew, he concludes:

And if you wrong us, shall we not revenge? If we are like you
in the rest, we will resemble you in that. If a Jew wrong a
Christian, what is his humility? Revenge. If a Christian wrong
a Jew, what should his sufferance be by Christian example?
Why, revenge. The villainy you teach me, I will execute; and
it shall go hard but I will better the instruction. [3.1.54–62]

He will out-Christian the Christians. To "better the instruction" is
tantamount to adding insult to imitation—which is the essence of
one sort of parody. In this context the bond of flesh virtually
parodies the eating of Christ's flesh in the Eucharist. In debating
with his foes at the trial, Shylock mimics their viewpoint, being
more faithful to the law than they: "I stand for judgment"
(4.1.103). One jibing meaning of his phrase is, "I represent or play
the part of judge."[14] And this is precisely the role of Portia-

Balthasar, and ultimately God himself. The diabolical usurer would make righteousness an evil weapon.

Playing judge, Portia and Shylock are opposites. Yet Portia at last gains the upper hand by adopting her rival's own strategy. She parodies Shylock. He disdains mercy, demanding literal execution of the bond. But Portia goes him one better: "This bond doth give thee here no jot of blood" (301). The opposition of the two "judges" dramatizes an assumption so basic to Christianity as to be nearly transparent:

> But Scripture teaches us nothing but charity, nor condemns anything except cupidity. . . . I call "charity" the motion of the soul toward the enjoyment of God for His own sake, and the enjoyment of one's self and of one's neighbor for the sake of God; but "cupidity" is a motion of the soul toward the enjoyment of one's self, one's neighbor, or any corporal thing for the sake of something other than God.[15]

Portia's play meets the conditions of charity: it is use-less, unselfish, liberating. The usurer's creative energies, however, are devoted to hoarding, bondage, and what Shylock calls "feeding." His use of the killing letter of the law mocks its spirit for the sake of selfish ends.

But here the picture seems to become extremely complex, if not contradictory. For all along we have been discerning irony in Shakespeare's manipulation of allegorical conventions. Shylock is no more the Devil than the clever Portia is actually Daniel (218) or Christ.[16] On the contrary, they are perplexing mixtures of qualities, even as the actions and motives of men usually combine "charity" and "cupidity" (which is why doctrine teaches that God must be the final judge over men). Let me briefly review some instances of individual complexity.

Autonomy, Parody, and Music

Portia and Bassanio enjoy an exceptional innocence. Returning to Belmont from Venice, however, they will be exposed to the vicissitudes of life as never before: hence the need for the ring compact, and renewed pledges of faith. Portia has always lived under her father's protection, gratuitiously fortunate in wealth and position. Magically joined, the lovers know one another on ideal rather than personal terms. As for Bassanio, he admits he has already squandered one stake in life. Henceforth he must be more realistic in matching his wishes to his resources. The lovers have arrived at a degree of openness, but they require worldly competence as well.

Unlike his Christian antagonists, who regard trade fatalistically, and Portia, who is gracious but cavalier about money, Shylock tries to be rational about business. (In this he has as much in common with Sir Thomas Gresham and the Tudor economic managers as he does with the usurer-bogeyman of popular lore.) Negotiating with Antonio, he takes a reasonable stance toward the requested bond, whereas Antonio is carelessly impatient to sign (1.3.175). Practicality is distorted in Shylock, surely, yet the virtue itself has merit. Despite his cruel mockery, he does bring clarity to bear on some of the unexamined assumptions the gentles make. "What should I say to you?" he demands of Antonio. "Should I not say /'Hath a dog money? Is it possible / A cur can lend three thousand ducats?' " (115–17). In this respect the Jew functions as a satirist, meaningfully challenging the motives and complacency of elite Venice. Like Portia, who pointedly evaluates her prospective lovers (1.2.32–108), he mistrusts mere appearances. However reluctantly, we are apt to find these critical voices refreshing.

To put these matters in perspective, we need to focus on Portia's last actions. For in the trial Portia confounds Shylock partly by imitating his literalness about the law.[17] As Shylock would overcome his foes through parody, so she transcends his viewpoint in turn, in a parody of him. He will provide no surgeon to stanch the blood because "I cannot find it; 'tis not in the bond" (4.1.257). Portia mimics him to stymie him:

> This bond doth give thee here no jot of blood;
> The words expressly are "a pound of flesh."
>
> [301–2]

And again: Shylock would be deaf to all voices but his own, sole judge over the defaulter's life. Portia counters with a law which exactly reverses things, so that Shylock's life now "lies in the mercy /Of the Duke only, 'gainst all other voice" (350). Nor is this the only time she tacitly "plays" Shylock.

In holding her new husband to his promise of fidelity, demanding the ring he has given away, "Portia gayly pretends to be almost a Shylock about this lover's bond. . . ."[18] In the theater men live only insofar as actors, through imaginative power, body them forth. And Shakespeare again and again plays upon imaginative sympathy—play—as a life-giving action, a form of resurrection. [19] Rather than simply annihilating the Jew, that is, Portia preserves certain valuable aspects or "parts" of him. In this instance she carries to Belmont some of his faith in the law, tempering it with love and her larger awareness of human frailty.

In themselves, individuals are incomplete. To become whole, they need to share in one another's lives. Through imagination, they may vicariously "become" one another, as the word "community" at root implies.[20] A fanatical miser or martyr would thwart such sharing. Those who would use play or "play the thieves for wives" (2.6.23), as the Jew and Lorenzo's guileful friends do, set imagination defensively on guard. Like the metaphors of trade and rings, play expresses the idea of unimpeded circulation and wholeness. This circulation harmonizes the relations between men, and also between men and nature; hence the restoration (or "resurrection") of Antonio's lost argosies from the sea. Within the personality, too, play dispels inhibitions and thereby releases into circulation feelings customarily "locked up" in the heart like Portia's image in its casket.

Music gives form to the spirit of play. It accompanies Bassanio's casket choosing and Portia's return to Belmont. In Lorenzo's rhapsody,

> the poet
> Did feign that Orpheus drew trees, stones, and floods;
> Since naught so stockish, hard, and full of rage
> But music for the time doth change his nature.
> [5.1.79–82]

Like play, music facilitates metamorphosis. Swayed by harmony, a given identity "doth change his nature." Orpheus married poetry to music, a power beyond speech, and in so doing participated with nature in a magical spell. The effect of that spell is of course wonder. When Portia makes her final revelations—"Speak not so grossly. You are all amazed" (266)—she shares Orpheus's ambition to turn all contradictions and "stockish . . . rage," at least "for the time," to wonder.

Meanwhile, in paradoxical harmony with this upswelling of music, the return to Belmont brings about a resurgence of satire and sensible foolery. Portia's jests about her infidelity with the "civil doctor" (259) bring critical wit to bear on the mortal frailties of love. Although she elicits "amazement," she is still the woman who apologized earlier for ridiculing her suitors: "In truth, I know it is a sin to be a mocker" (1.2.51). Shylock has been a sinful mocker insofar as malice rules him. Because she would serve love and not herself alone, by contrast, Portia's wit remains innocent.

The Play as Manna and Mockery

What emerges in the final scene, in sum, is a familiar opposition. Irreverent wit provides a salutary complement to Orphic rapture. In their ecstasy during the casket ritual the lovers were helpless to save Antonio from death. It takes Portia's shrewdness and daring to free him. At the close she declares, "You are all amazed." Yet from an ironic perspective "amazed" can mean not only wonderstruck, but also caught in a maze or befuddled. And in part, admittedly, Portia's revelations depend as much on trickery as on magic. Like the poet of the Sonnets, she tries to sustain these contradictory attitudes in play. Moreover, she is one of Shakespeare's first dramatic characters to do so. Like the ambiguous location of Belmont itself, the balance she strikes allows her to be both within and outside of the world of men and money. At once she participates in mundane life and transcends it. In her paradoxical "infidelity"—"by this ring the doctor lay with me" (5.1.259)— she mocks the worldly compulsion to possess love. For in seeking to lock up his wife as Shylock would Jessica, exploiting the marriage bond, the traditional cuckold resembles the miserly usurer. Portia's joke chastens the impulse to be a Shylock about love.

But there is another aspect of this opposition to be accounted for too. Presumably Shakespeare himself knew "it is a sin to be a mocker." Yet not only did he satirize the follies of the world which flocked to the playhouse, but he profited from it in the bargain. In Augustine's categorical terms, plays would ideally be use-less, created for the glory of God perhaps, but not for profit. Shakespeare, however, played for money. Like Shylock, he belonged to a much slandered profession—the London City Corporation monotonously tried to prohibit the theater, labeling it "ungodly" and its creators "rogues." In this context the grim conversion of the Jew might seem to play out a purge of satire. In Shylock scorn has become irrationally murderous:

> You'll ask me why I rather choose to have
> A weight of carrion flesh than to receive
> Three thousand ducats. I'll not answer that.
> But say it is my humor. Is it answered?
> What if my house is troubled with a rat,
> And I be pleased to give ten thousand ducats
> To have it baned? What, are you answered yet?
>
> [4.1.40–46]

Like Portia's initial contempt toward pious "sentences" and the casket ritual (1.2.11–23), the artist's scorn must come to serve the forms of play in order to thrive. Through its heroine, the play slyly contrives to present sinless mockery, associating it with her uncanny power to amaze. Satire comes to appear life-giving, as in Sonnet 100.[21]

"God be merciful to this realm of England," admonishes the Old Man in John Northebrooke's attack on the theater (1577), "for we begin to have itching ears and loathe that heavenly manna, as appeareth by their slow and negligent coming unto sermons, and running so fast and so many, continually, unto plays. . . ."[22] To this trite carping that playgoers "loathe that heavenly manna," Lorenzo's praise of Portia makes an apt retort. "Fair ladies," he exults in wonderment, "you drop manna in the way/Of starved people" (5.1.294). The "unthrift" lovers have been musing over poetic stereotypes of love (among them Pyramus and Thisbe), and have begun to bicker (1–24). Portia's "manna" not only refills their purses, but hopefully renews their imagination of love as well. Antonio also sounds refreshed: "Sweet lady, you have given me life and living" (286). Certainly now he has reason to relinquish his fatalistic judgment of the world as a "stage, where every man must play a part,/And mine a sad one" (1.1.77–79). A man must play, yet roles need not be imprisoning.

Manna is of course heaven's bounty, and Portia's role has something godlike about it. Self-conscious, uncannily knowing, she cannot help but stand subtly apart from her companions, as different as an actor-dramatist among simple actors. She loves, but her love transcends personal gestures, mediated by humor and the ritualistic bond of the ring. Were Bassanio less comically complaisant, she might seem to him as dangerously manipulative as Hermione does at first to Leontes. For that matter, we cannot be sure that harmony will persist once the closing "spell" is past.[23] It is a privileged moment, between darkness and the day: a moment charged with contingency.

In *Love's Labour's Lost*, where our inquiry into personal creation began, love is both an ineffable "judgment of the eye" and "common" sense sensuality. No force within the play reconciles these two opposed forms. The Princess at last retires to shut herself up in a mourning house, swayed by the will of her dead father. However, love frees Portia from her father's house. Her autonomy comes from her capacity to play, to transcend a fixed, inadequate role. But Portia escapes the sort of inner turmoil hinted at in the Princess's grief. Unlike Romeo and Juliet, she achieves her freedom without struggling against irrationality in herself or in society. In this respect at least her autonomy is sentimentally conceived.

In the following chapter we will meet another child of a dead father, but a father who literally haunts his offspring. He ordains a ritualistic test by which the youth may prove himself and gain a new identity—potentially a crown. But the youth is Hamlet; the ritual, revenge; and the endeavor "to be, or not to be" a fatal ordeal of passion and self-knowledge.

VIII. This Bodiless Creation Ecstasy:
Manipulation and Play in *Hamlet*

Shakespeare dramatizes Portia's autonomy through her mastery of roles. We imagine in her a heightened awareness which enables her to conceive and act out crucial "plots": a courtroom drama and, with the rings as props, a comedy of reaffirmed love. She takes a part in the drama she creates even as she sees beyond it, and thereby transcends it.

Like Portia, Hamlet plays out a movement toward autonomy. And like her, he sees beyond conventions. Yet for him the outcome is an agonistic "madness" and death. Seeking out his father's ghost, discovering in himself a depth "which passes show" (1.2.85), he suffers increasing alienation. To take his place in the world he must act out the will of a ghost, and attack a king, symbol of order and governance. To create, that is, he must take the role of murderer, and destroy.

Portia plays in order to actualize a vision of benevolent fortune. She has not only her father's will to guide her, but also the fertile and harmonious future she anticipates. For Hamlet, by contrast, the future looms as a dreadful gulf, and fortune is "a strumpet." Play itself holds a threat for him:

> Being thus benetted round with villainies,
> Or I could make a prologue to my brains,
> They had begun the play.
>
> [5.2.29–31]

Unable to fathom the play of events, he cannot freely choose roles. He cannot choose himself.

Guided by Portia, we are privy to truth at every turn. In *Hamlet*, however, our efforts to fathom Denmark's sinister mysteries complement Hamlet's own, and become an appreciation of his condition. Even as he struggles toward a spectral autonomy, we imaginatively discover with him, in cathartic awe, the universal darkness which rings the puny world of conventions, and reveals identity itself to be a precarious miracle.

"To the Manner Born": Manipulative Intimacy

Like Hamlet himself, audiences tend to fasten upon the crimes of Claudius as the "something" rotten in Denmark. Yet T. S. Elliot, for one, has pronounced the play a failure because the King's villainy seems inadequate to the Prince's extravagant passions.[1] Historically audiences themselves have been more haunted by the play than its revenge apparatus alone would warrant. Hence Ernest Jones and others have assessed Claudius's crimes in a larger psychoanalytic context in an attempt to account for the pressure of thoughts beyond the reaches of our souls. The Prince cannot destroy his uncle, the argument goes, because Claudius has accomplished what Hamlet must have unconsciously wished and feared to do: overthrow his father and win his mother's unqualified love.[2] Though the appeal to unconscious motivation may harrow up the soul and freeze the blood of positivist critics, Oedipal fantasies recur too often in Shakespeare to justify categorical dismissal of them. In what follows, however, I wish to examine Hamlet's passions in terms of a behavior pattern which pervades the play-world, and of which Claudius's subtle murder is but a symptom: the manipulation of intimacy for ulterior power.

When the Ghost beckons, Hamlet would confront it. But Horatio intercedes, warning that the apparition may "tempt" him toward the sea, the abyss which "puts toys of desperation,/Without more motive, into every brain" (1.4.75). Like an actor, the Ghost may "assume some other horrible form" and usurp the Prince's "sovereignty of reason" (72–73) as his own governance has been usurped. Horatio's prophetic dread invisions Hamlet a helpless spectator engulfed by an evil playworld. Yet though he cries out against external dangers, his language suggests he fears madness also. Behind his fear is a magical assumption, that the "play" of imagination will become horribly real.[3] He assumes *thoughts* of the Ghost and the sea to be agencies capable of overriding the motive-power of "every brain." Not Hamlet's life but his self stands imperilled. And yet, significantly, Horatio's well-meaning remedy itself would usurp his friend's will. He urges him to mistrust, even to fear, himself. Echoing Marcellus, he commands Hamlet, "Be rul'd. You shall not go" (81).

Now Claudius has just vowed that Hamlet shall not go again to Wittenberg. Laertes he has invited to adventure abroad "at thy will" (1.2.63). Hamlet he holds immobile. But then the King introduces us to the court with a monstrous, immobilizing sentence which obscures his own actions and desires with paradoxes— "defeated joy," "an auspicious and a dropping eye" (10–11)—and then terminates with the untoward predicate "taken to wife" (14). While "making" a dubious marriage in the utterance, the oration dissipates the action described. Like Hamlet's puns—"A little more than kin, and less than kind" (65)—this auspicious and dropping verbiage attempts to freeze irreconcilable public and priviate realities in an equilibrium of thought. Such an equilibrium however, is tantamount to paralysis.

Hamlet's desire to depart, like his claim to "that within which passes show" (85), would defy the control of his mother and "father." Hence they work to curb his will, pressing him into a politely impotent role. They would wheedle and shame him out of the troubling emotion they glibly label grief. "Good Hamlet" (68), of "sweet and commendable" nature (87), is in his independence "obstinate" (93), "impious and unmanly" (94), "incorrect" (95), "simple and unschool'd" (97), and so on. Yet even as Claudius conceals himself and dominates Hamlet, he solicits his love, imploring him to "think of us / As of a father":

> with no less nobility of love
> Than that which dearest father bears his son
> Do I impart to you.
>
> [107–12]

In these exchanges love is insidiously identified with dependence, obedience, and regulated public emotion. Intimacy itself is a performance: speeches and actions which "a man might play" (84).

Before we consider Hamlet's response to this seductive intimacy, let me introduce a more starkly touching and unwholesome instance of it, the sinister parting embrace Laertes forces on his sister. In the name of concern he robs her of will and in turn identity. In his advice to her he amplifies the court's sly hostility toward feeling. As if love is combat, he commands her "keep in the rear of your affection, /Out of the shot and danger of desire" (1.3.34). Like Horatio, he sounds as if he dreads loss of mental control, associating passion with the madness of "unmastered importunity" (32). Forthright desire he equates with lust. While he shrewdly perceives the Prince's "circumscribed" role (22), and that "his will is not his own" (17), Laertes can point to no cause but the abstract bogey "the danger of desire" (35).

Polonius, we gather, has abetted his son's anxiety about self-control. For the old man trusts no one, and seeks to gain leverage over others through use of trite imperative maxims and spying. Sparing no threats, Laertes plays out his father's lesson with Ophelia. Indeed, he sounds more like his father than a youth bound for adventure. "Be wary then; best safety lies in fear," he minces, "Youth to itself rebels, though none else near" (43). He casts Ophelia as a helpless child to be ruled by fear of her natural self. Yet blindly playing his father, he undermines the integrity of his own will at the same time. As Hamlet's father does, he becomes a hellishly frightening "watchman to the heart" (46) of his "child," an all-monitoring specter who condemns all the depraved passions he imagines under heaven. Like the Ghost, he departs with a warning: "remember well /What I have said to you" (84). To which, readily surrendering herself, his sister replies:

> 'Tis in my memory lock'd,
> And you yourself shall keep the key of it.
>
> [85–86]

In her affection lurks the germ of her eventual self-destruction.

Laertes violates his sister's heart, yet he seems almost innocently unaware of the harmful consequences for her and himself. However, in its most concrete image—the seizure of power by means of poison in a brother's ear—manipulation is artful and vicious. The murder symbolically focuses a wider and subtler corruption. Like Claudius's "leperous distilment," seductive words may poison the unwary or sleeping self. Ophelia would keep *her* brother's "good lesson" as a dreadful "watchman" over her implicitly sleeping heart. Hamlet himself obsessively construes his experience as dreams.

Yet Hamlet *cannot* be simply a victim. It marks his tragic condition that he cannot lose himself in sleep. From the outset, as aboard ship for England months later,

> in my heart there was a kind of fighting
> That would not let me sleep.
>
> [5.2.4–5]

At first, to be sure, he yearns to escape. For where the court would snare him in a rigid, impassive role, he has only the ill-defined prompting of "that within which passes show" to orient himself. To be truest or most real to himself, he must negate or at least hold apart from conventional reality as appropriated by the court. To be sane, as we shall see, he must appear "mad" to the court. Yet until he recognizes that paradox after the Ghost's revelations, he broods about "self-slaughter" as an escape from all conflicts.

In his first soliloquy, now literally isolated out of the public sphere, Hamlet wishes not for a confrontation with the sources of his anguish, but for bodily dissolution "into a dew" (1.2.130). He abjures all interest in the world, all desires. Yet his thoughts abruptly turn to the chaotic fertility of "things rank and gross in nature" (136), and his mother's remarriage. "Heaven and earth," he protests, "Must I remember?" (142). But what is the emotion he would suppress—disgust? despairing love? sexual anxiety? He would "not think on't" (146). A beast, he cries, "would have mourned longer" (151). But though anger and forboding fill him, he nevertheless keeps his suffering from crystalizing: "But break my heart, for I must hold my tongue" (159).

The abstract terms of Hamlet's soliloquies—being, not-being, heaven, earth—generate a nimbus of emotion that answers to any number of dramatic interpretations.[4] He obscures himself even in the act of expression. Similarly, his word play suspends the aggression which motivates it. His puns on "kin" and "kind" (65), and his insinuations about "seeming" (76) attack Gertrude and Claudius, but covertly. In this respect Hamlet's will to play is an act of self-suspension as well as self-assertion.

With this doubleness in mind, we might reconsider Hamlet's reaction to the Ghost. For awe and contempt mingle in him. At first the "questionable shape" intimidates him (1.4.43). But when Horatio warns against the danger (64), he scoffs, "Why, what should be the fear?" (64). And when he "explains" his risky pursuit by the tautology "My fate cries out" (81), invoking the absurdly poetical Nemean lion's nerve, his comrades understandably mistrust his judgment and follow.

Hamlet's doubleness has a manipulative quality. At once he is tormented yet aloof. He calls attention to himself even as he withholds himself. His life he despairingly calls worthless (65), yet efforts to save him stir his wrath. When Horatio intercedes, Hamlet threatens to "make a ghost" (85) of anyone who interferes. Like the word play he uses against the court, this apparent foolery counters "toys of desperation" (75) with verbal toys he can control. His jest obscures his meaning and the nature of his experience itself. But then, he refers to his "life" (65) and to his "soul" (66), not to the hopes and terrors by which we locate personal identity. Despite the urgency of the moment, he seems compelled to make very act an "act."

We may see what Hamlet's friends cannot, that his pursuit of the Ghost takes him closer to confrontation with himself. He wishes to believe he sees his father, his namesake and a model for him. Beseeching "Why is this? wherefore? What should we do?" (57), he seeks an answer which depends not only on the Ghost's identity, but on his own as well.

"Purpose is but the slave to Memory"

The Ghost first reveals himself to Hamlet as if summoned by his tirade against the "heavy-headed revels" of Claudius and, by extension, all Denmark (1.4.14–38). Hamlet's "explanation" of the festivity begins as a sermon, then transforms itself into an apology. A "particular fault" in a man otherwise "pure as grace," he maintains, may chance to damn the offender utterly in the public eye. But while Hamlet evidently identifies with those accused, sympathetic to their solitary natural flaws "wherein they are not guilty," his overtaxed, hysterical syntax blurs his logical focus. He conceives of an accusing watchman, to adopt Ophelia's image, which he calls "the general censure." Yet nowhere in the play do we hear any sign of will, let alone censure, in the public voice. He feels judged but cannot convincingly locate the judgment's source. And precisely as the Ghost enters, Hamlet's protest expires in the incoherent "noble substance of a doubt." The apparition, that is, literally appears when reason fails.

In a way the Ghost's first words tell all. Ominously, without need, he commands his excruciatingly attentive son to "mark me" (1.5.2). The command is pure emphasis. At once the voice is paternally authoritarian and theatrical.[5] Chided a second time— "pity me not" (5)—Hamlet mildly protests as much: "Speak. I am bound to hear" (6). But the Ghost directly crushes this self-assertion: "So art thou [bound] to revenge" (7). He goes on, advertising the thrills of a melodramatic "tale" which some nameless agency conveniently "forbids" him to unfold (13–20). As a tale-teller and father, the Ghost takes away even as he gives. He teases, he threatens. He wishes his son to act for him, yet gratuitously he insists upon the power of his tale to paralyze him, to "freeze thy young blood" and reduce him to a puny "fretful porpentine." When Hamlet tries to assume the desired heroic role, promising to sweep to revenge "with wings as swift/As meditation" (30), the Ghost rewards his theatrics while belittling him as a schoolboy: "I find thee apt" (31). He adds that only "the fat weed . . . on Lethe wharf" would decline revenge, virtually accusing Hamlet of inaction he is not yet guilty of (32–34).

The Ghost enacts that merciless and irrefutable judge whom Hamlet thought of as "the general censure." In his revelation he cries out for revenge and justice. Yet obsessively he recreates the crime itself, especially its secondary taint, "damnèd incest" (1.5.83). In his impotence he generates a righteous, self-intoxicating indictment (41–91). As he recreates his betrayal he invests it with superhuman reality and horror. Simultaneously he subjugates it to his verbal manipulation. No mere sinners have hurt him, but two monsters, a serpent-beast and an angel who "preys on garbage." It is a cruel and self-aggrandizing vision, a vision of motiveless cosmic evil.

The Ghost is of course partly a histrionic device and, we feel, partly a reflection of disturbed imaginations within the play-world. At the same time, however, he extends the singular pattern of behavior that underlies the play-world. Like the other parents in the court, the Ghost is deviously despotic in his need for control. *He* knows, *he* commands; *his* will must be preeminent. As a bodilessly spiritual Hyperion he would not allow "the winds of heaven/Visit [Gertrude's] face too roughly" (1.2.140–42). Such a love would have insulated the Queen from life, monitoring even her experience.

As his heroic rhetoric indicates, Hamlet would like to satisfy his ghostly father, and to join with him. Yet that figure repeatedly oppresses him, fixing him in a treacherous relation the way Claudius does, tolerating no initiative. Even as he appeals to to affection—"If thou didst ever thy dear father love" (1.5.23)—he proposes to shackle his son, to have him "bound" (7) to revenge. That bond helps to make Denmark a prison in Hamlet's eyes. The Ghost demands love, yet gives his son only his own outrage in return. Seduced into showing concern, made vulnerable, Hamlet finds himself mysteriously rejected in a manner that insinutates his inadequacy. He cannot be both a "fretful porpentine" and a heroic creator of new love and justice in Denmark.

The Ghost, then, imposes an impossible task. As he denies Hamlet positive goals, so he denies him useful, limited anger. Instead he demands a superhuman fury against Claudius, and no direct reconciliation with his mother: "Leave her to heaven" (86). His program makes no provision for healing Denmark or Hamlet. The Prince must desire nothing for himself, no ambition or passionate love, no dream of renewal.

In accord with the Ghost's apocalyptic vision Hamlet does promise to "wipe away" all traces of his natural self thereafter (96–111). He vows to make "thy commandment all alone . . . live / Within the book and volume of my brain." "Unmix'd with baser matter," the dross of human sympathies, that commandment will remain a poisonous void. To submit to the Ghost's will, he must become nothing. (Shakespeare reminds us of Hamlet's loss of self by making him sound like the Ghost whenever he is about to take action.)[6] And this is the basic paradox of his fate: he cannot succeed without wanting to live; he cannot want to live because he wants to succeed.

"To Double Business Bound"

How does Hamlet respond to the Ghost's manipulation? To put his predicament in perspective, let me recall Portia's initiation into life. Like the Prince, she despairs in her opening lines: "my little body is aweary of this great world" (1.2.1). Her will is "curbed by the will of a dead father" (21). But her father will eventually liberate her: his casket trial joins her to a husband even as it affords her new roles in life. Momentarily wonderstruck, she wishes to "exceed account" for her lover's sake (3.2.158). Though her former identity dissolves in this "ecstasy," new love orients her. Admitting herself to be "unschool'd" (160), she nevertheless "may learn" (161) and "can learn" (162). In fact she soon sets about mastering new roles. Released from the casket, her "image" comes into the world.

Now the Ghost would transform his child also. But in the words of his counterpart, the Player King, he would make his son "but the slave to memory" (3.2.183). He fills Hamlet with what to the conventional Gertrude appears "This bodiless creation ecstasy" (3.4.138). Yet for the Ghost, wonder is not a fulfillment but an instrument of coercion. "I could a tale unfold," he menaces, which "would harrow up thy soul," and so on for nine lines (1.5.13–22). He dominates his son by proscribing precisely the self-assertion his goal demands of him And of course that goal is the creation not of consensus and marital fertility, but righteous hate and destruction.

At first Hamlet seems bold in response. Rather like Romeo, he tries to grasp his new condition by vehement, naive conjuring. He would "wipe away" all traces of his conventional personality in a futile effort to identify completely with his father's will:

> I'll wipe away all trivial fond records,
> All saws of books, all forms, all pressures past,
> That youth and observation copied there,
> And thy commandment all alone shall live
> Within the book and volume of my brain. . . .
>
> [99–103]

Where Portia accepts her "unschool'd" condition (a word Claudius uses against Hamlet in 1.2.87), the Prince repudiates the school-boy "table of my memory" (1.5.98). He wishes to seize the truth, not learn, even though the Ghost's "I find thee apt" (31) casts him as an obedient pupil. He would fasten on words, on "thy commandment" which will, he says, dominate his consciousness (102). By his vow he would abandon his quotidian self, and substitute his father's spectral will for his own. Insofar as magical thinking allows, he wishes to become the father he has idealized as a god (1.2.140).[7]

In his awe the son would bypass the trials of self-knowledge that autonomy requires. Instead he would invoke an inhumanly pure hatred of Claudius. Of love and justice and healing he says virtually nothing. If we suppose that he makes his vows out of filial affection, we must concede that love to be a source of danger to him. For he cannot (and poignantly should not) give himself over to the spirit of his father, even though Claudius's vicious crime does require redress.

Grasping at absolutes—utter identification with the Ghost and hatred of his uncle—Hamlet behaves as if he can make himself and the King nothing. Conceptually, however, even "nothing" is something. In Shakespeare creation is an act of renewal: of reconceiving what exists. To hate absolutely is to conjure the forces of madness into play.

At this point we have located a flaw sufficient to account for an ordinary tragic hero. Yet the play and the Prince surpass simple tragic models. No sooner does the apparition vanish, for example, than Hamlet abruptly changes his role. With sacramental fervor he has pledged himself to the Ghost's "commandment." Now, however, he plays the fool in a way that deviously asserts his independence and makes light of spectral absolutes. With a slyness that reflects the manipulators around him at court, he thrusts at the Ghost as he has at his uncle. Mocking the Ghost as "boy" and "truepenny" (1.5.150) and "old mole" (162) for his comrades' benefit, he swaps roles with his formidable father. From awed submission he moves toward assertive play:

> I perchance hereafter shall think meet
> To put an antic disposition on. . . .
>
> [172]

Magnified by crisis, that is, Hamlet's earlier doubleness begins to look drastically complex. Rejoined by his friends, he riddles in an oracular voice one minute; the next, he jests about "this fellow in the cellarage" (151). He utters what may be "wild and whirling words" of madness (133) or intimations of "wondrous strange" things beyond philosophy's ken (164). And the contradictions intensify hereafter. He appears by turns committed to the Ghost and detached enough to challenge it as a "shape" of the devil, who may be exploiting "my weakness and my melancholy" (2.2.597).[8] One moment he apparently believes magically that "thinking makes [things] so" (251); the next, he seems rather to be self-ware, and complexly playing.

Hamlet disposes himself, then, in a strenuous equilibrium. To Horatio and the others, he is variously aloof and apologetic—"I am sorry to offend you, heartily./Yes, faith, heartily" (1.5.134). In insidious ways he is manipulative. Swearing his companions to silence, he emphasizes their impotence even as he excites their desire to aid him. Like his father, he intimidates by invoking unspeakable evils while precluding any remedial action. Making himself inscrutable, he nevertheless mobilizes the others to serve his ends. Awestruck himself moments before, he now causes his companions to gape in amazement. Even in his letter to Horatio, much later, he echoes his father's promise of a tale that would harrow up the soul: "I have words to speak in thine ear will make thee dumb" (4.6.20). Like a poet or seer, he looks to wondrous speech for power. His *use* of wonder, however, undercuts intimacy even as it binds his auditors to him. "So gentlemen," he summarizes with rueful warmth,

> With all my love I do commend me to you;
> And what so poor a man as Hamlet is
> May do t'express his love and friending to you,
> God willing, shall not lack. Let us go in
> together. . . .
>
> [1.5.182–85]

Speaking in the third person, he behaves as if he is interpreting to them an absent Hamlet who is beyond the reach of ordinary language.

In *Hamlet* as in no earlier play before us, things undreamt of in mundane philosophy radically pervade the play-world and human experience. There is no fairy wood, no walled garden in Verona or casket chamber in remote Belmont to shelter visionary awareness from chaos and evil. For Hamlet, in the Queen's pregnant phrase, "This bodiless creation ecstasy/Is very cunning in" (3.4.138). For Gertrude, ironically, her son's "ecstasy" is merely a sudden and special affliction. In what follows we need to probe further that profoundly equivocal ecstasy in order to learn more about the creative modality it bodies forth.

Manipulation and Self-Hatred

Hamlet tests Shakespeare's conception of creation as no earlier play had done. Its hero penetrates the mask of conventional reality. His "ecstasy," however, discovers not wondrous love, but deceit and madness and death. "Look you," he cries returning from the Ghost to his friends, "I will go pray" (1.5.130). But he can neither pray wholeheartedly nor play toward a consensus with others. Estranged from both spheres, he demands despairingly of Ophelia, "What should such fellows as I do crawling between earth and heaven?" (3.1.129). Though he struggles to master his condition, it becomes more insoluble: and the more insoluble, the more he strives to balance and preserve himself. Why does he find his will increasingly nullified?

To create we modify or re-create what exists. But creation is a twofold process: we assert a new order only by negating or "decreating" an old. Hamlet, significantly, would nullify the imperfect world. He would annihilate that "monster custom, who all sense doth eat" (3.4.161). Yet he cannot conceive, on a human scale, positive values and roles. Virtue for him is negative: the absence of sin, the abolition of marriage and other customary forms for affection, repudiation of "all the uses of this world." He commands his mother to "throw away" the "worser part" of her heart, and stipulates in cruel detail what she must *not* do, and *not* be. The role he forces on her ("Assume a virtue") remains nebulous. Though he urges her to despise her present self, he leaves any future redemption appallingly void (3.4.157–88).

Because he cannot or will not imagine love—whether love of justice or beauty or others, or love in the basic sense of pleasure taken in the existence of something—Hamlet cannot truly create. The play-world offers him no positive models. On all sides love *appears* corrupt or nonexistent, so we sympathize with him. Yet I stress "appears" because love is of course an act of belief or trust. Love, Shakespeare seems to say, and love will create love. Fear to love, and the self may embark on a destructive cycle of doubt, withdrawal, and madness. In part, Hamlet can take no decisive action because "his habitual feeling is one of disgust at life and everything in it, himself included. . . ."[9]

Self-disgust functions like the poison in the playlet, whose

> natural magic and dire property
> On wholesome life usurps immediately.
>
> [3.2.253]

When Horatio confesses to "a truant disposition," Hamlet tries to protect him from self-hatred while ambiguously protecting his own ear from the subject also:

> I would not hear your enemy say so;
> Nor shall you do my ear that violence,

To make it truster of your own report
Against yourself.

[1.2.169–73]

His metaphor (violence to the ear) describes the crime which destroyed his father. And the Ghost, we recollect, abhors the "blossoms" of sin which untimely death caught in him. He implies that with justice and the proper sacraments he would have gone perfect out of life. His murderer, "a wretch whose natural gifts were poor/To those of mine," exposed the reality of his flaws to him, and thereby exposed him to self-hatred. As in the player's oration, when the crash of "senseless" or unfeeling Ilium "takes prisoner Pyrrhus' ear" (2.2.468–71), so the collapse of an unrealistically idealized world penetrated the ear of the elder Hamlet with the poison, and took his life. Self-loathing registers even in his body's transformation as the poison takes effect:

a most instant tetter bark'd about,
Most lazar-like, with vile and loathsome crust,
All my smooth body.

[1.5.71–73]

He went helplessly

to my account
With all my imperfections on my head.
O, horrible! O, horrible! most horrible!

[78–80]

If we construe the Ghost as in some way a projection of Hamlet's own imagination, their encounter also may be seen to objectify the self-destructive process within him. For the apparition undermines him, imposing an insupportably negative task, exciting an inhuman idealism in him. "Father" and son mythologize human actions, making them impossibly angelic or demonic. They think not in terms of compassion and contrition—not of transformations—but in terms of annihilation. Such absoluteness is static; it denies time and the future. It fixes both father and son in the posture of martyrdom *whether or not* their revenge is carried out.

At the same time this idealism expresses Hamlet's ambivalence toward his father also. He has come to manhood with his heart, like his mother's, cleft in twain. For he has two "fathers": the Hyperion a child would emulate, and the hateful vicarious father Claudius. Returning from Wittenberg, he has found two grossly

175

imperfect individuals where he had esteemed parental paragons. An evil foster father has displaced the natural father, and tries to ingratiate himself with the son as he has with the "seduced" mother. In Hamlet's imagination, that is, Claudius and his victim present opposite faces of the same figure. If the Prince *could* be simply "mad," he could make Claudius a scapegoat, and thereby protect his love of his "exemplary" father. That he hesitates to trust his own imagination is therefore ironically heroic as well as self-disabling.

As Hamlet approaches action, his ambivalence threatens to surface. There is psychological logic in the timing of the prayer scene. Just as he has mistrusted the Ghost he has sworn to serve, so in spite of himself he seems partially to identify with the wretch he has sworn to kill.[10] Having confirmed his uncle's guilt and his own power through the "mousetrap" play, he suddenly espies the supposed monster on his knees, vulnerably beseeching grace. Spying, he is closer now to perceiving the doubleness in himself. His father, he concedes, was taken "full of bread, /With all his crimes broad blown, as flush as May" (3.3.80). His words could as well apply to Claudius. Though the moment is dizzyingly paradoxical (for one thing, Claudius cannot repent), Hamlet understandably fantasizes about catching his quarry in "some act/ That has no relish of salvation in't" (91). He would preserve the simple opposition between his "fathers" lest he face in himself an agony of irreconcilable feelings and self-disgust such as we overhear in Claudius:

> O limed soul that, struggling to be free,
> Art more engaged!
>
> [67–69]

In portraying his "fathers" to Gertrude, Hamlet grasps at absolute distinctions. One he makes godlike, with "Hyperion's curls"; the other, a "mildewed ear" and "a moor" (3.4.54–68). However, this "counterfeit presentment of two brothers" makes a distinction we in the audience cannot clearly see: nor is it certain that Gertrude herself does.[11]

Similarly, in his final apology to Laertes, Hamlet divides himself into opposing forces or "factions." Yet like the self-hatred he in effect describes, his speech undermines the meaning he creates:

> Was't Hamlet wrong'd Laertes? Never Hamlet.
> If Hamlet from himself be ta'en away,

And when he's not himself does wrong Laertes,
Then Hamlet does it not, Hamlet denies it.
Who does it, then? His madness. If't be so,
Hamlet is of the faction that is wrong'd;
His madness is poor Hamlet's enemy.

[5.2.225–31]

His repetition of his name (seven times in as many lines) emphasizes its form as a word, a sound: it insists on his identity and yet may call attention to his mysteriousness. Subsequently he exchanges fatal blows with Laertes, that mirror of him as an abused son. By "the image of my cause," Hamlet has said, "I see / The portraiture of his" (77).[12] The sinister staging of the duel, that final self-consuming climax, draws us back to the manipulative pattern in the play.

Manipulation, again, entails the use of love for the sake of aggrandizing power or control over life. A child such as Hamlet or Laertes has been learns to withhold his deepest, most natural feelings, stage-managing the image of himself he presents to others in order to protect himself from "use" and to gain some control over others. The Ghost blames all manipulation on Claudius: on the "witchcraft of his wits" and his "power . . . to seduce" (1.5.43–44). But "every major personage in the tragedy is a player in some sense, and every major episode a play."[13] Because manipulation so pervades the court, it goes unrecognized, like the "rank corruption" Hamlet senses "mining all within" (3.4.148). But when life is a performance, ever self-conscious, one outcome is that men blur their emotional reality for themselves and one another. Hatred and self-hatred become indirect and incalculable. In his fatuous parting advice to Laertes, Polonius so sharply separates the self from its social masks ("Give thy thoughts no tongue") that his most important precept ("above all, to thine own self be true") sounds by turns cynical or impossible (1.3.58–80).

Shakespeare places the defenseless Ophelia before us partly to expose by contrast the calculation and self-distortion of those around her. "As one incapable of her own distress," as the Queen puts it, she is openly pathetic in her suicide. The court, however, masks even her self-destruction by ordering a Christian burial for her. Given her father's exploitation of her feelings, we cannot miss the significance of the flowers she wears to her death. They include "long purples,"

> That liberal shepherds give a grosser name,
> But our cold maids do dead men's fingers call them.
>
> [4.7.169–72]

The name suggests her father's grasp on her soul, and also the forbidden sexuality he used to circumscribe her autonomy. Like Lear's flowery array, Ophelia's "fantastic garland" is an emblem of madness: of insight she cannot endure. Moreover, it is a garland she herself creates.

Because manipulation breeds insecurity, it encourages idealism as a means of orienting oneself. At the same time, however, men may use idealism to enhance their own power, as Polonius and Claudius and the Ghost do. They subject experience to value systems that flatter themselves and intimidate the spirit of love and play which might lead others toward liberating, incorruptible ideals. For Hamlet, after all, the dream of an ideal self is nearly as painful as his uncle's actual wrongs. Conversely, we are hard pressed to believe the murder of Claudius a sufficient resolution to his nephew's or Denmark's distress. For to fasten on the King's annihilation, as the Ghost commands, is to make him a scapegoat, a mythic figure whose death can vicariously redeem *all* corruption. Hamlet himself cannot believe that. In his antic, skeptical moods at least, he senses that every action may be an act. For him play threatens deception even as it promises, as in the "mousetrap," truth and release.

Identity as Magic and Play

The role "Hamlet" presents a sum of contending voices which commentators resolve into specific, sometimes incompatible portraits.[14] One difficulty is that the Prince himself reshapes the lineaments of his character from moment to moment. He is deliberately an actor, caught up in theatrical relationships with one and all. Yet because manipulation vitiates ordinary roles and treats play itself as an instrument of power, play for him is a fearsome prospect. He cannot trust the postures of sonneteering lover or "good child and ... true gentleman" (4.5.145) or even revenger, for each would entrap and disable him. Putting on an antic disposition, he holds himself apart from customary roles.

Hamlet's predicament, then, dramatizes in an extreme form a conception of identity we have met before. For Shakespeare, autonomy is not essentially a matter of self-expression, but rather a process of self-transcendence. It is not a particular arrangement of personal traits or virtues, but a risky awareness of the possibilities of being. However, in a world oppressed by spies and masks, autonomy becomes maddeningly contingent.

Mistrusting the many corruptible roles available to him, Hamlet yearns to leap beyond them all. Wishing to "wipe away all trivial fond records, / All saws of books, all forms, all pressures past," he seeks to transcend the uncertainties of "acting" (1.5.99). He would conjure a magical identity for himself, making his father's will so much his own that he would be virtually enacting *it* rather than playing out a self-directed part. In the delusive world of the court, however, magical belief is especially perilous, and he pulls back from it as he does from suicide in his soliloquies.

As time presses upon him Hamlet searches for a personal mode of action. But "bad dreams," the turmoil buried in his heart, make a prison of imagination's "infinite space" (2.2.252–56). His own will to revenge comes to seem a false show to him:

> Prompted to my revenge by heaven and hell, I
> Must, like a whore, unpack my heart with words
> And fall a-cursing like a very drab. . . .
>
> [580–82]

His imagery, strangely, echoes the Sonnets. A true lover might lose himself in his experience: might become what he plays. A whore, on the other hand, uses love for profit, and hence must remain aware of style: of the gap between what is and what seems.

Comparing himself to the actor playing Pyrrhus, Hamlet reflects bitterly on his own alienation. Seeing himself as a whore or drab, he makes his imagination the sort of "watchman to my heart" Ophelia suffered (1.3.46). He finds himself, as it were, spying on himself. In the court intimate life proceeds strategically, as a play begun before the Prince at least "could make a prologue to my brains" (5.2.30). As a result the false passions of real players may arouse a dread that all identity is a fabrication. The players' sham calls into question the substantiality of all emotion. "Is it not monstrous," Hamlet wonders with horrified admiration, "that this player here,"

> But in a fiction, in a dream of passion,
> Could force his soul so to his own conceit

That from her working all his visage wann'd;
Tears in his eyes, distraction in's aspect,
A broken voice, and his whole function suiting
With forms to his conceit? And all for nothing!
For Hecuba!

[2.2.545-51]

He dreads that identity is but "a fiction, a dream of passion" (545), and therefore "all for nothing" (550). Specifically he fears that no emotion is fundamentally real. Though he has the "cue for passion" (545), he can give it no adequate shape.

Hamlet's "monstrous" vision associates the basic experiences of identity with theatrical illusion. Exercising editorial control over his inner life, holding himself in abeyance, he fears that reality is but the caprice of "conceit" (546). If a man may force his soul to any conceit, then imagination is godlike in its freedom to form— and to falsify—the self. Identity would then be not substantive, but a creative action. Emotion, the vision implies, is fundamentally a condition of undifferentiated nervous arousal which an individual interprets to "make" love or anger or fright, and so on. Conventional wisdom, now as in the Renaissance, regards feeling as something concrete and particular, whether as a humor or a quantity of energy. With the altered emphasis natural to an actor-playwright, Shakespeare identified the genesis of emotion with interpretive acts: with art. In this perspective emotion is abstractive, dependent on behavior and future events to corroborate it. Which is to say that self-creation is predictive, and "proved" sane or mad by its adequacy to subsequent events. When the blood "speaks" in Bassanio's veins, in the ecstasy of the casket ritual, he and Portia construe that wordless "speech" as love. But it takes the ensuing trials, Shylock and the rings, to verify that love.[15]

Aroused by the Ghost's "tale," Hamlet construes his passionate awe as hatred of Claudius and devotion to his father. His imagination, however, proves tragically too narrow to satisfy actual circumstances. (The play leaves open the possibility that no human imagination could be equal to its enigmatic, evil world.) For one thing, the Ghost would bind his son to the past, denying him a personal future.[16] The Prince in turn "conceives" himself in incongruous ways. He loses sight of the future, and of himself as a potential, rightful king. Misconstruing, he is mad as all men, in some measure, must be.

Hamlet's vision magnifies individual autonomy and insecurity. If a man "conceives" himself, wittingly or not, then self-knowledge and a validating consensus become momentous. Yet where reason and consensus are untrustworthy, as in the Danish court, imagination's freedom comes to seem unbearable. Consequently a conception of identity which appears to relinquish magical thinking may actually provoke an anxious faith in such powers. In a different, comic milieu Portia's behavior reconciles magic and sense. Though hints of discord shadow her triumph, Shakespeare encourages us to trust the love and mirth we behold, and to wink at Portia's cunning management of all. But he protects her triumph from skeptical responses by inviting playful forbearance.

The great tragedies fight shy of such compromises. Hamlet, for example, endures irreconcilable visions of existence founded on magic and art-ful creation. He tries to conjure his will into form:

> I should 'a fatted the region kites
> With this slave's offal. Bloody, bawdy villain!
> Remorseless, treacherous, lecherous villain!
> O vengeance!
>
> [574–77]

Then abruptly he disavows this litany, scoring himself for an ass (578). Like the Ghost, he would use wonder if he could, wishing to display a passion whose potent words could

> Make mad the guilty and appall the free,
> Confound the ignorant and amaze indeed
> The very faculties of eyes and ears.[17]
>
> [557–59]

But his "shows" work, like all earthly things, including art itself, only within limits. His "mousetrap" exposes Claudius, but it cannot include all the audience in this new awareness, and cannot induce purifying madness in the "guilty" King. Similarly, his passionate "shriving" of his mother humbles her, but does not renew her spirit. Though his "prophetic soul" divines his uncle's ghastly crime, he cannot clearly see the distortions of intimacy poisoning all the court.

The Prince needs to integrate these opposed visions: to reconcile magical thinking and the equally chimerical ideal of absolute self-creation. Yet as he protests to the sophistical Rosencrantz, "by my fay, I cannot reason" (2.2.264). Awed by the player's "dream of passion," he recoils against his own impotent conjurations. However, he acts not to question, but to repudiate, himself.

His words seem to him a mere "act," a drab's curses. Though he scorns these artifices, he nevertheless goes on to invent roles for himself (rogue, peasant, slave, John-a-dreams, whore, drab, stallion) which he in turn repudiates: "Fie upon't, foh!/About, my brains" (583). As a result, what looks like self-examination leads not to self-knowledge but toward self-suspension or, ambiguously, self-transcendence. Throughout the speech he attentuates the reality of his feelings. And in a way he repudiates even his repudiations, for he turns abruptly to his "mousetrap" plot. But then, even his urgent wish for death, once clothed in words, becomes an entity ("that is the question") and loses the name of action (3.1.56). Hamlet remains alienated, in short, not because "reason panders will" (3.4.88) but because will becomes a drama of agonistic thoughts which supersedes the strife in his heart. In this sense "conscience" or self-consciousness "does make cowards of us all" (3.1.83).

Scourge and Minister: Fool and Priest

Hamlet, we said, mistrusts the conventional roles available to him. What roles, then, does he take? His inner conflicts about creation draw us to two opposed types of roles: those which affirm meaning and order, and those which are decreative. To the Ghost, for example, he swears that "thy commandment all alone shall live/Within . . . my brain" (1.5.102). Placing a "commandment" to hate before all else, his vow echoes (ironically if not blasphemously) religious vows. Soon he begins portentously riddling to his companions, like a seer. Lest we miss the oracular character of this riddling, Shakespeare has him tell the others that

> every man hath business and desire
> Such as it is; and for my own poor part,
> Look you, I will go pray.
>
> [130–32]

Prayer is of course the "business" of priests. Later, with Ophelia and his mother, he openly plays heaven's "scourge and minister" (3.4.175). "Confess yourself to heaven," he admonishes Gertrude, "repent what's past" (149). Her sin destroys the magical efficacy of prayer, and

> from the body of contraction plucks
> The very soul, and sweet religion makes
> A rhapsody of words.

[46–48]

He speaks as if words are corporeal, and can be murdered. Ophelia he harangues with the same homiletic outrage. In a grotesque parody of priestly service Shakespeare has him witness Claudius at prayer. Yet he ironically cannot, and would not, "hear" the confession Claudius tries fruitlessly to make. Invoking not mercy but murder and eternal damnation, he plays shockingly false to the priestly part implied.

Like Portia, Hamlet would re-create the law and renew justice. As a priest or prophet does, a judge acts to propagate an order which reflects heaven's (hence Portia's "quality of mercy" speech). With Gertrude he plays on the fearful relation of infirm human judgment to God's judgment and doomsday itself (70). These roles in turn color the role of poet or playwright as he adopts it to "set . . . up a glass/Where you may see the inmost part of you" (19). Staging the "mousetrap" he plays the joking clown, but "he is also like those improvising Old Testament prophets who, gathering a handful of dust or of little bones . . . presents to a bland generation a sudden image of their state."[18]

Nevertheless, Claudius's anguished cry could speak for his nephew too: "O, what form of prayer/Can serve my turn?" (3.3.51). Affirmation in this play is profoundly tenuous. The King's questioning prayer, for example, searches for grace, yet confounds itself by the unconscious bawdy quibble on "turn"— "what form of prayer can be exploited to excuse my lust." [19] Against his own affirmative roles Hamlet poses "antic" ones: madman, fool, skeptic, misanthrope, and others. Again, let me stress that his antic disposition presents not a positive alternative to flawed affirmations, but a negation of them. The opposed roles mutually condition one another. Sometimes one role uncannily subsumes another. To Ophelia he is "blasted with ecstasy" (3.1.160), whereas to her father and to us his madness reveals a method. Playing the fool as he does, Hamlet often deliberately obscures the deeper role of judge.

Opposite roles combine in Hamlet when, to use the King's ambiguous word, he "affronts" Ophelia. Indirectly he praises her beauty even as he damns "the power of beauty" to beget sin (111). In the celebrated quibble "Get thee to a nunnery" (whorehouse) he would save her in one meaning, deny her salvation in the other (121). So too, though he confesses his own vices, his exaggeration of them—and his tone toward Ophelia throughout—is disquietingly self-aggrandizing: "I am very proud, revengeful, ambitious; with more offences at my beck than I have . . . imagination to give them shape" (125). His words communicate man's loathing in the shape of heaven's love. Invoking salvation, he abets Ophelia's self-destruction. In the play's last act, and especially her burial, we can assess the consequences of these roles.

With the unwilled murder of Polonius, events can no longer be contained. Sent upon the sea, that favorite Shakespearean metaphor for contingency, the Prince undergoes "a kind of fighting" within himself which promises to free him from some of his sterile conceptions (5.2.4–11). Lying sleepless aboard ship, "worse than the mutines in the bilboes," he senses that he has been rebelling against necessity. He returns to Denmark, he tells Horatio, alive to "a divinity that shapes our ends," an ineffable meaning behind the face of things. Shakespeare does not show us Hamlet's transformation "at sea," but he does provide a dramatic equivalent in the scene which precedes, and apparently stimulates, Hamlet's recollection of the experience. I refer of course to the scene of Ophelia's "maimed rites" (5.1.213).

In the graveyard the Prince meets two fools, one symbolically named Goodman Delver, whose demeanors serve to evaluate his own. As if playing king of imagination's space, a dramatist, he invents scenes and voices using a few anonymous skulls as props. Specifically, he engages in bitter foolery; he scorns the forms of the human order as represented by the politician, the courtier, "Lady Worm," and the law itself. He dramatizes his own nihilism: not his suffering, but his refusal to concede even the reality of suffering.

The Clown's tireless quibbling, on the other hand, asserts that even Hamlet's nihilism is an artifice, however, negative, which can yet be fooled into verbal chaos. Asked "Whose grave's this?" (114), he riddles about death as a relinquishment of possession and "use." Asked at last if the grave is for a woman, he sallies, "One that was a woman, sir; but, rest her soul, she's dead" (131). Hamlet has been dramatizing with skulls, giving imaginative life. Imagination blurs the reality of death: "a woman" can be both a chapless scrap of rot and a living soul. The Clown forces a distinction. And his interlocutor marvels:

How absolute the knave is! We must speak by the card, or equivocation will undo us." [133]

This "absolute" speech restores attention to the elemental act of meaning the way his action—gravedigging, reuniting man and nature, dust and dust—makes palpable the ground of mortal existence. By contrast, Hamlet's roles and rhapsodies upon futility seem artful. He appears outfooled, as if he has yet to experience the Clown's "absolute" openness to the nothingness which conditions life: as if values must be founded on that openness to be more than empty gestures.

Paradoxically, the Clown is free of Hamlet's anxiety and disgust. "Has this fellow no feeling of his business, that 'a sings in gravemaking?" (66). Horatio proposes that "custom" has inured him to death. But the opposite is true: a fool is "by nature" spontaneous and therefore beyond customary order even as his riddles are beyond ordinary sense. Owing no allegiance to one invented order, he has no need to remake or manipulate other characters, no rigid self to defend against death and defeat. Being unself-conscious, he is close to Adam as well as to "Adam's profession" (31), free to live out his feelings, and profoundly open to play.

The Clown obliquely protests the hypocrisy subverting the reality of Ophelia's death. For us there is special resonance in his equation of self-destruction with self-defense (6). One of his songs glances at the idealism which has oppressed all of Hamlet's feelings, but especially his love for Ophelia:

> In youth, when I did love, did love,
> Methought it was very sweet,
> To contract-o-the time for-a my behove,
> O, methought there-a-was nothing-a meet.
>
> [61–64]

For Hamlet too, at times, there has been nothing meet. What the Clown points to emerges more concretely in the affectionate Yorick. For in one sense all of Hamlet's torment occurs in the void created by Yorick's death.

Yorick's skull restores to Hamlet memories of uncalculated play. As eulogized, he resembles an exuberant and affectionate father, with a healthy, "most excellent fancy," who "hath borne me on his back a thousand times. . . . Here hung those lips that I have kiss'd I know not how oft" (180–90). What dominates the recognition, however, is Hamlet's agony at the memory: "And now how abhorred in my imagination it is!" Revoked by death, Yorick's homely tenderness becomes for him one more fraud, akin to the false feelings which the court has long sought to make him "swallow." And he rejects the memory in an unmeditated reflex, a vomiting spasm: "My gorge rises at it!" It is a small but revealing crisis. Despite his wishful boast that "there is nothing either good or bad, but thinking makes it so" (2.2.248), he *feels* that love is treachery and he helplessly loathes it. The skull confirms mere emotion to him as a futile trick. Comparing the jester with the vainglorious Alexander, an authoritarian figure like the Ghost, he betrays the spirit of Yorick. The single figure of joy in the play is most real to him not as a cherishable memory, preserved in imagination, but as a decayed skull which Hamlet repudiates with epicene disgust: "And smelt so? Pah!"

Often Shakespeare's great women revalue experience and consecrate new meanings. We have encountered this pattern before. The Princess of France, Portia, Cordelia, Perdita: in different ways each promises to renew order and belief. Each has a priestly function.[20] In Hamlet's world, however, the guiding figures of the fool and priest—Yorick and Ophelia—are dead. In her madness Ophelia's speech

> is nothing,
> Yet the unshaped use of it doth move
> The hearers to collection; they yawn at it,
> And botch up the words to fit their own thoughts. . . .
> [4.5.7–10]

Hamlet himself has botched up her words to suit his own defensive thoughts. In a sense he rails at her as he spurns Yorick's memory, because his need for them, and their failures, are deeply rooted in the structure of the play-world. His vaunted imagination notwithstanding, he cannot live out the roles they have vacated.

Literally the vacancy Yorick and Ophelia create is their common grave, the hole in the stage, into which Laertes and possibly Hamlet hurl themselves. It makes a complex, cruel episode. Ophelia's competing "lovers" reach for her in death, where in life each has denied her. Laertes would possess her in a self-inflating, theatrical paroxysm of grief. And while Hamlet professes love, he acts only to chastise the show of love. Staging an absurd contest on behalf of that within which passes show, taking the transparent role "Hamlet the Dane," he "conjures the wand'ring stars," and would make them "like wonder-wounded hearers" (5.1.250). As in his vision of the player, he wishes vainly to *use* wonder. Yet he parodies Laertes too, as if he understands well abuses of poetry and love. Either way, as he rants his own love grows less, not more, immediate. Insofar as he sees Laertes as a mirror of himself (5.2.75–78), their clash objectifies an interior conflict such as he experienced at sea, when "in my heart there was a kind of fighting/That would not let me sleep" (4). His shipboard reconciliation to necessity also has an echo in the graveyard, in his vatic doggerel at parting:

> Let Hercules himself do what he may,
> The cat will mew, the dog will have his day.
>
> [5.1.286]

Woe in Wonder

What I am saying is that in addition to the political, psychological, religious, and other conflicts projected in the play—and mutually interacting with them—there is a conflict involving the dynamics of magical thinking and play. Hamlet returns to Denmark determined to keep himself open to necessity and wonder. And the play urges us to recognize his courage. His humility appears a truer form of negative creation than his will to destroy all the flawed world. "The readiness," he concludes, "is all" (5.2.215). Tacitly he acknowledges how finite even his ideals have been, and how impossible it is to make ideals absolute by force of will. By the inner action of making ready he would move from hatred to a new piety toward life. His deliberate failure to create a meaning he can act upon becomes the only possible assertion of meaning worth living for.

What makes the play tragic is the doubt which haunts Hamlet's readiness. While negative creation *implies* an absolute by pointing to the inadequacy of conventional meanings, it can prove nothing. The play keeps alive the possibility that Hamlet may be deceived or fatally incoherent. He is able at last, like a true fool, to abolish or decreate his sterile conceptions of what is. He knows what is not true. But he cannot create anew. He would maintain himself in pure potentiality. The closing action is as indefinable as Hamlet himself. Nullity and affirmation mingle in the paradoxes of "readiness," and the play loses its identity as a conventional revenge type even as its hero loses himself. Irony proliferates so thickly that like the fate of Rosencrantz and Guildenstern, whose "defeat/Does by their own insinuation grow" (58), the final slaughter appears mysteriously self-willed yet sourceless. To inventory paradoxes would be tedious; let me locate a few material examples.

Though Hamlet would accept the truth of his own deepest feelings as disclosed in "indiscretion"—"And praised be rashness for it" (7)—he regrets that voicing his love in the graveyard he "forgot" himself (76). He acts to kill the minor villains Rosencrantz and Guildenstern, answering manipulation ("do you think I am easier to be played on than a pipe?") in kind. He plays king to plot their deaths, but attains his role by forgery and stealth, unable to claim kingship before a public audience. He is a "player king" at best. But then there is a doubleness lurking in his every gesture. Some of his most noble poetry recalls the riddling Polonius: "If it be now, 'tis not to come; if it be not to come, it will be now" (213). "The fall of a sparrow" he makes the measure of providence, recollecting the fall of Ilium and of mankind, as well as the comforting words of Matthew 10:29. Such providence implies a divine resolution to earthly misery; it would preempt tragedy. Yet Hamlet's behavior admits no resolutions. He hints "how ill all's here about my heart" even as he minimizes that ill and the impending duel with Laertes as "but foolery" (204). We feel his uncertainty and pain in his disavowal of pain. Apologizing to Laertes, he makes himself "poor Hamlet," a beggar hounded by "Hamlet's madness" and innocent as a child (218–35). Despite its humility, his plea is fraught with legalistic self-justification. He cannot wholly be the beggar he claims.

But doubleness infects the court itself. Laertes connives to slay the one he pardons. Playing the polite child, wishing "some elder masters of known honor . . . to keep my name ungored," he consents to "receive . . . offer'd love like love" (236–44). His feint at affection, with its expedient "like love," blindly mirrors Hamlet's. As the stage directions describe their physical combat, *they play*. But they cannot, as Hamlet puts it, "frankly play" (245), even though they play for judges and can call aloud for "judgment" (272).

Assaulting one another, these "sons" resemble the child-actors accused of displacing legitimate players: "little eyeases, that cry out on top of question and are most tyrannically clapp'd for't" (2.2.336). The child-actors are "tyrannically clapp'd" in their roles as Hamlet was bound by the Ghost to revenge: with implied oppression. And so when the Queen "carouses," drinking poison, the pleasure she would take is in cosseting her son as she might an infant. She bids him "let me wipe thy face" (5.2.286), echoing his earlier vow to "wipe away" his childhood self. It is a bitter, even obscene moment. Her playful assumption of motherhood parodies thirsty sin ("carouses") and looses death upon the "family."

Loveless play poisons all those onstage. Even Horatio would in despair play "the antique Roman" by suicide. Like the King's "plots," the public masks and pretences of the court have passed out of control; they seem magically to have a life of their own. When Hamlet answers his mother "I dare not drink" (285), he speaks an uncanny truth. Gertrude likewise says more than she knows as she takes a drink and, inadvertently, her own life: "I pray you pardon me" (283). Her "suicide" eerily fulfills the Ghost's warning to her son: "O, step between her and her fighting soul" (3.4.113). Like the child-actors, who cannot write their own plays, those caught up in the manipulative pattern are both exploiters and victims. As Hamlet wondered about the child-actors, "Will they not say afterwards . . . their writers do them wrong to make them exclaim against their own succession?" (2.2.343). Not even Hamlet has come to understand how the will becomes turned against itself, almost as a thing apart. [21] Taunting Laertes for making him a "wanton" or willful brat, he associates manhood with aggression, and a spoiled child with the mere absence of parental intimidation (5.2.291). Unwittingly he provokes his alter ego to greater, fatal violence.

Only then, at the pressure of death, when "paternal" malice can no longer be denied, does Hamlet defy treason to attack the King. Then he vanishes into silence prophesying the election of Fortinbras with the visionary faculty of a dying man. At once he passes into his noblest moment and a chilling echo of the Ghost. For with his theatrical awareness of his life as a tale, and his promise of unspeakable marvels and truth, he haunts us as a man already beyond life: "Had I but time . . . O, I would tell you—but let it be" (328). At the same time his words insinuate that death itself may be unreal, an illusion. Twice he cries, "I am dead" (325 and 330), addressing all "that are but mutes or audience to this act" (327), as if he is only playing dead as he briefly did with Laertes in Ophelia's grave: "Be buried quick with her, and so will I" (5.1.273.). Calling death "felicity," turning Horatio from death, he acts generously yet also behaves as if he can preempt the inevitable, as if he can master "this fell sergeant Death"—his last accuser—by utterly submitting to him, making that inestimable will his own. We are audience, in short, to a bewilderingly rapid and multivalent "act."

Without denying the obvious significance of the conclusion—a purgation of evil, but in a maimed rite, at high cost—it remains to point out that Shakespeare is proceeding by negative creation. He has manipulated us into awed contemplation. We may "look pale and tremble at this chance," sensing a coherence in it which is undreamt of in our philosophy (5.2.326). Given Hamlet's imperfect understanding of the many "things standing thus unknown" (337), Horatio can "truly deliver" only a tale, one construction of reality (378). In fact he sounds a rather meretricious prologue to a new play: "So shall you hear/Of carnal, bloody, and unnatural acts," and so on (372).[22] (Again, "acts.") "His" play can scarcely be as comprehensive as the one which includes him, so that like a play within a play, his tale intimates an infinite series of possible tales regressing from the central, palpable mystery. But other uncertainties abound too, not least in Fortinbras. No political process in Denmark ensures future harmony. Claudius's defeat has ironically depended on his troubled nephew, a "questionable" Ghost, and finally on "this chance" outcome (326). After so much havoc the public world hastily consoles itself with tributes and new ceremonies

> Even while men's minds are wild, lest more mischance
> On plots and errors happen.
>
> [386–87]

We hear no voices bent upon understanding, no tolerance of mystery.

On the face of it the conclusion reassures us. "The masks drop off, and for the first time the characters confront each other without disguise." We are tempted to flatter ourselves that "through death, the conflicting worlds of 'seeming' and 'being' coincide."[23] But the play insists, as in Hamlet's vision of the player's self-creation, that we "conceive" reality. Without masks, without shape, a man would be lost in chaos or a visionary trance. The self would be a tempest of energy. Romanticism imagines a natural self beneath social masks. But beneath his mask who is Claudius? The horror of his attempt to pray is that he himself cannot fathom his own will. Who is Fortinbras? Or Laertes? Who, among his many masks, is Hamlet?

Let me reaffirm that the play's evident meanings *are* there, and important, even as they direct us toward more removed mysteries. But we must go one step further. Shakespeare's negative creation signifies an effort to set his play and audience free: to be faithful to the fulness of life itself. He manipulates us to feel what we do not know. Nevertheless, it could be objected that his art, or the picture of it I am presenting, is escapist. Wondrous art may appear to overstress self-conscious artifice, to distance us from common-sense reality, and evade the resolution of conflicts.[24] In nearly all the tragedies Shakespeare allows some glimmer of wonder (or mystification) that distances the soul from the pain which engulfs it. Lear dreams of being God's spies with Cordelia, an invisible audience to earth's follies and woes, protected by the prison which denies them life (5.3.7–19). In Lear's visionary cry, "Look there, look there!" at the moment of death we may find delusion and clues to a divine comic redemption held in poetic suspension (311). More clearly, at the death of Antony, Cleopatra cries: "O, see, my women,/The crown o' th' earth doth melt. My lord!" (4.15.62).

> There is a peace and effortlessness in "melt," as if there were no barrier between life and death, and one could flow easily into the other. . . . Rather than being resolved, the conflict between Egypt and Rome ceases to exist, and the hard, "visible shapes" of Rome are dissolved in an ecstatic, poetic reality. In this sense *Antony and Cleopatra* looks ahead to the mood of Shakespeare's last plays.[25]

As *Antony* looks, so must we. Specifically, we turn to the much misjudged *Pericles*, where tragedy passes into the magical sphere of the late plays, and Shakespeare renews and criticizes anew the uses of wondrous art.

IX. And Give Them Repetition to the Life:
Parodic Waste and Wonder in *Pericles*

In a way *Pericles* begins where *Hamlet* stops: with a speaker who wishes to recreate the past. At Hamlet's charge "to tell my story" (5.2.341), Horatio pledges to report all to "the unsatisifed" (332). His tale might transfigure the bewildering havoc which has convulsed the court. But his prologue is scarcely reassuring. "So shall you hear/Of carnal, bloody, and unnatural acts," he vows, "Of accidental judgments, casual slaughters," and the like (372). This could herald a racy revenge melodrama with a glibly edifying resolution. Art threatens to usurp life. Potentially Horatio's tale implies countless other tales, the recollections which we call history, each one further dissociated from the core reality. Yet already we have experienced, and been moved by, one such story: the play *Hamlet* itself.

These problems and paradoxes dominate *Pericles* from the outset, but with a consumingly parodic cast.[1] In Gower's art dissociation is comically rampant. Not only is his tale the remote work of "mine authors" (1.pro.20), but he himself is oddly dislocated from the fictional reality. Time interposes between his age and ours, and between his age and the play's no less. Onstage he stands before walls posted with the expressively severed heads of suitors who failed to fathom Antioch's riddling, evil "art." Yet Gower evinces no emotion relevant to "yon grim looks" whatever (40). From death he addresses us, in the third person, an unaccommodated voice chattering doggerel out of a gap in time and space:

> To sing a song that old was sung,
> From ashes ancient Gower is come,
> Assuming man's infirmities,
> To glad your ear and please your eyes.
>
> [1–4]

With its motives placed at the rhetorically prominent opening and close of the sentence, this genial archaic formula makes bold to clarify things as a prologue customarily does. Yet the speech undercuts itself by facetious repetition ("sing . . . song . . . sung") and tautology ("To glad your ear and please your eyes"). We cannot merely take him seriously. But then how should we respond?

Like Quince's prologue to *Pyramus*, Gower's assemblage of clichés creates more mystery and uncertainty than it dispels.[2] For example, nothing in the play warrants the declared "purchase" of making men "glorious" (9). In the self-justifying Latin slogan "Et bonum quo antiquius eo melius" (10) he appeals to authority. Whereupon he perfunctorily contradicts himself, meekly flattering us:

> If you, born in those latter times,
> When wit's more ripe, accept my rhymes,
> And that to hear an old man sing
> May to your wishes pleasure bring,
> I life would wish, and that I might
> Waste it for you, like taper-light.
>
> [11–16]

Come "from ashes" yet not "in" life ("I life would wish"), Gower is a sort of ghost. As in Hamlet's rumination that to die is perchance to dream—neither to be nor not to be—he hovers between existence and oblivion, suspended in art, sustained by the power of our imaginations.

Gower wastes his speech in used-up platitudes even as he would waste his life anew for our wishes, and perhaps even as the private theater's taper-light (the experience of art itself) must as last come to nothing. His condition parodies one consequence of the creative life: the artist's anxiety about isolation and exhaustion after a life given to—wasted on—imagination. Gower would willingly sacrifice himself again to win our praise: he accosts us as an artist-beggar craving renewed connection with life at any cost. In this posture he allows Shakespeare to satirize the servility latent in the artist's relation to his patrons.[3]

But if Gower is obsequious, he can also be outrageously didactic. His self-effacement gives way to an equally incongruous certainty as he tries to fix the play-world in his demonstrative grasp: "This Antioch, then . . ." (17). To name Antioch or anything "fairest," as he does, is vulnerable praise, and absurd when followed by an account of the city's immorality. But he characteristically construes reality in clichés. The King's daughter looks "as heaven had lent her all his grace" (24); two lines later we hear the father "her to incest did provoke (26). Her depravity Gower makes a pat matter, the tautological consequence of "bad child! Worse father!" (27), and "custom" (29). The joke of course is that custom falsifies Gower's own relation to the life of the play. His sententious reflex imposes judgments as ruthlessly as Antiochus wields law to keep suitors from overcoming his evil "custom." Yet there is a complementary joke here too: Gower is only bringing art, however bad, which pleases us.[4]

The prologue entices and stymies us as the riddle does the Princess' suitors. Gower concludes in the typically dubious syntax of his idiom, flattering us that we can verify or judge his truth: "What now ensues, to the judgment of your eye /I give, my cause who best can justify" (41). We must be committed to adventure yet critically detached as well. For recomposed "from ashes" (2), "assuming man's infirmities" as easily as a costume (3), Gower is insubstantiality incarnate. We behold a world projected by imagination: specifically, a world "conceived" in rigid conventions. Once we perceive that, we begin to venture (as Pericles himself does) toward the unknown.[5]

A World Consumed by Artifice

Like Gower, the figures who meet in Antioch are estranged from life. They exist in comically flat roles, operated by the laws of romance. In the old manner they insistently identify one another by name, defining every motive and action. Stereotype dictates the theatrical action even as the King's riddling law does the characters'. Just as Claudius tries to control Hamlet by manipulating roles, so Antiochus deploys "actors" in a cynical rite: "Bring in our daughter, clothed like a bride" (1.1.6). The Princess can only impersonate a bride.

Pericles blindly participates in the mock bridal. It measures his vulnerability that he takes at face value the stock hyperbole which his rival uses to deceive him. Competitively groping for grandiloquence, the Prince deems the Daughter's face "the book of praises" (15), a weary trope which makes praise an inventory of formulae in an effort to encompass all permutations. In his reply to the tyrant's warning he shows himself a creature of formulae, incapable of praise (and love) as a profound experience (41–52). In this speech life is, as he insists, "but breath, to trust it error" (46). For his virtues are as bloodless as they are noble and fastidious. His bequest of a "happy peace" (50) sounds feebly anticlimatic. However exemplary, his resignation is inappropriate. Surely marriage involves the will in the "earthly joys" (49) he politely renounces. Desire alone can justify the trial it has presumably brought him to. Unlike Bassanio, however, he cannot risk himself joyfully for love. He fixes instead upon death.

Presenting himself in a flurry of placative words, Pericles is more truly like "sick men" (47) than he knows. Like a character in search of an author, he obeys the dictates of romance convention, passively expecting guidance. He would be "son and servant" (23) to the gods who "have inflam'd desire in my breast" (20). When he applies his wish for a father to Antiochus,

> *Antiochus.* Prince Pericles—
> *Pericles.* That would be son to great Antiochus,
>
> [25–26]

the tyrant ignores the wish, keeping him "Prince," captive to courtesy and custom. Like Hamlet, the Prince first discovers evil in a powerful father figure. Hamlet's feelings toward Ophelia and Gertrude have an analogue in Pericles' rivalry with Antiochus for a woman who is at once "mother, wife, and yet his child" (69). We might go so far as to entertain Pericles' resignation and flights from danger as a parody of Hamlet's tortuous inaction.[6]

While marriage promises to end Pericles' alienation, the riddle would keep men baffled by what Gower calls "awe" or wonder (1.pro.36). The riddle exploits dissociated meanings in order to perpetuate alienation, securing more and more lies and beheadings. While it feints at joining ordinarily separate roles (mother, wife, and child), it relies on the dislocation of natural love to fool suitors:

> I am no viper, yet I feed
> On mother's flesh, which did me breed.
> I sought a husband, in which labor
> I found that kindness in a father.
> He's father, son, and husband mild;

> I mother, wife, and yet his child.
> How they may be, and yet in two,
> As you will live, resolve it you.

[1.1.64–71]

The premise is that reflex propriety will blind suitors' imaginations. Because it steals the Princess' voice, the riddle literalizes the usurpation of life by formula and "art." As in Bassanio's trial, only a soul truly open to play can penetrate the riddle.

Even if the bride does long to be freed from her father (as she professes), Pericles offers no help. Though he has the sensitivity to guess the truth about her, he priggishly judges her (72–86). His indignation is no more convincing than his "inflam'd desire" for her was. He sounds petulant: "Being play'd upon before your time,/Hell only danceth at so harsh a chime" (84). He imagines her as passive an instrument as he himself is: a "fair viol," ideally "finger'd to make man his lawful music" (82). He limps to an insipid conclusion: "Good sooth, I care not for you" (86).

Like Hamlet, the Prince suddenly finds himself in a political and Oedipal nightmare. To protect himself, he turns to righteous self-disablement and sham. Abandoning his posture of "bold champion" (61), he offers to "keep shut" his "book of all that monarchs do" (94). His response is ruinous. Inwardly he behaves as if he has a special moral potency. Outwardly, however, he becomes a craven actor hiding behind platitudes, and hiding from himself as well as from his rival.

As a whole, the scene argues that false relations among men turn life into a bad play. Even when the characters try to "act," they remain trapped in unauthentic roles, Antiochus no less than the Prince. Evading painful truth, they blind themselves to increasingly formulaic recreations of reality. One result is that words come to direct and fuddle the will. Pleading to be allowed to escape in silence, Pericles speaks as if his tongue is a creature independent of his head and ruled by Antiochus: "All love the womb that their first being bred:/Then give my tongue like leave to love my head" (107). His "to love my head" is eerily playful, a joke about keeping still and hence loyally keeping his head from the executioner. Ludicrous word play likewise shadows the King's reply: "Would that I had thy head!" (109). Unwittingly he signals not only a wish to murder Pericles, but also envy of the wits by which he defeated the riddle. Like the despot's unfulfilled promise to confide his mind's "private actions" to Thaliard (154), the play on "head" comes to nothing. Like Thaliard's anachronistic pistol, such language distances us from the literal action.[7] Words appear to play pranks on their users, making comedy bloom in threats, for example, and thereby complicating our responses.

Fleeing Antioch, Pericles flees from conflict within himself too. For safely home, he is tellingly beset by melancholy. Even he finds his dolor odd, customary ("so used a guest") yet unfathomable (1.2.2). Trying to rationalize it he envisions himself "but as the tops of trees" in relation to his subjects, the roots (30). His metaphor describes as well his separation from the roots of his own nature. (In his complaint that care "makes . . . my body pine" (32) we might hear another stray, silly pun in the midst of gravity.)

Pericles brings a callow and demoralized imagination to the problem of a hostile father figure. He feels "too little to contend" (17) against Antiochus, believing the tyrant can magically "make his will his act" (18). Not actual force, but an ability to "look so huge, / Amazement shall drive courage from the state" (25) is what gives the despot his power.[8] Actually the overawed will of the "son" determines his fate. He dreads to retaliate. Yet as his abdication of his throne makes plain, Pericles cannot understand himself in order to heal himself. Hence the irony of his escapist relationship with Helicanus, who "speak'st like a physician" (67).

By playing tyrant to Helicanus, the Prince reveals a fantasy that has been influencing his behavior. Their exchange is a wish-fulfillment of the original crisis at Antioch. Offering up his life to indict flattery, Helicanus takes a role Pericles has yearned to play. In addition, however, their scene enacts a fantasy of achieving power through self-effacement or martyrdom. For the Prince rewards his lieutenant's readiness to die—even eagerness: "I have ground the axe myself" (58)—by making him a ruler in his stead. It is as if at Antioch Pericles wished that his meekness alone could win the "bride" and cause his menacing rival to vanish graciously, installing him in his place.

Bearing a "message" of murder, Thaliard caricatures communication. He brings to Tyre lethal feelings he cannot personally "mean." He acts the villain for Antiochus as Helicanus acts the endangered prince for Pericles. Thaliard reveals conventional obedience to be amoral: "if a king bid a man be a villain, he's bound" (1.3.8). His faulty timing and release from his oath are miracles on the order of Pericles' arrival in Tharsus. Will stands twice mocked, for though Pericles acts for the wrong reasons, his flight issues in good fortune.

In Tharsus convention is implicated again in the paralysis of will. Cleon's comical reflex invites didactic tales of woe to insulate him from his grief. Once more art is an instrument of escape. Cleon sees his city enervated by surfeit (1.4.21–31). A craving for "inventions" to liven cloyed palates first usurped natural appetite (40). Riches reduced the populace to sated dependence on artifice, as the glut of literary conventions onstage would be cloying to us were we not aware of the parody. With deprivation, the idle dissociation of desire in Tharsus has become horrible. Intimate relations collapse, mothers "ready now / To eat those little darlings whom they loved" (43) even as the Princess of Antioch has appeared "an eater of her mother's flesh" (1.1.130).[9]

As if verifying Cleon's plea that even noise is preferable to silent resignation, Pericles declares on his arrival that word of the famine has reached "as far as Tyre" (1.4.88). Nevertheless, when the grateful city blesses him, he declines their homage, still unable to accept his own potency. Moments later, Gower tells us the Prince once more returns to the sea and uncertainty. He ventures into "the shipman's" sphere, "with whom each minute threatens life or death" (1.3.24). As so often in Shakespeare, the sea is a space beyond conventions, where Pericles can, and must, risk coming to life no less than death.

Shipwreck and Perseveration

The drastic scene changes which keep Pericles in flight from himself also keep our attention unsettled. Like the characters, we understand nothing in depth. The play's structure, that is, imitates its sense. Gower reappears confidently offering, like the manipulative Antiochus, an illusion of meaning. Yet his characters are crude abstractions. His claim that we have seen Antiochus "his child iwis to incest bring" (2.pro.2) smacks more of theatrical huckstering than of truth. Yet like Pericles, we find ourselves playing along with a peremptory playwright: "Be quiet, then, as men should be" (5). As an audience to Pericles, believing he speaks holy "writ" (12), Tharsus burlesques our relation to Gower. And while Pericles is no more responsible than Gower ("Pardon old Gower—this 'longs the text" (40)), Tharsus itself escapes the burden of autonomy by conscripting a savior in whom it invests all authority.

Vainly the populace wishes to "build his statue to make him glorious" (14).[10]

The audience-playmaker relationship which metaphorically pervades the play is ambivalent. All too readily playmakers turn tyrant, and audiences parasites. For no autonomy exists to stabilize character. Tharsus would evade responsibility by exalting Pericles' "writ." Pericles himself has cringed before Antiochus. Helicanus, we are told, has dealt with those "living like a drone / From others' labours" (18) by striving "to killen bad, keep good alive" (20): an overreaction. The point is that assertion and effacement may alternate violently in the same character if no firm identity underpins his roles. This applies to villains, too: Thaliard, the pirates, and Boult, among others.

As he flees, Pericles severs himself from one place and role after another. His escape from human irrationality (Thaliard's "message") only brings him to the sea where, says Gower, that grand playmaker "fortune, tired with doing bad, / Threw him ashore, to give him glad" (37). Fortune's gratuitous desire "to give him glad" recalls Gower's intent "to glad your ear" (1.pro.4). Yet fate is merely bored with cosmic tedium, "tired" of its customary catastrophes. Stripped of unhappy roles, the Prince washes up as a stranger on an alien shore, "reborn" as Thaisa will later be. As if the farce of an escapist repeatedly exiting and being thrown back onstage were not enough, Gower's understatement ("And here he comes") and the deadpan stage direction *"Enter* Pericles, *wet"* insist on the comedy of the shipwreck.[11]

Pericles enters railing timidly against the heavens, protesting the lot of "earthly man" (2.1.2). His puny defiance makes an amusing echo of the outcast Lear, and the fishermen function rather as Lear's fool does. They moralize that in society "the great ones eat up the little ones" (28), recalling Pericles' fear of Antiochus and the cannibalizing of children in starving Tharsus. The notion of whales swallowing men suggests the way Antiochus overwhelmed Pericles, and the fisherman's remedy, to be swallowed in a church belfry and clamor until vomited up, comments on the Prince's temporizing silence and his taboo on showing anger toward the authority figure.

Trying to explain his predicament, Pericles resorts to a hilariously incongruous trope which envisions him (more truly than he knows) a tennis ball played on by the elements. Warned that without a worldly role such as fishing he "wilt starve, sure" (68), he delivers an oration that negates him and itself. Want, he claims, "teaches" him to confront "what I am" (72). But his answer, "A man throng'd up with cold" (73), is true on a level he cannot appreciate. Figuratively he is indeed cold. He experiences no wonder, no deep emotion. On the contrary, after reaching safety his first expression was "a pretty moral" (35)—frigid and banal praise of the fishermen's piety. Meekly he solicits his own burial, more sympathetic toward dead decorum than toward his living self. There is nothing tragic about his condition inasmuch as he loves life so little death seems to him agreeable.

Then the rusty armor surfaces. The armor provides him a role, the worn-out role of knight. It dramatizes the exacerbated idealism which has befuddled him from the first: an idealism deriving like the armor itself, we may gather, from his father. Pericles' idealism stymies his will as it does Hamlet's. It demands lifeless, rigid perfection, and fractures reality into antinomies: in this instance Pericles' dead "real" father is as flawless as the usurping "father" Antiochus is evil. Because it materializes from outside the personality, the role of knight never becomes altogether genuine for the Prince.[12]

Simonides suggests the ideal father Pericles lost; he counterpoises Antiochus. Instead of oppressing his "son," Simonides chastises his excessive modesty (2.3.13–17). He speaks of art and identity, holding that men succeed by actively becoming "labour'd scholars" of self-creation:

> In framing an artist, art hath thus decreed,
> To make some good, but others to exceed;
> And you are her labour'd scholar.
>
> [15–17]

Whereas Antiochus brags like the rival poet of the Sonnets, disguising his daughter and himself in false praise, Simonides uses art to foster connections.[13] But pure benevolence is as gratuitous as pure malice; it leaves the Prince himself unchanged. When he presents himself as "the mean knight" with the device on his shield of "a withered branch that's only green at top" (2.2.43), recalling his self-conception at Tyre and (unwittingly) the sorry truth that he is dead at root, the King solemnly echoes Pericles' earlier fatuous judgment of the fishermen: "A pretty moral" (45). In playing out the "jealous father" interlude, he abruptly transforms his threat of punishment into a blessing:

And being join'd, I'll thus your hopes destroy;
And for further grief—God give you joy!

[2.5.85–86]

Pericles acquires a bride, then, not through mutual understanding
with her, or through an enlightened commitment of his own
feelings. Rather, he comes to love thanks to a capricious, magical
blessing. Such a conclusion might suffice for a routine romance,
but not for Shakespeare.[14]

Repetition and Rebirth

Once Tyre summons Pericles back toward responsibility, he passes
into Gower's distancing narrative again, and thence into a symbolically significant storm. As if releasing his hero to find himself,
Gower relinquishes his control over his tale as well: "what ensues
in this fell storm /Shall for itself itself perform" (3.pro.53). The
remark might be taken as a definition of autonomy: will enacted
"for itself" becomes a self. And only now, for the first time, does
the play shed the constraints of exhausted literary convention and
start to come alive. Even Gower's narration becomes incipiently
dramatic, drawing on folk art, coming close to the lyrical music of
Shakespearean songs:

The cat, with eyne of burning coal,
Now crouches fore the mouse's hole. . . .

[5–6]

Says Gower, "I nill relate, action may /Conveniently the rest con-
vey" (55).

Exposed to the stormy sea, symbolically the realm of contingency and the unconscious, the Prince and his bride undergo a
shipwreck of identity. A father has created their marriage. Assent-
ing to marriage the lovers have sounded like docile children: "Yes,
if't please your Majesty" (2.5.90). Now at the midpoint of the
play decorum can no longer contain experience. A "storm" erupts
and dissociation pervades the scene. Night defeats vision; the
seaman's pipe (authoritative music) is reduced to "a whisper in the

ears of death,/Unheard" (3.1.9). Yet while birth and death take place around him Pericles personally undergoes no "sea-change" at all. To be sure, concern for Thaisa seems to inspire a new poetry in his voice. Clinging to piety, however, he describes rather than experiences his suffering. Emphasizing this fearful detachment, Shakespeare has Lychorida voice the anxiety at the heart of the scene. If the new babe "had conceit" of its birth (16), she warns pityingly, it would die. Yet on one level the storm objectifies Pericles' own unconscious turmoil about coming to life. One reason the tempest so terrifies him is that he has long shunned the passions and energies it expresses. He quickly agrees to the sailors' superstitious "custom" (83), though it means casting Thaisa into the depths. Tellingly, he does not take the infant to him, but orders: "Lay the babe/Upon the pillow" (67). His later abandonment of Marina will bear out his incapacity for deep attachments. He is still more child, so to speak, than father.

Thaisa's "death" in childbed complements her husband's crisis. She has been the lovely but dependent royal daughter. Like her resurrection as an uncompromisingly (even defensively) chaste priestess, her death to motherhood suggests she cannot follow her new roles through to autonomy. It is revealing that the only tenderness we witness between husband and wife—in fact, the only words which pass between them—is in Pericles' "priestly farewell" to her (69). By releasing him, that is, her demise permits affection to surface.

Critics usually sense the play's poetry coming to life at this point—and with reason. Unaware, Pericles intones a rite which will be magically fulfilled by Thaisa's recovery. Speaking as if his wife still lives, the Prince uses the play's language of resurrection. His invocation of "the belching whale," for example, calls to mind the fishermen's "Jonah joke" (62): the fisherman would be in a belfry when swallowed, so that the bells would cause the whale to belch him up in a sort of resurrection (2.1.36–44).[15] Though Pericles imagines the whale and the "humming water" as monuments, as if the sea and its music were as lifeless as the other monuments in the play (3.1.63), his language has unforeseen resonance. Comically "belched" ashore, Thaisa will in fact revive. Cast into "ooze" (60), she enters a realm without customary boundaries, a realm like the uninhibited poetic imagination, in which things reveal astonishing connections with one another, and destruction and renewal merge. Marina's birth, then, coincides with the birth of poetry in the play, even as the word "fresh" makes the first of its increasingly rich appearances. In a homely, comic, yet movingly wishful way, the play itself is at last coming to life. Marina's birth and her mother's regeneration provide a reflexive mirror of that artistic process.

In his credo Cerimon professes that immortality attends "virtue and cunning . . . /Making man a god" (3.2.26–31). As the playwright plays "the gods" to audience and actors, so Cerimon touches the "hundreds" who "call themselves / Your creatures, who by you have been restor'd" (44). With Thaisa, the physician-mage (his name suggests "ceremony") invokes the play's resurrection language. He vows that the sea's "belches" delivered up the windfall coffin, naming Thaisa "fresh" as Pericles did Marina (58 and 84). Yet this magic has a suspect, comical side.[16] Cerimon's credo ironically gives new life to hoary ("dead") commonplaces about art. The scroll promises to give the Queen an identity, yet leaves her exemplary and abstract. Though he bids her "Live, and make / Us weep to hear your fate" (108), we hear nothing—pointedly, she has a "relapse" (117).

Withdrawn from the sea, both Pericles and Thaisa give themselves over to resignation. He leaves Marina and would lose himself in penance. To Cerimon Thaisa offers thanks, yet explicitly adds "that's all" (3.4.16), as if she fears a sexual advance or a burdening intimacy. And temporarily she too vanishes from the play.

Art Whored and Redeemed

As an artist without peer "absolute Marina" (4.pro.31) will bring autonomy into the play-world. Her music, the language beyond earthly sense, "made the night-bird mute" (26). She becomes a source of "general wonder" for jaded souls (11). Her birth literalizes the inception of art as a living idiom just as the plots against her life express the dangers latent in conventionality. Like Antiochus, for example, Dionyzia reduces praise to an instrument of vanity and rivalry. She would *make* her own daughter "peerless" (40) by destroying Marina to recreate her as a cynical cenotaph, an impotent artifact.

The brothel scene develops prostitution as a metaphor for the conventionalizing process. It degrades love to an "act" both theatrical and mercantile. Dehumanized by "use," the "creatures" (4.2.6) of the brothel become, like love itself, commodities "with continual action . . . even as good as rotten" (8). Like the ships that ply the play, "A strong wind will blow [them] to pieces, they are so pitifully sodden" (18).

From our vantage point the brothel is also the theater, where art goes whoring for profit and pleasure. The "qualities" (45) which make Marina exploitable are theatrical virtues: a good face and speech, and "excellent good clothes" (47). The Pander worries professionally that she may be "raw in her entertainment" (55). Advertising her, Boult operates as an artist, relishing his verisimilitude and manipulative skill with his audience. He thrills at visions of the magical materiality of his words: "There was a Spaniard's mouth so wat'red that he went to bed to her very description" (101). Like a love-mongering sonneteer, he exults that "I have cried her almost to the number of her hairs; I have drawn her picture with my voice" (93). The Bawd in turn advises Marina to play-act at inherently counterfeit love: she must pretend to do "fearfully" what she commits "willingly" (118). She should exploit sentimentality, "staging" pathetic scenes of weeping, for "pity begets you a good opinion, and that opinion a mere profit" (121).

If she is to survive, Marina must live beyond the audience's grasp as well as the plotters'. Otherwise she would shrink into the usual idealized heroine. Like the sea, she must exceed confining shores. Hence the allusive joke Shakespeare contrives for Marina's epitaph at Tharsus. Without realizing its larger meanings, Dionyzia labels Marina "Thetis' birth-child" (4.4.41) which "earth, fearing to be o'erflowed . . . on the heavens bestowed" (40). As a result the living sea makes "raging battery upon shores of flint" (43). The image suggests not only the emotional deadness afflicting individuals in the play-world, but also the larger "flinty" resistance of created forms such as society and myth to the flux of reality. The epitaph ironically testifies to the revitalized language Marina has made possible. The "bad art" of the play's opening has generated artifice so false to life that its dissociation might strike us as a type of comic madness. Now, however, words have begun to point to a coherent, if parodically indirect, truth behind appearances.

Thinking his daughter dead, Pericles himself plays dead, as it were, vowing to become utterly silent. Like Thaisa, he has as yet no language for truth and feeling, and cannot "live" onstage until

Marina's creation is complete. In despair he renounces all social conventions, determined never "to wash his face nor cut his hairs" (28). At once his withdrawal is saintly—"He puts on sackcloth" (29)—and childishly rebellious.

With Marina's birth, a benign magic begins to appear behind the manifest absurdity of the play-world. Language begins to seem telic in ways that its users cannot control. Urging Marina to walk by the sea with Leonine, for example, Dionyzia rhapsodizes that the sea air "pierces and sharpens the stomach" (4.1.29). Her metaphors betray her murderous intent. For Marina, on the other hand, language is magically liberating. Answering, she vows with clairvoyant innocence: "I'll not bereave you of your servant" (32). So too, as she re-creates the storm of her birth for Leonine, real danger materializes: he announces his intent to kill her. But he is a criminal bound by forms, and commands "say your prayers" first (67). And her entreaties function like prayers: instantly the pirates rescue her.

At once the pirates are merely renegade merchants akin to the brothel entrepeneurs, and agents of "the great pirate Valdes" (98), a master as shadowy and teleological as the gods within the play-world, and also a comic avatar of the playwright's will. So while they do sell Marina into whoredom, the pirates at the same time preserve her virginity. Though savage in demeanor, they behave with droll piety, testifying to her chastity in the voices of bumpkins or obsequious tradesmen: "O, sir, we doubt it not" (4.2.41).

The brothel uses up words as it does virgins. For whoring—to "taste gentlemen of all fashions" (77)—nullifies discrimination. The brothel puts "absolute" words, the medieval ideal, to mercantile, bourgeois use. The Pander calls for "fresh" whores (10), debasing a quality associated with "this fresh-new seafarer" Marina (3.1.41) and Thaisa's resurrection (3.2.84). Subsequently his meaning founders in unintended ambiguity—"credit" (4.2.29) gives good repute and credibility an unsavory financial dimension in his use—and sinister euphemisms such as "commodity" (30). When Boult prepares to assault Marina and she tries to divert him by speaking personally to him, he deflowers her plea, in effect, by bawdy word play:

Marina   Prithee, tell me one thing first
Boult.   Come now, your one thing.

[4.6.154–56]

Marina riddles, playing the fool through "virginal fencing" (58) to keep free of debased meanings. At the same time she commits herself to efficacious words by defining them soundly and anew. Eventually Boult will in fact complain she makes "our swearers priests" (12). Resisting the Bawd, she deems herself "an honest woman, or not a woman" (4.2.84), and deplores her vulnerability to stereotype by lamenting "that I am pretty" (68). Urged to "note" Lysimachus (4.6.49), she uses the word so it signifies not calculation but respect. To the word "bound," which means coercion to the Bawd, she restores the notion of lawful service (54–56). Quibbling with Lysimachus, she prods him to acknowledge the magic of language. He "cannot name" her trade (ostensibly whoring) "but I shall offend" (68), as if to speak the word is to enact it. By playing with meaning until her "trade" loses its corrupted significance, she frees the word and herself. (67–75).

Her "conversion" of Lysimachus is a series of ironic surprises. Though accused of conjuring, of using "holy words" on him (132), she has not tampered with reality at all. For we discover that the lecherous lord in the Bawd's mind has never existed.[18] He rewards Marina with gold as he might a poet, not for pretty rhetoric, but because her words *could*, he believes, "alter" his mind (104). Paradoxically, it scarcely matters that her power may be illusory. She elicits wonder, liberating in others a will to praise life. Lysimachus "ne'er dreamt" her speech could change him. In that power of transformation lies her potency: it is analogous to the potency of the dramatist's speech, the play proper, for the audience's imagination. For souls who weather a sea-change or, like the penitent Pericles, quest for their true selves at sea, Marina is a guide. Lysimachus hits on this role, with its marvellous potency-in-impotence implied in his term "serve": "Faith, she would serve after a long voyage at sea" (43).

Recognition as Renewal

Aboard Pericles' ship, "staleness," the triumph of convention, has extinguished the Prince. Affirming that mock death by trying to impose meaning on it, Helicanus opens the curtain to the Mytilenian visitors, advertising Pericles as a sort of medieval *exemplum* of misfortune. As the Bawd did Marina, he makes him a paragon. Even the source of Pericles' sorrow has become an artifact, a "tale" and "too tedious to repeat" at that (5.1.28).

Since the Prince lies "not destitute for want,/But weary for the staleness" (56), life needs "fresh" meanings. At length he equates his daughter's speech with food and feels "hungry" (111) for it. Instead of devouring one another, as Tharsus has done, parent and child corroborate each other. Freeing his feelings, her words accomplish the rebirth of self he blunderingly intimates in a fortuitous image: "I am great with woe, and shall deliver weeping" (105). Marina releases in him long-denied, natural wishes. Her reward is, as Lysimachus promised, "such pay/As thy desires can wish" (74). For reality itself has come to seem capable of sustaining human wishes.

Revealing herself, Marina protects her singularity. She "names" herself in a relation to the Prince, yet a maid "that ne'er before invited eyes,/But have been gaz'd on like a comet" (84). Her revelation enacts what it means, not "inviting" us to appraise a routine paragon, but seeking to baffle us. Whenever Pericles grasps at her identity, she parries him. Like the Princess in Antiochus's riddle, she exists beyond customary sense. Yet her verbalized self is no mere disguise. Her words are irreducible signs pointing to an inexpressible meaning. She is a woman not

> of any shores,
> Yet I was mortally brought forth, and am
> No other than I appear.
>
> [102–4]

Her "mortally brought forth" means not "humanly" alone, but "through death" also. For death is the way to birth, and for child as well as mother, inasmuch as Marina too is only now coming fully into her "own" life. Asked where she lives, she replies, "Where I am but a stranger. From the deck/You may discern the place" (113). She indicates a specific yet unbounded place, beyond the stage and the theater. She wishes a connection to the world which will relieve her alienation without "prostituting" her soul: she wishes for family, and love.

For the Prince, recognition comes in an angry reflex: "when I did push thee back . . . was when I perceiv'd thee" (125). Marina's plea links this hostile sign with a failure of self-knowledge: "if you did know my parentage/You would not do me violence" (98). For Pericles *is* her "parentage" without realizing it. Yet this is the first time he has allowed expression to his anger, and it makes a sort of liberation for him. He must repudiate in order to embrace. [19] Because she makes herself vulnerable, he can strike at, and through, her. Her role is implicitly sacrificial; her weakness is her strength. Paradox so radically qualifes motivation in their inter-action that love makes itself felt as an extrarational force.

In Pericles Marina would find "the man that can, in aught you would,/Resolve you" (12), a true king who can reintegrate individ-ual and social life. Having pursued chimerical, unexamined ideals hitherto, Pericles has never achieved the role. Now, uttering non-sense syllables akin to a child's first speech ("Hum, ha!"), he pushes Marina away (82). Openly childlike, he can at once initiate the mutuality of questions, and the active sympathy of an audi-ence. He will "credit" or reward her story as Lysimachus did in the brothel, willing to "credit" or trust her. Once corrupted, the word now signifies an act of belief and praise (121). To give audience to another's voice is now, in a new way, to enhance the value of the tale and the telling. [20]

To enhance our wonder, paradox infuses Pericles' awakening. Ecstatically the Prince swears that if Marina's tale

> prove the thousandth part
> Of my endurance, thou art a man, and I
> Have suffered like a girl.
>
> [134–36]

All told, her role does prove equal to his, and unexpectedly it appears he *has* "suffered like a girl." What's more, given a boy player in Marina's part, she is indeed "a man." But then, the scene admonishes us that now all the play's excesses somehow match reality. As a comedy self-consciously deployed by a playmaker-god, the play even justifies his frantic conviction that she has been sent "by some incensed god" (142) to inspire the world to laugh at him. He imagines her as the allegorical lady Patience "smiling/ Extremity out of act" (138). Since she is truly herself, her smile can win him out of his old false role or "act." After all, she stipulates herself "daughter to King Pericles/If good King Pericles be" (177)—that is, not simply "if he still lives," but also "if he is now truly himself, the king."

When he does claim himself by name, Marina kneels to him. She confirms a hierarchy in the play at last. Thereafter he sheds his sackcloth for a new role in "fresh" garments (212). To Helicanus he pronounces her "thy very princess" (216), then turns to another ruler, Lysimachus, and the social world, saying: "I embrace you" (220). It is then, with "a great sea of joys" upon him (191), nearly as "wild in . . . beholding" as Lear with Cordelia (221), that he hears music not vouchsafed to the others. Having had to "die" to live, he goes "madly" to lucidity. Learning to *hear* others, he now experiences the wonder which music objectifies. In the last of these familiar antinomies, having understood his waking as "the rarest dream which e'er dulled sleep/Did mock sad fools withal" (160), he must genuinely sleep to wake from his lifelong hallucination.

As slumber finally takes Pericles out of "character," the gods themselves put an emissary onstage: Diana. She charges him to become a responsible artist of his own experience. At Ephesus he must give his misfortunes "repetition to the life" (244). Her command bids him summon from the past dead or denied experiences, and bring them to life, as the play does, through art: to "perform my bidding" (245) and "awake and tell thy dream" (247).

"To Hear the Rest Untold"

What's past, as it turns out, is prologue. For the act which recovers the lost Thaisa is an "act" of drama:

> Hail, Dian! to perform thy just command,
> I here confess myself the King of Tyre;
> Who, frighted from my country, did. . . .
> [5.3.1–3]

We could be listening to the prologue to a command performance of an old play. Already the marvellous restoration of Marina has hardened into a plot detail. As a kind of play-within-a-play, the recitation itself appears transcended by its context, the discovery of Thaisa in the priestess' "voice."

Calling Thaisa to be "buried/A second time within these arms" (45), he summons back to the service of life both the woman and the once-dead word "buried," which earlier gave conceptual "being" only to death: "when I am dead . . . pray see me buried" (2.1.76).[21] Charged with ambiguity in the scroll coffined with

Thaisa—"Who finds her, give her burying" (3.2.77)—the word eventually fulfills its latent meaning of love. As the play approaches pure ritual, the "act" becomes the thing itself. Will and wish become congruent with the word, and the word at last "lives."

Yet the reunion emphasizes the need to accommodate risk in the intimate order of experience. In no sense does the play conclude with an "embrace." The characters have only a moment (in the pun, only "a second time") embosomed together before the motion of life resumes. We do not see them loving together onstage, nor can we feel certain that each will ever after resist the self-effacing impulse to be buried—in a sinister sense—in the other: consigned to psychic oblivion, as so often before. The word's richness offers menace as well as hope. The Prince's last speech, for example, records a father's death (painful but inescapable adjunct to autonomy) and one generation's succession to the roles of another. Yet the play's experience gainsays his glib disposition of two kingdoms and all the future.

In dramatic terms, risk is reflected in the interpenetration of comedy and seriousness. Tolerant mirth attends Pericles' solemn promise of "nightly oblations" (5.3.71) to Diana, expecially in light of Thaisa's worries about her "sanctity" (30) and "licentious ear" (31). In a broader perspective, though the "gods can have no mortal officer/More like a god than" Cerimon (63), and though Thaisa testifies to his "letters of good credit" (78), the man who may "resolve" all things (62) is, in Pericles' suggestive words, a "Reverend appearer" (19). And indeed Cerimon carries "the rest untold" offstage with him (85).

Like the players, we too must follow a reverend appearer out of grace, into contingency. For Gower has the last disrupting word, and his voice has regressed to the form of his prologue. And now his pat didacticism sounds complexly inappropriate to us. Pericles' "honour'd name" (97), he tells us, acquires a magical potency that precipitates irrational mob vengeance against Cleon and his family. Worse, the gods "seemed . . . content/To punish" Cleon's innocent family (101), though the murder of Marina never actually took place. The moral nullifies whatever "credit" the gods might have won from us.

But then, Gower's absurd judgment cautions us implicitly to suspend our own judgments. We may be startled to perceive that with antic perversity the comforting term "reverend appearer" suits Gower aptly. Fatuously pious and an apparition, he too would "lead's the way" (85). As a venerable author, he too "hath letters of good credit" (78). In bringing to life the characters of the old romance, he directly parodies the resurrection artist Cerimon. "From ashes . . . come," he burlesques the story's miraculous salvation, gulling us while reminding us of our own imaginative complicity. His illusions would fail "unless your thoughts went on my way" (4.pro.50).

Gower disengages from the play not only its audience, but also its author. After a life of postures, Pericles comes to himself by learning to play, absolved by wonder and love from the illusionism latent in play. Yet wonder is evanescent in a fallen world; an embrace is, after all, a gesture. Therefore Shakespeare offers us Cerimon to consecrate the self's new journeys on the seas of time. Yet he also provides us the clownish Gower. Neither ennobling conviction nor comic detachment is alone in adequate response to being. As a conjuring act, a sacramental contrivance, the play requires its creator to be both priest and antic cheat, maker and unmaker: as are Marina and the riddle's Princess, Diana-Thaisa and Dionyzia, Simonides and Antiochus. To achieve its visionary stasis and stand independent of its mortal creator, the play must incorporate forces of mutability and dissolution. As a result, wishing for life "that I might waste it for you" (1.pro.15), Gower makes art sacrificial. Since his creation is both a potent action and merely play, energy expended into thin air,

> Thus time we waste, and longest leagues make short;
> Sail seas in cockles, have and wish but for't.
> [4.4.1–2]

As in the quibble on "waste," in the enactment the drama annihilates time even as, from the standpoint of "use," we squander the measurable substance of our lives. In its form the play sacrifices itself. It does "use" the bad play of acts one and two, redeeming such sorry stuff in vital theater. Yet the play repeatedly relinquishes the conceptions it embraces, wasting characters and artistic devices another dramatist might have taken seriously. So that as Gower observes, life fulfills itself by preempting its own end, cheerfully dissolving itself: "Now our sands are almost run;/More a little, and then dumb" (5.2.1).[22]

Pericles boldly mimics not the manifest world, but our imaginings of that world. As parody, it brings us to an imaginative equilibrium repudiating what is *not* true, while implying an affirmation of unnamed values. The Prince's flattery at Antioch calls into question the nature of true praise. Falsely conventionalized ardor indirectly exposes the lineaments of authentic love. Because it can only *imply* an ideal, however, parody generates an ambiguity both liberating and treacherously expedient. The play cannot *be* anything at all; it can only revive us, as Marina does its hero. At once it panders to, and chastens, wishful longings in us. It envisions no comfortable rationality or theology, yet it satirizes failures of reason and religion. Because it so radically questions man's myth-making, the play seems to put into critical perspective even the conception of tragic awe.

Art promises all and nothing at all. The chap who congratulates himself on his redemption by Marina by swearing "I am out of the road of rutting for ever" belies himself inasmuch as "rutting" is the nature of roads (4.5.6). Earlier his cohort vowed we shall "never hear the like" of Marina in "such a place as this" once she departs (2). But "this" is the theater as well as Mytilene. The Gentlemen are only partly right about art. For while time appears to deny the power of wonder to alter us, and mutability seems about to seize the incomparable Marina once the play is up, the life of the Gentlemen's words for us now mocks their negation and swears anew to the efficacy of art.

X. This Is Some Changeling: The Seacoast of Bohemia Revisited

Acting out his dream vision at Diana's altar, Pericles gives his fortunes "repetition to the life." Ritually reenacted, past sorrows now issue in a joyful consummation. Yet there is no repose in this magic. Those reunited embrace only to vanish offstage as the motion of life resumes. Gower returns with an epilogue reminiscent of the vicious conventionality of the opening scenes. He reports a world as susceptible to unreasoning brutality as to magical revelation. Hence the poignancy of Pericles' wish that his ecstasy release him from the play:

> You [gods] shall do well
> That on touching of [Thaisa's] lips I may
> Melt and no more be seen.
>
> [5.3.42]

As in Cleopatra's cry at Antony's death, "O, see, my women, the crown o' th' earth doth melt" (4.15.62), Pericles' "melt" predicates not annihilation, but a metamorphosis that would dissolve all conflict. So Hamlet wishes to "melt" and be "resolved" into a dew (1.2.129). For him "not to be" is to sleep, "perchance to dream" (3.1.65).

These examples envision death as a trancelike suspension of consciousness. Rejoining Desdemona after a storm at sea, Othello yearns to stop time, to preserve his "absolute" joy:

> If it were now to die,
> 'Twere now to be most happy; for I fear
> My soul hath her content so absolute
> That not another comfort like to this
> Succeeds in unknown fate.
>
> [2.1.187–91]

Later he kisses the sleeping Desdemona, pledging: "Be thus when thou art dead, and I will kill thee,/And love thee after" (5.2.18). He behaves as if death is but life apotheosized. Bidding Desdemona to "be thus," he associates death with playing dead, as Romeo and Juliet do. Then there is Lear, who would play dead to the cares of life, and "unburden'd crawl toward death" (1.1.39). His confused motives, however, rapidly confound him. In his mania he exults: "I will die bravely, like a smug bridegroom" (4.6.200). Yet when he next appears, the bridegroom's "die" has become a deathly sleep and an ecstasy of torment:

> You do me wrong to take me out o' th' grave.
> Thou art a soul in bliss; but I am bound
> Upon a wheel of fire. . . .

[4.7.45–47]

In the comic context of *A Midsummer Night's Dream*, ecstatic love and deathlike sleep combine as the medium of magical transformation. The lovers "die" into a rebirth. Entering the fairy wood, the Athenians not only escape an intolerable conventional reality, but also open themselves to deeper experience. Like the unquiet ghosts Puck heralds, though "spirits of another sort" associated with regeneration (3.2.388), the fairies themselves inhabit a sphere between life and death. They objectify the imagination's ability to transcend (or play dead to) ordinary mortal existence. As "shadows" or actors (5.1.412) the fairies express a basic fantasy about the power of impersonation and play. For like Shakespeare's figures of the fool and magician-priest, they transcend customary selves, able to manipulate appearances at will: invisible.

Everywhere in Shakespeare we find characters who acquire potency (or dream of acquiring it) by disguising themselves. Portia, for one, assumes a new identity to effect her will. Like the Duke in *Measure for Measure*, Rosalind in the Forest of Arden, or *All's Well's* Helena, Portia becomes psychologically invisible to achieve mastering insight.[1] Once outside herself, she sees into Bassanio and others with the privileged acuteness of a spy. Variations of this fantasy abound in Shakespeare, as we have seen. Lear would play "God's spies" with Cordelia; Navarre's courtiers wish for immortal omniscience as "living art"; exiled from Milan to a magic isle, Prospero cultivates supramundane faculties.[2] In *Hamlet*, the concealment of one's inner life serves a compulsion to dominate others, and perverts intimacy throughout the court. What links these many diverse forms of behavior is an implicit belief that become insubstantial, suspended, the self gains invulnerable freedom and potency. This fantasy underlies the efficacy of Puck and Ariel and, in different ways, the play-deaths of Juliet, Falstaff, Hero in *Much Ado*, and Cleopatra. In *The Winter's Tale*, finally, the fantasy facilitates Hermione's escape and triumphant "resurrection."

To conclude this study, let us return to the seacoast of Bohemia where, in a sense, we began. Specifically I propose to analyze the death of Antigonus and discovery of Perdita in light of the fantasy sketched above. To a reader expecting a compendium of all the truths gleaned so far, such an ending may seem inconclusive—as if, like Antigonus himself, we make our exit pursued by a bear. Yet the analysis I have in mind will reflect the goals of both parts of this book. For in unexpected ways, the old counselor's demise is radically a part of the play's "magical" structure; at the same time, it illuminates the conception of identity as a creative endeavor which has been our immediate concern.

Antigonus as Changeling

Leontes has two individualized counselors, Camillo and Antigonus. They are foils to one another, permutations of a single role. When Camillo flees, Antigonus replaces him, only to be supplanted as counselor and husband on Camillo's return. Symbolically, Leontes' "madness" drives out good counsel, leaving a henpecked and irresolute old man whose weakness mirrors the King's. For vacillating between hate and compassion toward the "bastard" infant, Leontes confesses: "I am a feather for each wind that blows" (2.3.153). Antigonus is no less unstable. One moment he is slyly amused by the King's mania (2.1.198); the next, he is cowering abjectly.

Commanded to poison Polixenes, Camillo disobeys in the name of conscience. In daring to disclose Leontes' plot to his intended victim, Camillo counteracts the failures of communication that have bedevilled the opening scenes. The grateful Polixenes vows: "I will respect thee as a father, if / Thou bear'st my life off hence" (1.2.461). His language ironically glances at Antigonus, who bears off Perdita, and at Leontes, who precipitates his own son's death. Camillo acts the nurturing father.

By contrast, Antigonus is comically unable to muster integrity or nurture. Unwillingly he takes the infant Perdita to be abandoned, "though a present death/Had been more merciful" (2.3.183). As a father to his own daughters he is also untrustworthy. Overeagerly he offers to "geld" them if the Queen's faithlessness be proved (2.1.147). Where Camillo resists tyranny, his alter ego is self-denying, even to the point of impulsively offering to sacrifice himself.[3] "I had rather glib myself" than tolerate illegitimate offspring, he vows (149)—although his daughters' and his self-castration are absurdly beside the point.

Antigonus's references to castration reflect Leontes' fears about cuckoldry, just as his inability to control his wife parodies Leontes' terrors. As the King scoffs, "He dreads his wife" (2.3.79). Indeed, he becomes the object of her curse:

> For ever
> Unvenerable be thy hands, if thou
> Tak'st up the Princess by that forced baseness
> Which [Leontes] has put upon't.
>
> [76–79]

And on the seacoast of Bohemia her curse fulfills itself. Interpreting his shipboard dream to mean that Perdita is "indeed the issue of King Polixenes" (3.3.43), Antigonus does take up "that forced baseness" his wife warned against. Moments later the bear fatally descends on him.

Like the bear in *A Midsummer Night's Dream*, this bear may be seen to objectify irrational anxiety. For the old man is cruelly divided against himself. Leontes has forced him to play false to his "heart so tender" (2.3.132) and his "tenderly officious" instincts (158). The King wagers, "what will you adventure to save this brat's life?" (161). The implied answer is, his life: an old life risked, sacrificed for a new. At sea, brought to the paradoxical seacoast of Bohemia, Antigonus beholds in a dream what he cannot face, that he acts "against [his] better disposition" (3.3.28). He is intolerant of dreams and the hidden depths of experience they intimate. To him "dreams are toys" (39). While "Camillo, the text hints to us, has been Leontes' assistant in covert immoralities," Antigonus has kept himself artificially innocent.[4] He denies absolutely the possibility of evil, in the Queen and in himself no less. He represses all his potential anger toward his unjust king. And it is just such a dissociated, irrational rage which in the figure of the bear tears him apart, as it were. On one level, that is, the encounter dramatizes Antigonus's inner crisis, and thereby echoes the onset of Leontes' madness.

This is not to deny the comic aspects of the bear business. In all likelihood the scene cannot be staged without admitting humor and awareness of artifice. But then, as we saw in chapter three, the interplay of incompatible responses (sympathy and detachment, fear and laughter, among others) is a basic means of eliciting wonder. What is more, Shakespeare is at pains to keep this scene "ungraspable," I suspect, because it initiates a profound transformation.

As the bear drives the courtier back toward the sea, a storm and the sea itself momentarily put all in flux. As the Clown portrays it, "I am not to say it is a sea, for it is now the sky; betwixt the firmament and it you cannot thrust a bodkin's point" (82). With its bedlam roaring of men and weather, this dissolution of the horizon suggests madness and loss of consciousness. The landscape appears to dissolve, and our tragic expectations begin to follow suit. As a tale told by a clown, full of bears and fury, Antigonus's demise exceeds seriousness. More to the point perhaps, if we are sensitive to the symbolic logic of the play, his death is also a liberating transformation. The bear frees energies which in the courtier and in Sicilia itself are suppressed. "The spirits o' th' dead/May walk again" (16).

By all accounts, the scene is tacitly one of regeneration. The Clown "met'st with things dying," the Shepherd "with things new-born" (109). What is lost, in the Oracle's terms, already begins to be recovered. It can be argued that Antigonus's death, "one of the two irreversible tragedies of the play (the death of Mamilius is the other), is partially responsible for a sense of sobriety that obtains even at the play's close, when Paulina points out that all are revived and reunited but [Antigonus]."[5] But is this an irreversible tragedy? When Paulina does belatedly miss her husband, she compares herself to an old turtledove who will "lament" for him till she is "lost." Leontes reacts to this conspicuous self-sacrifice with anything but heavy sobriety: "O, peace, Paulina!/Thou shouldst a husband take by my consent" (5.3.132–36). So Paulina is to have the good counselor Camillo as her mate.

Paulina's marriage is restored: but what of Antigonus himself? There is a joke implied, I think, when he vanishes crying "I am gone for ever" (3.3.58). For instantly the old Shepherd enters, and then the Clown. And as we shall see, it is as if the bear has disintegrated the sophisticated Sicilian into his natural elements. The old Shepherd actually continues Antigonus' role, but as a wish-fulfillment version of it. Not only does he bear off the babe to safety as a surrogate father, he is rewarded by gold to boot. Later we learn that he exercises his authority without the burden of a shrewish wife. The Clown, on the other hand, might be taken to fulfill the courtier's smothered tendency to play the fool. We have heard Antigonus jest about henpecked husbands (2.3.108–11). Scorned for his "ignorant credulity," he has retaliated against the King by quipping in an aside that Leontes' proclamation of the Queen's guilt will raise his audience "to laughter" (1.2.198). But Antigonus cannot openly fool, whereas the Clown can. Indirectly chided by the Shepherd for not aiding the mariners, the Clown jests: "I would you had been by the ship-side to have help'd her; there your charity would have lack'd footing" (3.3.106–8). With comic wonderment he accepts events beyond human control. He compares the foundering ship to a cork thrust into a hogshead, for example (92), and is even capable of sympathy for the bear.

But Antigonus' death symbolically releases creative forces on another level as well. In Shakespeare, creative action proceeds by the disruption and renewal of convention: phases repeatedly dramatized by the roles of fool and priest. As we have observed in Hamlet, Marina, and others, a given character's relation to these roles may intimately shape his destiny. When Leontes praises Camillo for having "priestlike . . . cleansed by bosom" (1.2.237), he is seeking "priestly" corroboration of his idée fixe, Hermione's treachery. When Camillo demurs, the King damns him as liar.

> or else a fool
> That see'st the game play'd home, the rich stake drawn,
> And tak'st it all for jest.
>
> [247–49]

This intolerance of fools is as ominous as it is arrogant. It anticipates Leontes' desperately rigid defiance of the oracle, "great Apollo's priest" (3.2.126). Only years later, awakening his faith inside her chapel (5.3.94–97), does Paulina enact a priestly complement to the shrewish "fool" she played earlier to penetrate his tyrannical delusions. She confirms and consecrates his renewed love by her "magic."

Antigonus, by contrast, is benignly impotent. He does fool, but only in timid asides, without seriously challenging the King. On Bohemia's seacoast, when the Mariner wrongly argues that "the heavens with that we have in hand are angry"—presumably referring to the "bastard" babe (3.3.5)—Antigonus agrees, acting the servant of the gods, a misguided priest: "Their sacred wills be done" (7). With that, he abandons the infant. At once the bear attacks him and he flees as he has been psychologically fleeing dangers all along. Then the rustics enter.

The Clown plays out the openness to experience characteristic of the "true" fool. To him, all is possible: he imposes no self-serving judgments on reality. To him all the elements in the catastrophe—bear, nobleman, ship, storm—are equally part of nature. The Shepherd, on the other hand, evinces a priestly concern with meaning and values. At every step he interprets things to the Clown. "But look thee here, boy," he adjures. "Now bless thyself . . ." (109). He exits with an equally pious promise to "do good deeds" (131). Nevertheless, from his moralistic stereotypes about youth's follies (59–63) to his parodic association with Christ the shepherd, he is a comically imperfect figure—as Antigonus himself is. His "let my sheep go" (120) "insists on the parodic effect of the entire episode. This shepherd is no saint; given a choice between duty and gold, he knows which to follow. The Clown, too, expresses more curiosity than compassion. . . ."[6]

We perceive, then, that Antigonus's demise is radically qualified by its imaginative context in the play, as if Shakespeare himself construed it, consciously or not, as a play-death of the sort we treated at the start of this chapter. The old man is not so much annihilated as transformed. The bear itself is an agent of rebirth as well as death, for "in folklore the bear is one of the most common symbols of immortality and resurrection, because of its habit of winter hibernation."[7] Significantly, the Shepherd's first remark recapitulates the hibernation motif:

> I would there were no age between ten and three and twenty,
> or that youth would sleep out the rest; for there is nothing in
> the between but getting wenches with child, wronging the
> ancientry, stealing, fighting. [59–63]

In effect, the Shepherd wishes youth would play dead. Such a "hibernation" would prevent youth's rebellion against authority and tradition, but also its growth toward autonomy. Such a sleeper would create nothing. This solution to the conflict between authority and creative autonomy may remind us of Antigonus, who has declined to live out dangerous emotions. It is apt that distressing truths come to him as he sleeps on board ship. Though Hermione's ghost adjures him to weep over the babe, he is unable to give his feelings life: "Weep I cannot" (51). Yet even earlier Antigonus shared the Shepherd's complaint against youth's willfulness. He has threatened to "geld" his daughters: age "fourteen they shall not see / To bring false generations" (2.1.147).

Time as Creator

Shakespeare of course may or may not have been wholly aware of the symbolic logic and patterns of association evident in the seacoast metamorphosis. What claims our attention are the patterns themselves and their antecedents in his art. We might reflect at this point that as an actor Shakespeare seems to have been struck by the innumerable "reincarnations" an actor may undergo. One man in his life plays many parts: an actor compounds that multiplicity of identity. He can "be" anyone. In imagination he is potentially all men past, present, and future. This somewhat giddy perspective matters to us because Antigonus's transformations may be understood to continue beyond the rustics' exit. In the figure of Time the process of re-creation proceeds.

Time usually earns the grudging tolerance of critics as a clarifying device. Yet the information he conveys already exists more unobtrusively elsewhere in the play.[8] And like *Pericles*' Gower, the more he speaks, the more his auditors are apt to wonder. For his speech may create as much uncertainty as it resolves. He distances us from the opening action of the play, and from the emotional responses we have felt appropriate. Just as Antigonus becomes a remote, anonymous figure in the Clown's recital, so Sicilia and the threat of tragedy recede almost to nothing in Time's tale. Like Antigonus and the Shepherd, this old man ("Father" Time) is both comic and serious at once. Like Gower, he is atavistic yet brings the future into being too, inviting us to step back from our present selves in an effort to embrace the scope of his meanings. Which is to say, Time makes us self-conscious; he reminds us of mystery and what we cannot grasp.

Symbolically, again, the sophisticated courtier Antigonus undergoes de-composition in death, yielding to simpler figures which express with wishful clarity the basic rhythms of creation stifled in the Sicilian. But these figures, the Shepherd and Clown, yield to a still more fundamental avatar:

> I, that please some, try all, both joy and terror
> Of good and bad, that makes and unfolds error,
> Now take upon me, in the name of Time,
> To use my wings. Impute it not a crime
> To me or my swift passage that I slide
> O'er sixteen years, and leave the growth untried
> Of that wide gap, since it is in my pow'r
> To o'erthrow law and in one self-born hour
> To plant and o'erwhelm custom. Let me pass
> The same I am ere ancient'st order was
> Or what is now received.
>
> [4.1.1–11]

As David Young has pointed out,

> Time's omnipotence is established . . . but a question lurks around the matter of his identity. The speaker is making his gesture "in the name of Time," so that he is an emblem of Time and someone who assumes that guise, not so much the actor taking the role as the artist who also "makes and unfolds error" and who has a similar privilege to use his wings.[9]

The supposed "crime" (4) is an artistic violation of the "laws" of narrative unity. Yet imagination, especially the artistic imagination, exceeds such conventional laws and limits. It is only linear reason which decrees sixteen years a "wide gap" (7). Like imagination, Time has the radical power "to plant and o'erwhelm custom" (9). Hence he is himself immutable: "The same I am" (10).

As an avatar of the artist, then, Time is no mere dealer in artifacts, but a dynamic will perpetually destroying and recreating what exists. He will "make stale/The glistering of this present, as my tale/Now seems to be to it" (13). Yet despite this threat of mutability, he is also mysteriously purposeful, ordained to "try all" (1) and unfold "error" (2). Though "it is in my pow'r/To o'erthrow law" (7), Time is yet unfathomably lawful.

We are beholding, I think, a familiar Shakespearean paradox. By identifying with Time, "playing" him, the artist assumes time's transcendent potency. Instead of defying change and disorder, the creator seeks to accommodate them in his art and self. Such a wish—and it is a magical wish—is reflected in the desire to conceive absolute, "living art" which we have met again and again in Shakespeare.[10] In the equivocal person of Time, magic and play merge, and imagination discloses its immortal longings.

But what has this to do with Antigonus? What relation does Time have to the seacoast metamorphosis? Beginning with the old courtier's dream and death, it is as if we are following a symbolic unfolding of the inner processes of identity. Time offers us a glimpse of the ambiguously transcendent creative energy which Shakespeare repeatedly envisions at the core of personality. Like Oberon the dramatist-king of shadows, Puck, and related figures, Time operates at the furthest verge of rationality, where man's and nature's creation join. Antigonus is in effect "rended" to reveal basic processes behind the sophisticated masks Sicilia deems reality. He is reabsorbed into the play as mortal man is reassimilated into nature's rhythms.

We should not be surprised that this metamorphosis harbors sharply ambivalent meanings. The bear and storm for example, suggest that nature revolts if a man falsifies himself. Denying his love, acting out "unintentional" aggression toward the infant, Antigonus courts his own destruction. Yet these pivotal scenes also dramatize the rewards of sublimation and escapism. Justifiable hostility toward deranged authority turns into a fantasy about an enigmatic creative force (Time) that is omnipotent, and which imagination can impersonate or vicariously "become." Time plants and overwhelms custom—tyrants included. What need then for rebellion? The play offers no model of direct, reasoned resistance to "mad" authority.[11] Its characters succeed by flight (Camillo), secret maneuvers (Hermione, Paulina), or a gift of personal grace as gratuitous as the oracle (Perdita and Florizel).

To identify with Time is to cultivate a chimerical energy. As slippery a character as he is, we recognize in him the root ideas behind the fantasy of playing dead which we treated at the start of this chapter: a vicarious but invulnerable potency, emotional withdrawal, and visionary transcendence. He exists beyond life and death, beyond anxiety and violent passions and inhibiting human laws.

As Time passes across the stage, we "see through" the shallow reality which Sicilia conceived. At the same time we see through the tragic structure of the play's opening, and espy other possibilities beyond that. The transformation, in other words, depends partly on a change in ourselves. Time urges us to let him give his scene "such growing/As you had slept between" (16). Our sleep would itself be akin to the fantasy play-deaths I described earlier. If we imagine as bidden (19), our reward will be wonderment: to behold Perdita "now grown in grace/Equal with wond'ring" (24). If earthly experience seems dangerous and inadequate to our needs, Time holds out the consolation of magical imagining.

Epilogue

But Shakespeare is of two minds about consoling visions in art. He remains acutely critical of Time even as he plays Time before us. As we saw in chapter three, his intimations of an ineffable order behind the play-world are crucially open-ended. Parody qualifies the allegorical and emotional meaning of the action. The personage Time is not only the abstract process of time, but also a verbose, shifty old man, and a satirically revived anachronism. Like allegory itself, he promises sense: yet he is an obscurantist too. We cannot surrender our imaginations to Time's command anymore than Sicilia's counselors might yield to Leontes' peremptory fantasies. For Time's ability to "try all" (4.1.1) comes to nothing in his apology for leaving "the growth untried" (6) in his tale. Though supposedly omnipotent, he depends on our "patience" (15), and hence flatters us as "gentle spectators" (20):

Of this allow,
If ever you have spent time worse ere now;
If never, yet that Time himself doth say
He wishes earnestly you never may.

[29–32]

This is the polite, wheedling voice of the artist-as-epilogue, pleading for our sufferance, slyly reminding us that we participate in his vision by choice.[12] It teases us about metaphysics and pretensions which otherwise might bedazzle us.

In parody, as in allegory, an image at hand implies an ideal on another plane. But parody proceeds by negation. It mocks what is deficient or false at hand; its affirmation is indirect, tacit, unparticularized. For Shakespeare, this negative disposition was appar-

223

ently a fundamental mode of imagination. In unlikely lands such as the seacoast of Bohemia or Prospero's isle, or in figures such as Gower, Time, Ariel, or Puck, life is stylized not merely for clarity's sake, or to free the imagination, but also to express the insufficiency of human understanding. For overtly fantastic things routinely subside into fictive stereotypes. The parodic sense can free us to question the ephemeral nature of our comprehension. Time amuses us, yet we also momentarily share his widened perspective.

As an act of negative creation, parody resembles conjuring. It may direct us toward, and articulate, things inexpressible. In its local ironies it suggests humane, stoical skepticism. Yet Shakespeare also shows us parody playing itself out in the forms of belief, as an act of faith. Not the parodic content, but the act itself, comes to seem an expression of the deepest intuition and wishes.[13]

That wishes are not omnipotent Shakespeare well knew. Yet to the end of his work he explored the kinship of magical thinking and play. He saw that a man cannot live merely as a mask, by purely rational manipulation of self and others, or utterly stripped of masks either. Magically invested, art renews the old human dream of integrating the personality on the ground of immediate experience, in nature, in an ecstatic condition such as Adam is supposed to have enjoyed. Shakespeare, however, keeps us actively disposed between ideality and skepticism, involvement and detachment, just as he himself is always in the process of negating his own creation, testing its limits, reaching beyond it. This equilibrium allows the artist and his audience both to be and not to be "in" an insoluble reality.

Hence the ruefulness which seems to attend wonder even in the romances. There is no repose in absolute love. And yet once alerted to the inadequacy of convention, the heart may find little repose short of absolute love. In Shakespeare we rarely hear any language of unmediated tenderness or pain or hatred. In wonder and madness his characters come closest to it—I am thinking of Lear's bloodcurdling "Howl, howl, howl, howl!" Such moments are perhaps the greatest ones in his art, and they move us deeply. But we never entirely forget the interposing forces of creation that distance us from the thing itself.

To look upon man as a creator is to contemplate the possibility of his apartness, his estrangement in the universe. By that contemplation, however, we come to value poetry which attempts to reconcile magic, play, and conventional understanding in an integrating vision. This is one reason why Shakespeare's epilogues often stir such pathos in us when ambassadors of the play seek to keep alive irreconcilable attitudes, wishing us to applaud and break the spell of art even as our applause confirms the spell's ongoing vitality.

Appendix

Ritual and Drama

Drama as we know it bears only vestigial resemblances to sacred rite. There are forms of performance, however, in which the demarcation is not yet so complete. As the tropes which became the nucleus of medieval religious drama evolved within the Mass, for instance, they remained sacramental. Enacted not by actors but by priests, a trope such as the *Quem quaeritis* only incidentally depicted the discovery of the Resurrection. Rather it reaccomplished that discovery anew, just as the Church year as a whole reenacts the life and sacrifice of Christ.

For worshippers taught to believe earthly life the flicker of a dream, and the reality of the spirit absolute, impersonation must have been an ambiguous concept. In the theological notion of *figura* divinity could reveal itself in avatars estranged in time and space, yet one in God. As *figura* Abraham and Moses at once could be historical personages and transcendently the Lord himself.[1]

Performed, nearly all the extant tropes become a revelation, an experience of wonder. To the demoralized wayfarers in the *Peregrini* the Lord disguises himself as a priest, breaks bread before them (as in the Eucharist to come in the Mass), and disappears. Whereupon the wayfarers intone: "Heu! miseri! ubi erat sensus noster quando intellectus abierat?[2] The amazed question ("where were our senses when we did not comprehend?") leads not to an awareness of role-playing or impersonation, but to the recognition of the insubstantiality of human wits and the shapes of this world in the sight of God. Sung or chanted, the question has the force of an incantation. It celebrates the incapacity of the rational self, and encourages mystification.

226

On one level these early liturgical dramas teach a common lesson: conventional understanding must yield to the absolute reality of the Word. Since the drama itself also does reveal the Word and move the beholders to awed assent, the rite's meaning *is* its action. A magical simultaneity makes the Word "live." In this light the harsh repudiation of the Jews in the *Peregrini* has a dynamic function. Not merely villains in the Crucifixion story, the Jews serve as a model of conventional doubt hardened against revelation. With the urgency of prayer the choir vows:

> Credendum est magis soli Mariae veraci
> Quam Judaeorum turbae fallaci.³

Reinforcing the abstract lesson (that mankind must resist "all the lying host" of unbelief to follow the solitary, even unlikely, voice of truth) is the action, willed by all the participants, of "casting out" that worldly self-conscious mentality from the ceremony.⁴ (I am reminded of Sonnet 125, in which we saw the poet struggling to banish inimical consciousness as a false witness to his love: "Hence, thou suborn'd informer! A true soul / When most impeach'd, stands least in thy control.")

As long as liturgical drama commanded its audience's belief in the corporeal and causal force of the Word, it was an efficacious act of praise. In a thirteenth-century *Conversio Beati Pauli Apostoli* a "voice from aloft" strikes blind the scoffing Saul on the road to Damascus. Not persuaded but transformed by the voice itself, Saul falls in a fit, "quasi semi-mortuus." Recovering, he addresses the congregation, and challenges the "Jews"—doubters—to open their hearts to the Word. The performance then culminates in a concerted act of praise, a *Te Deum laudamus.*⁵

While we cannot precisely determine how fully men believed in the magical powers of language, the recurrence of the idea in religious drama and elsewhere suggests that at the least we can say men wanted to, and thought they should, believe it. God's voice remakes Saul. In the Chester *Fall of Lucifer*, one of the Corpus Christi cycles, Deus sweeps the usurping angel from his throne merely by announcing his will:

> Thu Lucyfere, ffor thy mekyl pryde,
> I bydde the ffalle from hefne to helle. . . .⁶

The word itself re-creates Lucifer.

In the Sonnets the disruption of conventional awareness induces wonder. In turn wonder may lead to a conviction of transcendence and love, or to madness and destruction. These possibilities are latent in ritual drama also. Because it actualized the inner, spiritual world as the preeminent reality, ritual drama needed no less than liturgy to regulate the intense wishes and fears it aroused. The worshipper who renounced his sinful worldly self during the Mass could confirm his spiritual rebirth in formal praises. Yet even within the Church, despite its conservative forms, such complex psychic processes sometimes faltered.[7] Such dangers loom vividly in the Corpus Christi play. For when Christ directly pleaded in helpless agony with onlookers who were called upon to play the vicious witnessing mob at Golgotha, the horror of his torment must have had an impact unequalled in the Gospel narratives.[8] The spectators' role required them to "pulle of Jhesus clothis, and betyn hym with whyppys . . . tyl he is alle blody."[9] Credible stories have come down to us of actors engulfed by their roles: of player-Christs who went mad, or were "forgetfully" speared to death on the Cross in the intensity of the enacted persecution. Presumably such catastrophes were possible because the spectators' passions could momentarily supersede reality itself. In the hands of religious reformers, certainly, such tales were propaganda tools. As in the Sonnets, we may be dealing primarily with fears of madness and violence. Historically true or not, the popularity of such tales betokens a fascination with—and some belief in—the preternatural potency of imitation.[10]

All these performances express a wish that the world of myth and material reality become fused. The religious context alone cannot account for the wish. Needless to say, the Church itself repeatedly condemned magic and "idolatrous shows." Official hostility, in fact, reaches back toward Tertullian's *De spectaculis*, which bolstered the Roman state's eventual repression of drama.[11]

Some of the "spectacles" which Tertullian attacked were ambiguously magical forms, not religious but rather fundamentally dramatic—which increases their significance for us. Certain Roman mimes, Martial tells us, were designed to introduce in the amphitheater the actual execution of a criminal. On a lavishly realistic set, with real trees, animals, and birds, the condemned man might take the role of a mythological hero such as Daedalus or Orpheus. As stage hands maneuvered a "magic forest, like the garden of the Hesperides" toward this Orpheus, he approached it singing. As in the myth, his song "charmed" the (trained) tigers and lions before him. In the midst of this pastoral pageantry a bear suddenly appeared and seized the hero, tearing the man to pieces.

Vicious as they were,

the principle of these mythological dramas lay in the search for an ambiguity between the imaginary and the real. This is shown in startling fashion in the trait which consists in making the actor, whose very essence is to *represent*, perish in flesh and blood. What is found here, not represented but "reified," namely, transformed on stage into a thing, is what belongs . . . to the domain of the imaginary: mythological legends or fabulous history.[12]

In such a performance the actor's death disrupts the boundary between artifice and reality. For an instant myth and imagination fuse with the objective world. The story and the intricate props

lose their quality of fiction. By a mechanism analogous to that of "transference" the agony of the actor confers on what was false a sort of *reality in the second degree*, the mystery of which excites the mind. It is at the same time "true" and "false," even as the actors "live" and "mime."[13]

Were the mimes' creators manipulating reality merely for the sake of a "mystery . . . which excites the mind," the mimes would have been—in a horrible way—parodies of ritual. Given the pervasiveness of magical thinking in Roman culture, however, we may suspect that for those witnessing it, the mime was not without preternatural implications. What matters for us is the mime's effort to induce wonder in the spectators. Its illusionism seeks to baffle the mind by disrupting conventional discriminations between true and false, imagination and reality. In this way, however nihilistic it may or may not have been, the mime was concerned with transcendence.

Notes

Part One

Introduction

1. Stanley Edgar Hyman, *Iago: Some Approaches to the Illusion of His Motivation* (New York, 1970), p. 4.

2. Caroline Spurgeon, *Shakespeare's Imagery* (Cambridge, 1935), p. ix.

3. Madeleine Doran's *Endeavors of Art* (Madison, 1954) comprehensively records the justifying intellectual maneuvers of Renaissance aestheticians, notably in its chapter on "Verisimilitude," pp. 53–74. I am aware that there are startling exceptions to my "rule," among them Minturno, who conceded that "great praise is due the poet who wins for feigned things a faith filled with wonder" (Doran, p. 408). But as Minturno's juxaposition of "wonder" and "faith" may indicate, Renaissance critics as a group are strongly motivated toward certitude and the rationalization of art.

4. In *Shakespearean Metadrama* (Minneapolis, 1971), James L. Calderwood argues at length that the plays "are not only about the various . . . thematic issues with which critics have so long and quite properly been busy but also about Shakespeare's plays. Not just 'the idea of the play' . . . but dramatic art itself . . . is a dominant Shakespearean theme, perhaps his most abiding subject" (p. 5).

What Calderwood calls "metadrama" Sigurd Burckhardt designates "intrinsic interpretation" in *Shakespearean Meanings* (Princeton, 1968); more restricted than these is Lionel Abel's *Metatheatre: A New View of Dramatic Form* (New York, 1963); a metadramatic perspective is implied as well in Kenneth Burke's 1951 article on *Othello*, Leslie Fiedler's "Shakespeare and the Paradox of Illusion," in *The Collected Essays of Leslie Fiedler* (New York, 1971), Anne Righter's *Shakespeare and the Idea of the Play* (London, 1962), Philip Edwards' *Shakespeare and the Confines of Art* (London, 1968), and Herbert Wiesinger's "Theatrum Mundi: Illusion as Reality," in *The Agony and the Triumph* (East Lansing, 1964).

5. *King Leir*, Malone Society Reprints, edited by W. W. Greg and R. Warwick Bond (1908), 11. 1232–33.

Chapter One

1. Readers have boldly rationalized the Sonnets from the start. John Benson's 1640 edition advertises them as "SEREN, cleare and eligantly plaine, such gentle straines as shall recreate and not perplex your brains, no

intricate or cloudy stuffe to puzzell intellect, but perfect eloquence." In the many autobiographies conjectured from the Sonnets their "recreation" has gone on apace.

2. See Heinz Werner, *The Comparative Psychology of Mental Development* (New York, 1948), pp. 337–76., and Ernst Cassirer, *Language and Myth* (New York, 1946). In chapter 3 of *Totem and Taboo* Freud calls the controlling principle of magic "omnipotence of thought" or "the over-estimation of psychic processes as opposed to reality." In neurosis, he points out, it is not the reality of the experience but the reality of the thought which underlies symptom formation. A conscious or repressed death wish, for example, may lead to as much guilt as an intentional act. It should be noted that Freud is disposed to emphasize the pathological potential of magical thinking. For a survey of magical forms of belief in Renaissance England, see K. V. Thomas, *Religion and the Decline of Magic* (New York, 1971).

3. See also Stephen Booth's *An Essay on Shakespeare's Sonnets* (New Haven, 1968), p. 14: "Perhaps the happiest moment the human mind ever knows is the moment when it senses the presence of order and coherence—and before it realizes the particular nature (and so the particular limits) of the perception. At [that] moment . . . the mind is unlimited. It seems . . . about to grasp a coherence beyond its capacity. As he reads through the 1609 sequence, a reader's mind is constantly poised on just such a threshold to comprehension."

4. In *Themes and Variations in Shakespeare's Sonnets* (New York, 1966) J. B. Leishman acknowledges the singularity of the Sonnet's hyperbole, yet in the end he argues the familiar view that even Shakespeare's "most unprecedented . . . conceptions . . . may be related to . . . traditional *encomia*," and were "almost certainly not arrived at as the result of a deliberate attempt to say something . . . he hoped had never been said before" (p. 177).

5. By itself the liabilities of "naming" explain to a great extent why we know so little about the "real" identities of the personae in the sequence—assuming Shakespeare ever had specific people in mind.

6. Critics have long been wont to regard Shakespeare's complicated or perverse syntax as a sign of immature technique. In forcing language beyond ordinary syntactical limits, however, the poet has a means of accommodating multiplicity within the order of meaning. In effect, he preempts multiplicity, wishing to create something akin to formless form. Cf. "composed wonder" in Sonnet 59.

7. In "The Poet as Fool and Priest" (in *Shakespearean Meanings*) Burckhardt perceives that certain poetic devices such as ambiguity and repetition have a disruptive function, loosening the bonds of convention and thereby enabling the poet to renew the integrity of his language by reaffirming its "absolute" meanings. Even so just a critic as L. C. Knights, writing about the Sonnets in *Explorations* (London, 1946), complains that Shakespeare's ambiguity sometimes fails to "unify" or enlarge his meaning, as if ambiguity ought only to "make sense." Burckhardt understands Shakespeare's drastic awareness of language as a response to the difficult proposition that "when all is 'said and done,' the poet *acts* by *speaking*" (p. 46).

8. By the phrase "conceptual conventions" I mean to suggest Shakespeare's recognition of the latent "artificiality" of all our conceptions of the world. To the extent that Renaissance artists customarily conceived the truth of art as a function of its "artifice" and formal properties, as Rosemund Tuve maintains in *Elizabethan and Metaphysical Imagery* (Chicago, 1947), one measure of Shakespeare's uniqueness is his appreciation that artifice may be necessary to truth yet also inescapable and inadequate.

9. With its more fluid, rhetorical rather than logical punctuation, the 1609 quarto makes the point clearer still, so I have quoted the quarto text

Notes

here. While the quarto may have been carelessly printed, as many editors maintain, the interpretive punctuation in modern editions is one more sign of the critical effort to rationalize the Sonnets.

10. A vivid instance of one sonnet redefining another occurs when in Sonnet 106 the poet vows that all past praises "name" the beloved as prophecies/Of this our time, all you prefiguring." Sonnet 107 then avers that

Not mine own fears nor the prophetic soul
Of the wide world dreaming on things to come
Can yet the lease of my true love control,
Supposed as forfeit to a confined doom.

Chapter Two

1. Quotations are from M. M. Mahood's chapter on the Sonnets in *Shakespeare's Wordplay* (London, 1957), p. 103. I don't mean to endorse the points argued in these passages.

2. Negative creation bears some resemblance to the mystics' Via Negativa, and the theologians' apophatic mode of argument, which presupposes that the inexactness of language makes negative language about God less faulty than positive. The power of the negative also governs the Zen exercise in which the novice meditates upon what God is *not*, systematically "emptying" his mind of conventional concepts (God is not a tree, a stone, a cloud, and so on). What remains to be contemplated is presumably God.

Negative thinking also has a euphemistic function, to prevent offenses against the powers which prevail in the spiritual world. Hence the Hebrew name for God, "That-which-cannot-be-named." While the prohibition that Orpheus not behold Eurydice literalizes his wonder as he leads her out of death, when he does grasp for reassurance and control by looking at her, he brings about the punishment of death. In a different way the example of Orpheus illustrates the magical power of the negative in attempts to propitiate fate by sacrifice or self-negation. Like Orpheus, the poet of the Sonnets could be said to enjoy a deathless love so long as he sacrifices direct personal and sensual possession of his beloved.

3. Compare *Romeo and Juliet* (2.3.27–30):

Two such opposed kings encamp them still
In man as well as herbs—grace and rude will;
And where the worser is predominant,
Full soon the canker death eats up that plant.

4. *Poetry of the English Renaissance*, edited by J. William Hebel and Hoyt H. Hudson (New York, 1929), p. 887. Cf. George Puttenham's *Arte of English Poesie*, which begins with a comparison of the poet-creator to God, "who without any travail to his divine imagination made all the world of nought."

5. Lest it be imagined that magical thinking is remote from us, it is worth mentioning that this disruption of magical belief is a common—and comic—subject in cartoons, wherein a character runs off a high place into thin air. For an instant his intense wish to fly sustains him, until he looks down and becomes self-conscious about his position. His concentration interrupted, he plummets to earth.

6. Another, commensurate reading would view the "knife" as the beloved's virtue, in danger of losing its power to inspire praise.

7. Hebel and Hudson, p. 886.

8. See Anne Righter, *Shakespeare and the Idea of the Play* (London,

1962), pp. 92–93. The ambiguity of these terms allows them to suggest painting or any other artistic "imitation" as well.

9. In his espial of the mind's "idols" the judicious Bacon echoes this concern with the limits of perception, sometimes employing the same metaphors. For example, "there are idols which have migrated into men's minds from the various dogmas of philosophers, and also from wrong laws of demonstration. These I call *Idols of the Theatre*, because in my judgment all the received systems of philosophy are but so many stage-plays, representing worlds of their own creation after an unreal and scenic fashion. . . . And in . . , this philosophic theatre you may observe the same thing which is found in the theatre of the poets,—that stories invented for the stage are more compact and elegant, and more as we would wish them to be, than true stories out of history" (*Novum Organum*, I, 44). Shakespeare is concerned with "idols" on behalf of the truth of praise ("Let not my love be called idolatry"), Bacon on behalf of reason. Yet both share a mistrust of art that reaches back to Plato's warnings that the artist will readily sacrifice truth to form.

10. Mahood, p. 99.

11. In his well-known essay on this sonnet in *Some Versions of Pastoral* (New York, 1935) William Empson exhaustively rehearses its ambiguities. Interestingly, he discerns in the poem "the feeling that life is essentially inadequate to the human spirit," although he relates this feeling to pastoral: "a good life must avoid saying so."

12. In *The Play and Place of Criticism* (Baltimore, 1967) Murray Krieger speaks of "the magic unpredictability of poetry's spell." In the Sonnets, we "are beyond the limited world of wit—but not beyond the world of art. . . ." (P. 36.)

Chapter Three

1. Lily B. Campbell, *Shakespeare's Tragic Heroes* (London, 1930), p. 109. The play's "dominant idea" is supposedly "that those who balance passion by reason are not Fortune's puppets. And such is the lesson of tragedy" (p. 147).

2. From a letter to George and Tom Keats, December, 1817.

3. What Polixenes yearns for, Jaques in *As You Like It* ridicules:

> Ducdame, ducdame, ducdame,
> Here shall he see
> Gross fools as he
> An if he will come to me.

Amiens: What's that "ducdame"?
Jaques: 'Tis a Greek invocation to call fools into a circle. [2.5.50–55]

4. Primitive magic, for example, does not sharply differentiate the spheres of subjective and objective phenomena: magical powers are believed to pervade all things. Primitive man commonly evaluates dreams and illusions as real, and "in the realm of magic this belief becomes an active conviction that the dream and vision are magically effective realities. It is because of this similarity between the inner world of man—that is, his ideas and his personal strivings—and the world of outer events, that in the magic sphere the wishes, intentions, and thoughts are even reality itself." Heinz Werner, *The Comparative Psychology of Mental Development* (New York, 1948), p. 339.

5. Johan Huizinga, *Homo Ludens* (Boston, 1955), pp. 15, 25.

6. Joseph Campbell, *The Masks of God* (New York, 1959), I, pp. 21–22.

7. See Jackson Cope's summary of Ortega's position in *The Theatre and*

Notes

the Dream (Baltimore, Md., 1973), pp. 4–8; also his comments on Artaud and Northrop Frye, pp. 8–12.

8. In *Magic and the Decline of Religion* K. V. Thomas identifies many of the forces in Renaissance English culture working to diminish and sublimate magical beliefs: ranging from a proto-scientific spirit to a persisting dread of daemonic potency (pp. 641–68). For an account of the Puritans' drastic attacks on magic and magical (usually Papist) religion, see pp. 51–77.

9. For interested readers I have provided an Appendix with a brief sketch of some pre-Shakespearean dramatic forms which are, ambiguously, rituals.

10. Stephen Orgel, *The Jonsonian Masque* (Cambridge, 1965), p. 6.

11. Orgel, p. 10. Orgel includes extensive passages from the masque.

12. Orgel, pp. 13–17.

13. The phrase is Orgel's, and corresponds to his useful hint that the Esquire's role entails a "sort of artistic self-consciousness, whereby the virtue or power of a figure is dependent on his ability not to take himself or his world seriously."

14. Just this theme of course came famously to light within a few years of Davison's masque in the English Faust-book and, thereafter, in Marlowe's *Faustus*, which must have been nearly contemporary with *Proteus*. Faustus echoes the aspirations the Esquire voices ("All things that move between the quiet poles / Shall be at my command"), and in his indulgence in perverted praise he invests a fallen queen, Helen, by comparisons with myth and nature. The roles he imagines for himself are theatrical and self-aggrandizing and restlessly Protean. He would have profane love of a queen "make me immortal with a kiss."

15. That Hermoine is herself doomed to "die" a prisoner ironically transfigures her words—one more indication of the possible dangers of playing in such an unnatural atmosphere.

16. M. M. Mahood comments on Leontes and playing (pp. 149–50), as does Joan Hartwig in a study which appeared after my own argument was complete, *Shakespeare's Tragicomic Vision* (Baton Rouge, La., 1972), pp. 106–9. Within the purview of tragicomedy Miss Hartwig's account of wonder tends to corroborate mine. For a more detailed analysis of the interpretive process by which certain Shakespearean characters may be seen to "create" themselves, see my chapters on *The Merchant of Venice* and *Hamlet* in part two.

17. Mahood, p. 154. In *Fables of Identity* (New York, 1963) Northrop Frye observes that "Leontes' state of mind is a parody of the imagination of lover and poet" (p. 115).

18. See M. C. Bradbrook, *The Growth and Structure of Elizabethan Comedy* (London, 1955), especially her remarks on Lyly (pp. 71–76) and the Poet's War (pp. 104–17).

19. See *Volpone* (3.7.14011.) in the C. H. Herford and Percy Simpson edition of Jonson (Oxford, 1937), v, pp. 81ff.

20. Herford and Simpson, IV, p. 205. "Formal" not only implies a claim to authority, but also means "regular" or "conventional." "Shapes" is a common synonym for actors (cf. Sonnet 53, which raises these issues, in chapter two). "Conjuring" speaks for itself, although it is interesting that Jonson, who deemed *Pericles* "a mouldy tale," took a jaundiced attitude toward magical creation—however secretly ambivalent *The Alchemist*, say, reveals him to have been.

21. In *Shakespeare's Last Plays* (London, 1938) E. M. W. Tillyard observes that the masque in *The Tempest* is "executed by players pretending to be spirits, pretending to be real actors, pretending to be supposed goddesses and rustics" (p. 80).

22. Hartwig, p. 108.

23. See also Auerbach's essay on *figura* in *Scenes from the Drama of European Literature* (New York, 1959), pp. 11—76. Perdita has functional similarities to Portia, whose role meets the requirements for *figura* (see chapter seven).

24. See G. Wilson Knight, *The Crown of Life* (London, 1965), p. 101. More broadly, in "An Interpretation of Pastoral in *The Winter's Tale*," *Shakespeare Quarterly* XXII, 2 (1971), Philip M. Weinstein finds "a conflation of realism and symbolism in the Pastoral Scene that not only ballasts the symbolism . . . but also limits, even indicates the inadequacy of, that symbolism" (p. 97). In *The Winter's Tale: A Study* (London, 1947), S. L. Bethell sees the play's dramatic awkwardness as "a deliberately comic underlining of a deliberately crude technique" (p. 49).

25. See J. H. P. Pafford's Arden edition of the play (London, 1963), p. 150. Julio Romano scandalized Rome as well as Jupiter; he illustrated the sex manual to which Aretino contributed sonnets (its caption: *"In quanti diversi modi attudini e posituri giaccino i disonesti uomini con le donne"* or "in how may various ways, attitudes and positions loose men lie with women"). Shakespeare's joke adds liberating and complex comedy to a complexly solemn rebirth of love.

26. Shakespeare has many ways of reinforcing the illusion of an autonomous playworld. In a theater without a curtain or footlights to demarcate the formal beginning, end, and internal scene divisions of a play, certain dramas may appear to exceed the temporal bounds of the action we witness. We seem always to be catching in midcourse a larger, integral action which has preceded us and will continue after. On another level, the master metaphor of life-as-drama leads to a conception of the play as "a little world which refuses to be static, to accept the limitations of mimetic form; a little world which mocks aesthetic objectivity as it incorporates the theatrum mundi into itself" (Abel, p. 168).

27. C. L. Barber, *Shakespeare's Festive Comedy* (Princeton, 1959), p. 15. Cf. Barber's elusive but appropriate remark in his Laurel edition of the Sonnets (New York, 1962) that the poems "ask for a special sort of attention because in them poetry is, in a special way, an action" (p. 11).

28. John Holloway, *The Story of the Night* (London, 1961), p. 19.

29. James L. Calderwood, *Shakespearean Metadrama* (Minneapolis, 1971) p. 141. This passage applies to *A Midsummer Night's Dream* the notion of a marriage of minds as the poet's goal, following Burckhardt's elaboration of the concept in "The Poet as Fool and Priest" in *Shakespearean Meanings*.

Part Two

Introduction

1. The quote is Kenneth Burke's, in Stanley Edgar Hyman, *Iago: Some Approaches to the Illusion of His Motivation* (New York, 1970), p. 61.

2. Sigurd Burckhardt develops the connection between artistic and regal ordering in *Shakespearean Meanings* (Princeton, 1968), pp. 3—21, as does Harold E. Toliver in "Shakespeare's Kingship: Institution and Dramatic

Notes

Form," in *Essays in Shakespearean Criticism*, edited by Calderwood and Toliver (Englewood Cliffs, N.J., 1970), pp. 58–82.

3. Cf. Sonnet 121, "'Tis better to be vile than vile esteemed," in which the poet defies utterly the reproach of "others' false adulterate eyes" and, godlike, vows "No, I am that I am. . . ."

4. A fine illustration of priestly functions in terms of the Renaissance notion of the *magus* appears in Albert Cirillo, "As You Like It: Pastoralism Gone Awry," in *English Literary History* XXXVIII (March 1971), 19–39.

5. In *1 Henry IV* Falstaff's famous incantation praising "sweet Jack Falstaff, kind Jack Falstaff, true Jack Falstaff" and so on "aggrandizes an identity," as C. L. Barber puts it. Barber goes on to point out that Falstaff magically equates himself with "all the world" (*Shakespeare's Festival Comedy* [Princeton, 1959], pp. 212–13).

Chapter Four

1. Cf. Philip Edwards, *Shakespeare and the Confines of Art* (London, 1968), p. 37. "In this play Shakespeare refuses the 'proper' ending. . . . The impulse, in his early years, to write an anti-comedy is very closely akin to the wish to enclose the stuff of tragedy within the kernel of comedy."

2. The quote is from Frank Kermode's New Arden edition of *The Tempest* (Introduction, p. 1).

3. Cf. the praise of the Queen in *The Masque of Proteus*. Shakespeare's parody of such worshipful rhetoric suggest the play's connections with court circles. Cf. Richard David's New Arden edition of the play (Introduction, p. xliii). The King's "immortal" tomb becomes complexly satiric when we recall the contemporary craze for aggrandizing monuments. See Lawrence Stone, *The Crisis of the Aristocracy* (New York, 1967), pp. 186, 263–64, and 324.

4. Cf. Leontes' attempts to silence Paulina, who takes refuge in the comic role of shrew. Leontes has wrongly conjured up a war against his own affections too.

5. See Anne Righter on the player-king (*Shakespeare and the Idea of the Play* [London, 1962], pp. 102–24), and James L. Calderwood on *Richard II* (*Shakespearean Metadrama* [Minneapolis, 1971], pp. 149–86).

6. We might hear "eye" as a pun too: beauty is realized not by the "base sale of . . . tongues," but by the "I" or whole person. The language of the passage presages that of the brothel scene in *Pericles*, as chapter nine will show.

7. Since Longaville enters at this point it is possible that the King wishes only to dispose of incriminating evidence. The Folio punctuation, which I have used, makes "I'll drop the paper" a complete sentence, as much an answer to the question preceding as a antecedent to the next line. Also, by *vicariously* presenting his love the paper will "shade" his folly from disclosure.

8. Literally of course there is no new oath sworn here, but this speech does commit the courtiers to their new goal.

9. In Sonnets 129 and 144, among others, the poet wars against the huge armies of the world's desires, but on behalf of purely spiritual love.

10. Analogous to this is the deceptive fulfillment of the uncanny prophecies Macbeth conjures through the witches.

11. *The Merchant of Venice* might be said to present a ritual (the casket scene) in which such a ghostly will is satisfied and exorcised. Cf. my remarks on *Hamlet* also.

12. That these same two personae for the creator preside over *The Winter's*

Tale through the Oracle and the cunning Autolycus seems to me to reinforce the structural similarities between the two plays.

13. Shakespeare apparently took the flower names not from nature, but from Gerard's *Herbal* (1597). See Richard David, p. 184n.

14. It has often been noted that the song parodies the medieval *débat*.

Chapter Five

1. P. Siegel, "*A Midsummer Night's Dream* and the Wedding Guests," in *Shakespeare Quarterly* IV (1935), 139–44, comments on the concept of love as mystery. More substantial is the treatment of love in Paul Olsen's "*A Midsummer Night's Dream* and the Meaning of Court Marriage," in *English Literary History* XXIV (1957), 95–119.

2. Analogous is the hunt in *Love's Labour's Lost*, wherein the Princess, for similar symbolic ends, "must play the murderer" of the deer.

3. Cf. *The Medieval Stage* (Oxford, 1903), where E. K. Chambers reports a pre-Christian ritual in which villagers dance together through all the doors in their community (*I*,119). The dance, I take it, allows them to enter concretely into one another's "interior" lives, but in a ceremonially regulated way.

4. See Northrop Frye's familiar essay "The Argument of Comedy," in *English Institute Essays*, 1949, pp. 58–73.

5. It is worth bearing in mind that in many of the Sonnets the poet and his beloved symbolically flee from a rigidly conventional world into a magical sphere.

6. C. L. Barber, *Shakespeare's Festival Comedy* (Princeton, 1959), p. 140.

7. When Lysander bids Hermia "take the sense . . . of my innocence," we might take him at his word, subtracting "sense" from "innocence," hearing the word as "in no sense."

8. The same fate overtakes Helena and Hermia. Complex mockery dogs Helena's inflation of their misbegotten love:

> We, Hermia, like two artificial gods,
> Have with our needles created both one flower,
> Both on one sampler, sitting on one cushion,
> Both warbling of one song, both in one key. . . .   [3.2.203–19]

9. Knighthood functions as a deceptive solution to the need for an effective masculine identity in such diverse plays as *King Lear* and (as we shall see) *Pericles*. Stricken by the love-potion, Lysander woos Helena by vowing "to be her knight" (2.2.144).

10. It may be objected that Egeus is too much a type to warrant any psychological interest. However, he participates in a pattern which recurs time and again in Shakespeare, with increasingly subtle psychological insight. Cf. the treatment of old Capulet in the chapter that follows, and the adumbration of the pattern in the Princess's feelings about her father in *Love's Labour's Lost*. More compelling still are the examples of Lear and Brabantio and, in a happier way, Prospero.

11. Of the mechanicals' dramaturgy Barber says: "the clowns forget . . . that a killing or a lion in a play . . . is a mental event. Because, like children, they do not discriminate between imaginary and real events, they are literal about fiction. But they are *not* unimaginative: on the contrary they embody the stage of mental development before the discipline of facts has curbed the tendency to equate what is "in" the mind with what 'outside' it" (pp. 150–51).

Notes

Bottom's transformation literalizes *for us* the "naturalizing" tendency of the magical mentality.

12. Among other meanings of "passion" the Oxford English Dictionary gives: "an eager outreaching of the mind towards something." It is just such an outreaching that playlet and play alike seek to incite.

13. Calderwood points out (p. 147) that "The final graciousness of the dramatist Oberon is to sacrifice his own play for the sake of those on whom it has bestowed its blessing. Thus when he has brought all the lovers into a charmed sleep he creates for them one final illusion:
    When they next wake, all this derision
    Shall seem a dream and fruitless vision."

14. The notion that "real" death makes the most compelling performance—a lighthearted jibe here—is grimly literal in the Roman mimes, treated in the Appendix, pp. 228–29.

15. Cf. Wyndham Lewis, *The Lion and the Fox* (London, 1927): "Over against the fortunate central person is always another figure, or impulse, that contradicts his power and happiness. This propitiatory figure is a sort of periapt or *paratonerre:* his function is to forestall adversity, and guarantee (should the dark powers look at the small human figure of authority with jealous eyes) that the *hubris* is not there, or that there is a factor of disillusion always present to prevent too dangerous and overweening an insolence. The jester is thus there *for luck*" (p. 130).

16. I cannot resist pointing out that Shakespeare's humor and good sense stand out the more plainly in contrast with some of the bear-avatars in contemporary popular culture—for example, a pamphlet presenting the "true and most dreadful discourse of a woman possessed with the devil; who in the likeness of a headless bear fetched her out of her bed and in the presence of seven persons most strangely rolled her through three chambers and down a high pair of stairs on the 4 and 20 of May last 1584 at Ditchet in Somerset." A May rite twice over.

Chapter Six

1. *If* we felt this contrivance to be paramount, Shakespeare might appear to be as tyrannical as Egeus, and his play but as a form in wax. To prevent just this "tyranny," he brings on disruptive death to close *Love's Labour's Lost.* Contrivance similarly haunts the Sonnets, as in 35, wherein the poet ruefully confesses that "to thy sensual fault I bring in sense."

2. This awareness, we recall, is the central "trick" in *Proteus.* It will occupy us in a far more profound way in *Hamlet.*

3. Cf. Lear's "Come not between the dragon and his wrath" (1.1.121) and Othello's "Now, by heaven,/My blood begins my safer guides to rule" (2.3.196–97). In both instances ostensibly powerful men try to use their anger as a social weapon, dramatizing it for others rather than directly experiencing it themselves.

4. In *The Power of Satire: Magic, Ritual, Art* (Princeton, 1960) Robert C. Elliott provides a valuable account of the origins of belief in the destructive force of words. Of the fallen Timon, a believer in magical curses like Lear, he says: "Timon's language takes on the incantatory tone of a prophet. He tries to preempt the full power of the archaic curse . . . to confound the hated creature man. It is as though Timon were . . . attempting to change the world through the power of language" (p. 165). In defense against their own magical belief, children today still chant (magically!):

> Sticks and stones
> Will break my bones,
> But names will never hurt me.

5. The connection between insecure "grasping" and resentment of play is vivid in the tight-fisted Shylock, who decries masques and "Christians with varnished faces" to his daughter. Whatever we think of Jessica's elopement itself, masks and play appear as means to liberation and love.

6. Playing dead recurs almost obsessively in Shakespeare, from Hermione and (penitentially) Leontes, to the poet in Sonnet 73 ("That time of year thou may'st in me behold"). Kings Lear and Ferdinand of Navarre play dead to the world and women (Lear makes a point of declaring that he will "unburthened crawl toward death") to win "immortalizing" love, although neither bears actual rejection with appropriate indifference. Puck's love potion plays out a version of this fantasy, making the lovers "dead" to themselves and susceptible to renewal. Chapter ten explores this fantasy.

7. Harry Levin, "Form and Formality in *Romeo and Juliet*," *Shakespeare Quarterly* XI (Winter, 1960), 8. Levin's essay is in general vastly more judicious than those which plug for the lovers' moral superiority and the pleasant "greater good" their deaths bestow on Verona. Cf. J. Lawlor, "*Romeo and Juliet*," in *Early Shakespeare* (London, 1961).

8. While Lady Capulet can rhapsodize about the "gold clasps" that lock the book Paris is (1.3.93), the lovers' most abstract and literally inconceivable tropes should be understood in the context of relinquishment. Cf. Juliet's invocation (3.2.21—25):

> Give me my Romeo; and when I shall die,
> Take him and cut him out in little stars. . . .

9. The fantasy takes numerous forms in Shakespeare: in *Love's Labour's Lost* the women promise to welcome back their suitors after a year's death-like penance; Othello would murder Desdemona to love her in "heaven" ("Be thus when thou art dead, and I will kill thee, / And love thee after"); Leontes receives his wife from death, as does Pericles; in *Twelfth Night* Viola recovers a drowned brother; in *The Tempest* virtually all the lives in the play are restored to life thanks to the gifts of Prospero's imagination.

10. Of this passage (3.2.45—50) M. M. Mahood says: "excuses are scarcely needed since this is one of Shakespeare's first attempts to reveal a profound disturbance of mind by the use of quibbles. Romeo's puns . . . at Friar Lawrence's cell are of the same kind" (*Shakespeare's Wordplay* [London, 1957], p. 70).

11. In *Love's Labour Lost* the Princess's desperate renunciation of her freedom might be understood in this light. In *The Winter's Tale* rejection leads Perdita to rebirth as an incomparable queen.

12. A tomb is, significantly, death conventionalized. Presumably the gold statues of the lovers will adorn the tomb—in the context of the Sonnets' repudiation of ornament, a biting irony.

13. As a play on words ("an artificial knight") the phrase locates in Romeo the same compulsion to idealize oneself which entraps Juliet. Also see note 9 in chapter five.

14. That the Friar's potion functions like Oberon's might warn us that he impinges on the role of playmaker. It is noteworthy that in directing all the action of *Measure for Measure* the Duke assumes the guise of a friar.

15. The Friar's wish for the lovers to play dead in Mantua and return triumphant presupposes some prodigious labors. He plans

> To blaze your marriage, reconcile your friends,
> Beg pardon of the Prince, and call thee back
> With twenty hundred thousand times more joy
> Than thou went'st forth. . . .   [3.3.145]

Notes

16. Many a commentator has bowed to the claims of fate in the play, some following F. Boas's moot deduction that fate's preeminence over the lovers' will makes the play no tragedy (*Shakespeare and his Predecessors*, 1896). In *Not Wisely But Too Well* (1957), F. Dickey would have us believe fortune the vehicle of divine justice!

Chapter Seven

1. Wolfgang Clemen, *English Tragedy Before Shakespeare* (London, 1961), p. 143.
2. Maurice Charney, *How to Read Shakespeare* (New York, 1971), p. 91.
3. See E. Pearlman, "Shakespeare, Freud, and the Two Usuries," in *English Literary Renaissance* II, (Spring 1972). Pearlman notes the pun on "stones" and adds: "Jessica has in fact absconded with the family jewels in the sense of her father's generational and sexual capacity. Her exogamous marriage has deprived him of heirs; metaphorically Shylock has been sterilized" (p. 224).
4. Cf. the association of "furnish" with costuming and ornament in *Much Ado* (3.1.102): "I'll show thee some attires, and have thy counsel/Which is the best to furnish me to-morrow."
5. The editors of the *New Cambridge Shakespeare*, for example, depict Bassanio equipping "himself to go off and hunt an heiress" (p.xxv).
6. William Empson, *Some Versions of Pastoral* (New York, 1935), p. 114.
7. In his chapter on the play in *Prefaces to Shakespeare* (Princeton, 1947), II, Granville Barker comments on its fairy-tale quality and the "emancipating" role of Bassanio as prince to a sleeping beauty. See also Freud's "The Theme of the Three Caskets," in *The Collected Papers of Sigmund Freud* (New York, 1959), IV, chapter 15.
8. Sigurd Burckhardt, *Shakespearean Meanings* (Princeton, 1968), p. 210.
9. Although his terms for the "living" image ("counterfeit," "shadow") could apply to a visual imitation of life such as painting, they are virtual synonyms for "actor" and invite us to associate their "demigod" creator with the dramatist Shakespeare. If we take "this shadow" to be the boy actor impersonating Portia, we have a familiar Shakespearean joke about the inadequacy of art to the "substance" of imagination and—since Bassanio has repudiated gold and silver for "meager" lead—a sly jest about the insubstantiality of substance also.
10. Burckhardt, pp. 207–11.
11. The notion of cannibalism as a magical acquisition of powers is of course commonplace in anthropology; it should not be forgotten that the idea obtains in the Eucharist. This connection of feeding and power underlies Lear's rage against his "pelican daughters," since the pelican proverbially fed on its parent's blood. In *Othello* Shakespeare's Venetian gentry once again need the help of an alien whom they scorn, and the alien boasts of his familiarity with "the Cannibals that each other eat,/The Anthropophagi. . . ."
12. In *Enter Plato* (New York, 1965), Alvin W. Gouldner analyzes the structure of friendship in Hellenic society, which in its competitiveness and the narrow role allotted to women resembles the society in the play. Gouldner contends that insofar as competitiveness threatens to undermine friendships, "homosexuality may be seen as enabling Greek men to resolve their ambivalent orientation to men and to establish close relationships with some of them" (p. 61). Most recent of many commentators to perceive Bassanio's and Antonio's "love" as incipiently homosexual is Leslie Fiedler, in *The Stranger in Shakespeare* (New York, 1972). Rather than identify any character as

240

homosexual, I would prefer to focus instead upon the social dynamics Shakespeare has imagined, and the compensatory quality of the love arising therefrom.

13. Pearlman, p. 218.

14. Cf. Hal's use of "stand for" in *1 Henry IV*: "Do thou stand for me, and I'll play my father" (2.4.418).

15. Saint Augustine, *On Christian Doctrine*, translated by D. W. Robertson, Jr. (New York, 1958), p. 88.

16. Portia meets many of the conditions Auerbach elucidates for a *figura* Of Christ. Interestingly, Marlowe's antic Jew Barabbas is far more nearly an atavistic Vice or stage devil than Shylock is.

17. Burckhardt, p. 233. The melodramatic excitement of such a strategy apparently echoed the mood of many actual court cases. Cf. Lawrence Stone: "The very deficiencies in the machinery of the law, its great cost, its appalling slowness, its obsession with irrelevant technical details, made it an admirable instrument for the sublimation of the bellicose instincts of a leisured class. Sixteenth-century litigation combined the qualities of tedium, hardship, brutality, and injustice that tested character and endurance, with the element of pure chance that appealed to the gambler . . ." (*The Crisis of the Aristocracy*, p. 118). For contemporary audiences, that is, the court contest may have suggested another form of the wagering with fortune that opens the play.

18. C. L. Barber, *Shakespeare's Festival Comedy* (Princeton, 1959), p. 187.

19. This, it will be recalled, is the point of the "statue scene" in *The Winter's Tale* (cf. chapter three).

20. Play is thus a benign sort of "cannibalizing" in which one takes into oneself parts of another just as the cannibal thinks to acquire the qualities of another by eating him.

21. The poet seeks to invoke his muse's "fury" or potency:
Rise, resty Muse, my love's sweet face survey,
If Time have any wrinkle graven there;
If any, be a satire to decay
And make Time's spoils despised everywhere.
Give my love fame faster than Time wastes life. . . .

22. John Northebrooke, *Treatise Wherein Dicing, Dancing, Vain Plays or Interludes, with Other Idle Pastimes . . . Are Reproved*, ed by J. P. Collier for the Shakespeare Society (London, 1843).

23. If we can trust a suggestion of Leslie Fiedler's, Gratiano's last words are both a pledge of fidelity and an allusion to a widely known bawdy joke extant in a fabliau called "Hans Castorp's ring." "While I live I'll fear no other thing," says Gratiano, "So sore as keeping safe Nerissa's ring" (5.1.306–7). And "in Hans's dream, the Devil slipped a magic ring on his middle finger, promising that so long as he wore it, his wife could never betray him" (p. 136). Awaking, Hans found his charmed finger in his wife's vagina. In the joke, that is, magic is a delusive dream, and love trustworthy only when palpably grasped in the rude flesh: a grotesque parody of love-making itself.

Chapter Eight

1. T. S. Eliot, "Hamlet and His Problems," *The Sacred Wood* (London, 1920). Eliot aptly observes that an inexpressible emotion dominates Hamlet, but he proceeds to draw unfruitful conclusions.

2. Ernest Jones, *Hamlet and Oedipus* (New York, 1954). Norman N.

Notes

Holland's *Psychoanalysis and Shakespeare* (New York, 1966) has a useful survey of theories.

3. Cf. the rationale behind the "mousetrap." In the presence of a "cunning" scene, says Hamlet, "murder, though it have no tongue, will speak/With most miraculous organ" (2.2.589). In illustrating magical thinking in chapter 3 of *Totem and Taboo*, Freud points out that in neurosis an evil thought may seem as real—and produce the same guilty reaction—as an intentional evil deed.

4. See Stephen Booth's "On the Value of *Hamlet*," in *Reinterpretations of Elizabethan Drama*, edited by Norman Rabkin (New York, 1969), which analyzes a self-confounding process in the play's language such as we discerned in the Sonnets. Booth minutely demonstrates a "nonlogical coherence" in the "to be or not to be" speech (pp. 164–71). In *Every Artist His Own Scandal* (New York, 1964), Parker Tyler too sweepingly argues a similar point: "The irony of the famous soliloquies is in their bare statements as made: anyone who can juggle the subjects of life and death, spirit and body, in such a masterful way is simply making them interchangeable with each other and thus, intellectually, absurd" (p. 103). In *The Development of Shakespeare's Imagery* (Cambridge, Mass., 1951), Wolfgang Clemen reminds us that Hamlet's habitual rich imagery cannot be reduced to simple statements without falsifying the meaning (p. 111).

5. See also Lionel Abel, *Metatheatre: A New View of Dramatic Form* (New York, 1963), pp. 46–47.

6. Cf. Hamlet's macabre lines about the witching time of night,

When churchyards yawn, and hell itself breathes out
Contagion to this world. Now could I drink hot blood,
And do such bitter business as the day
Would quake to look on. [3.2.378–82]

Ironically he recapitulates his faith in words as deeds:

How in my words somever [Gertrude] be shent,
To give them seals never, my soul, consent! [388–89]

7. The cruel inverse of this fantasy of "becoming" is Shylock's cannibalistic threat. So Hamlet, calling himself the "beggar that I am" (2.2.270), later threatens Claudius that "a king may go a progress through the guts of a beggar" (4.3.30).

8. As a synonym for actor, "shape" recalls the anxiety aroused by the Devil's parodic powers which we treated in relation to Shylock in chapter seven.

9. A. C. Bradley, *Shakespearean Tragedy* (New York, 1956), p. 105.

10. See Francis Fergusson, *The Idea of a Theater* (Princeton, 1949): "The actual crime was that of Caludius; but in the playlet the guilty one is nephew to the King. This could mean . . . a direct threat by Hamlet to Claudius; it also means that Hamlet (who had . . . assured Ophelia, that . . . "I could accuse me of such things it were better my mother had not borne me") had granted Claudius, in advance, that he too is at least poentially guilty. Neither Hamlet nor Shakespeare seem to rule out a Freudian interpretation of the tangle . . ." (p. 123).

11. Booth, p. 171.

12. It could be argued that the Prince can kill Rosencrantz and Guildenstern without remorse because they function as alter egos objectifying the craven, obedient child in himself.

13. Maynard Mack, "The World of *Hamlet*," in the *Yale Review* XLI (1952), 515.

14. Cf. Rolf Soellner, *Shakespeare's Patterns of Self-Knowledge* (Columbus, 1972): "Even attempts to formulate Hamlet into a sterile prototype of a

malcontent avenger have produced astute descriptions of the scintillating and contradictory nature that make him, as E. E. Stoll has it, 'both vindictive and high-minded, active and reflexive, ironic and pathetic, merry and melancholly, indecent and decorous, insolent and courteous, cruel and tender, both suspicious and crafty . . .' " (p. 177).

15. In this light we can understand some puzzling transformations. In *Richard III*, for example, Lady Anne construes herself a grieving and outraged widow in a formulaic incantation (1.2.1–32). The despised Richard meets the funeral and sets about reinterpreting her feelings to her. At once he plays the fool to open up her closed meanings, and vows an incalculable love for her. The recreation of her hate as love appalls him as it does Hamlet, however, as a proof of debasing mutability: "yet to win her, all the world to nothing."

16. In *Dream in Shakespeare* (New Haven, 1974), Marjorie B. Garber points out that the Ghost pleads for a "return to an Old Testament world as well as to a world of epic values and heroic wrath." But she also notes that he speaks the obsolete language of early tragedy burlesqued in "Pyramus and Thisbe" (p. 97). That is, the deadness of the past registers in the dramatic form itself. For Hamlet and *Hamlet* alike, a new and more self-aware "art" is necessary. It is worth recalling that the relation between futurity and self-creation dominates *Love's Labour Lost* as it does, say, Sonnet 107, "Not mine own fears nor the prophetic soul. . . ."

17. "Hamlet repeatedly attempts to control . . . the entire external world through the manipulation of language. In so doing he asserts the primacy of the imagination, the dream state of creation in which 'words, words, words' are greater than and different from the mere 'matter,' they contain" (Garber, p. 96). This (magical) perspective on his thinking at once reconciles and criticizes two opposite and oversimplified views: that he is a "slave of passion" (Lily Campbell); that he is over-intellectual (Coleridge).

18. Fergusson, p. 122. Fergusson, among others, recognizes Hamlet as an incipient Prospero: a magician-artist manqué (p. 131).

19. Cf. "turn" in *Taming of the Shrew* (1.2.169).

20. To the "churlish priest" Laertes vows: "A minist'ring angel shall my sister be" (5.1.235). In *The Shakespearean Imagination* (New York, 1964), Norman N. Holland calls the mad Ophelia "almost a goddess of the spring" (p. 168), a role which presages Perdita's. An illustration of priestly functions (Rosalind as a *magus* figure) appears in Albert Cirillo, "*As You Like It*: Pastoralism Gone Awry," in *English Literary History* XXXVIII (March 1971), 19–39. Most relevant to my argument is Burckhardt's "The Poet as Fool and Priest," in *Shakespearean Meanings*. In the following chapter we encounter other figures of the artist-priest, *Pericles'* Marina and Thaisa.

21. A striking instance of this dissociation is Macbeth's discovery of his own urge to murder: "Is this a dagger which I see before me,/The handle toward my hand?" (2.1.33). As in magical thinking he perceives a wish—here, an evil one—as an independent force.

22. Cf. J. V. Cunningham, *Woe or Wonder* (Denver, 1951), p. 33.

23. Charles R. Forker, "Shakespeare's Theatrical Symbolism and Its Function in *Hamlet*," *Shakespeare Quarterly* XIV (1963), 229. The intermingling of artifice and truth is not reductive, but expansive. The "being" is, after all, only another sort of "seeming"—what Hamlet equivocally calls "this act" (5.2.327).

24. What Joan Hartwig says of the late plays is relevant here: "The double awareness of being simultaneously involved and removed is not a matter of being 'toyed with' by the playwright. . . . It directs us toward an ethical reassessment of what art may be allowed to do. We are forced to look beyond the limitations we ordinarily impose on art as an imitation of life, to look at

the transparencies of the artifice as legitimate containers for meaning that cannot finally be reduced to the forms of expressive art" (*Shakespeare's Tragicomic Vision* [Baton Rouge, La., 1972], p. 7).

25. Maurice Charney, *Shakespeare's Roman Plays* (Cambridge, Mass., 1961), p. 141.

Chapter Nine

1. For treatments of the textual problems which have bedeviled criticism of the play, see F. D. Hoeniger, Arden edition, *Pericles* (London, 1963), p. liii, and Ernest Schanzer's New American Library edition (New York, 1965), pp. xxiff. Schanzer convincingly hypothesizes that Shakespeare took over a clumsy manuscript probably "by some very minor playwright" and rewrote the last three acts (p. xxvii). For reasons that will be evident, I agree with G. Wilson Knight in *The Crown of Life* (London, 1965) that after many rereadings "one begins to suspect some especial purpose in the passages of stilted verse" (p. 33). That purpose seems to me parody. Like Hamlet with the players, Shakespeare was intensely interested in the meaning and metaphor of "bad art."

2. In *A Natural Perspective* (New York, 1965) Northrop Frye claims that Gower "stands for the authority of literary tradition . . . and is there to put us in as uncritical a frame of mind as possible" (p. 31). Efforts to make the play a didactic allegory are hard pressed to account for its bold absurdities. Cf. Howard Felperin's "Shakespeare's Miracle Play," *Shakespeare Quarterly* XVII (1967), 363.

3. It is appropriate to recall the players' licenses declared them to be legally servants or retainers of a lord. The exploited condition of the child-actors in *Hamlet* is also relevant in this connection.

4. Cf. Schanzer: "*Pericles* seems to have been one of Shakespeare's greatest stage successes. The fact that the Quarto text was reprinted five times between 1609 and 1635 alone bears witness to its popularity" (p. xli).

5. In "Shakespeare and Romance," in *Later Shakespeare*, Stratford-upon-Avon Studies 8 (London, 1966), Stanley Wells argues that Pericles stories were so common that the audience's familiarity with the tale permitted Shakespeare to play upon their expectations, emphasizing the limits of their preconceptions. This seems congruent with his usual practice, and the likeliest explanation of his adoption of such tales as subject matter in the first place.

6. In a play that opens with a ghost, it is intriguing to encounter lines reminiscent of *Hamlet*. Cf. Pericles' "The blind mole casts/Copp'd hills toward heaven, to tell the earth is throng'd/By man's oppression" (1.1.100) and Hamlet's sobriquet for the Ghost, "old mole" (1.5.162).

7. In "Word and Picture in the Final Plays," also in *Later Shakespeare* (London, 1966), Francis Berry points out that in the play "present" is always being made "past," distanced, "thrown back by the framed picture" (pp. 86–92).

8. Cf. the Ghost's ability to "harrow up the soul" of his son in a similar perversion of wonder (1.5.13–22).

9. Cannibalism as a "consuming" of another's identity echoes in the image Pericles later uses as Marina gradually "gives" her true identity to him: she "starves the ears she feeds, and makes them hungry/The more she gives them speech" (5.1.111). The image, like the relationship, redeems an earlier, destructive form. Tharsus may well have satirized the excesses of some English aristocrats at the time of the play's debut. In *The Crisis of the Aristocracy* Lawrence Stone describes a society "even more obsessed with status

than with money" (p. 108), and given to outrageous conspicuous consumption, including banquets of fabulous variety and "stupendous cost" (p. 256).

10. It is perhaps not unnecessary to recall the satiric use of statues in *Love's Labour's Lost* (1.1.2), *Romeo and Juliet*, *The Winter's Tale*, and *Hamlet* (5.1.291).

11. Recent studies have acknowledged the play's kinship with the early comedies in some cases, but declined to pursue the matter. Cf. W. B. Thorne, "*Pericles* and the 'Incest-Fertility' Opposition," *Shakespeare Quarterly* XXII (1971), 43. In "*Pericles, Prince of Tyre*," *Shakespeare Quarterly* XVII (1967), John Arthos manages to take note of the play's artifices while seriously maintaining that they "lend something of the usual power of romances, suggesting the . . . East and the mysteries of strange oceans" (p. 258).

12. As a means to sublimation and escapism, knighthood had far-reaching satiric implications for contemporary England. In Lawrence Stone's words, "the nobility were losing their nerve. As their utility in war declined, they tried to protect their position by a romantic and artificial revival of the chivalric ideal . . ." (*The Crisis of the Aristocracy*, p. 131).

13. In a tale told by Cicero and Quintilian, "Simonides" is the father of lyric poetry and mnemonics.

14. By "calling attention to the limitations of the comic formula in this self-conscious way, the playwright is also suggesting that the comic resolution alone is not sufficient to resolve the tragic complications which man faces." Joan Hartwig, *Shakespeare's Tragicomic Vision* (Baton Rouge, La., 1972), p. 44.

15. In *All's Well* lust is compared to a whale devouring virgins (4.3.203). Insofar as the metaphor is basically "about" the "consuming" power of irrational passions over the passive personality, it applies to Pericles himself. The self can drown in irrationality, so to speak, and yet be "belched up" again, for all its fears.

16. Contemporary magicians or cunning men were often notorious confidence tricksters. K. V. Thomas cites one example after another, including "the case of the Venetian physician in London in the reign of Edward VI who was confronted with an unconscious patient; well aware that the man was in no real danger he declared he would perform a miracle by raising him from the dead, and duly did so" (*Religion and the Decline of Magic*, p. 208).

17. In its incongruous superstitions, allegorical hints, comic moralizing, Christian anachronisms, and pious hypocrites (such as the brothel-keepers), the play takes a complex attitude toward orthodox religion. In *The World Turned Upside Down* (London, 1972), Christopher Hill asserts that "Most men and women in seventeenth century Britain still lived in a world of magic" (p. 70), yet he also corroborates findings of significant religious skepticism in *Religion and the Decline of Magic:* "Mr K. V. Thomas has collected a number of . . . examples under Elizabeth and the first two Stuarts [of] denial of the resurrection, of the existence of God (very common in the diocese of Exeter at the end of the sixteenth century). . . . He emphasizes how wrong it is to describe all such . . . expressions of irreligion as 'Lollardy', and expostulates with embarrassed historians who dismiss them as the products of drunks or madmen" (p. 21).

18. Joan Hartwig summarizes some of the uncertainties attending the conception of Lysimachus (P. 53n.). Though she believes the play more didactic than I do, to my mind Miss Hartwig's chapter on *Pericles* is exceptional for its appreciation of Shakespeare's humor. The brothel scene "comically underscores the miraculous power of virtue. . . . This scene . . . presents a comic referent for the serious enactment of wonder which is to follow in *V.i.*" (p. 53).

19. Variations of this pattern are crucial in *Love's Labour's Lost,* Oberon's treatment of Titania in *A Midsummer Night's Dream,* and of course *Lear.* Significantly, though Hamlet desperately purges his feelings against Ophelia and his mother, for him the pattern comes to nought. Leontes' behavior, on the other hand, might be said to consummate the pattern.

20. Cf. *The Taming of the Shrew*: "I call them forth to credit her" (4.1.91).

21. The couplet which closes Sonnet 146 illustrates the reverse process, vowing that the beloved will bring death to the word "death" and thereby with "Death once dead, there's no more dying then."

22. "Waste" and satire dominate the argument of Sonnet 100, as mentioned in chapter seven.

Chapter Ten

1. Cf. Ulysses' strategy for escaping Cyclops. Commanded to reveal his identity he replies craftily, "I am Nobody."

2. In *The Orphic Voice* (New York, 1971), Elizabeth Sewell describes the magical character of Lear's thought (5.3.8–19) in terms applicable to Prospero and his island: "This is fatidic or Orphic speech. It begins to gather up the universe . . . here is language as fairytale or prelogic, and as prayer, and in union with music. There is an astonishing sense of space, the heavens, the tides with humanity flowing with them, the vision of the world as a seat of mysterious royalty of which scattered and conflicting news may be got by language and from various messengers, of vast secrets yet to be discovered, and all this from a prison as small and enclosed as any one single human organism which is yet in relation with the whole of creation, in its metamorphic death as well as in life" (p. 167).

3. This dilemma somberly echoes the burlesqued loyalty tests of Thaliard, Helicanus, Leonine, and Boult in *Pericles.* At Hermione's "death" the process is reversed: her suppressed self-assertiveness is liberated in the behavior of her alter ego Paulina.

4. J. I. M. Stewart, *Character and Motive in Shakespeare* (New York, 1969), p. 35. Stewart bases his argument on notes to 1.2.237 and 2.1.52 in Dover Wilson's New Shakespeare edition.

5. Marjorie Garber, *Dream in Shakespeare* (New Haven, 1974), p. 171.

6. Joan Hartwig, *Shakespeare's Tragicomic Vision* (Baton Rouge, La., 1972), p. 128. Unfortunately Miss Hartwig's didactic emphasis produces a moral judgment of the Clown which overlooked the liberating aspects of a "fool-ish" viewpoint.

7. Garber, p. 172. See also the Arden edition of the play, which glosses Hermione's "bug which you would frighten me with" (3.2.92) by relating "bug" to bugbears and bogeys.

8. For example, see Nevill Coghill, "Six Points of Stage-craft in *The Winter's Tale,*" *Shakespeare Survey* 11, p. 35.

9. David Young, *The Heart's Forest* (New Haven, 1972), p. 142.

10. The poet "plays" or identifies himself with Time in Sonnet 115, for example:

> Alas why fearing of Time's tyranny.
> Might I not then say now I love you best,
> When I was certain o'er incertainty,
> Crowning the present, doubting of the rest:
> Love is a babe, then might I not say so
> To give full growth to that which still doth grow.

(1609 punctuation.) Like Time, who gives his scene "growing," the poet would nurture a "babe" who "still doth grow." The word play on "still" produces a paradox of constancy or integrity within change.

11. Some recent studies have brought new sensitivity to the troubled relation of play to conceptions of history and political power. Important formulations of the problem are Sigurd Burckhardt's chapters on *Julius Caesar, King John,* and the Prince Hal trilogy in *Shakespearean Meanings;* James L. Calderwood's "*1 Henry IV:* Art's Gilded Lie," in *English Literary Renaissance* III (1973), 131–44; and John W. Blanpied's " 'Unfathered heirs and loathly births of nature': Bringing History to Crisis in *2 Henry IV,*" in *English Literary Renaissance* V (1975), 212–31, as well as " 'Art and Baleful Sorcery:' The Counterconsciousness of *Henry VI, Part 1,*" in *Studies in English Literature* XV (1975), 213–27.

12. Cf. Puck at the close of *A Midsummer Night's Dream:*
   If we shadows have offended,
   Think but this, and all is mended,
   That you have but slumb'red here
   While these visions did appear.
   And this weak and idle theme,
   No more yielding but a dream,
   Gentles, do not reprehend.
   If you pardon, we will mend.   [5.1.412–19]

13. This wishful disposition resembles religious faith. But what Northrop Frye observes about *The Tempest* in his Pelican edition of that play (Baltimore, 1959) applies here: "*The Tempest* is not an allegory or religious drama; if it were Prospero's great 'revels' speech would say, not merely that all things will vanish, but that an eternal world will take their place" (p. 18).

Appendix

1. See Erich Auerbach's essay on *figura* in *Scenes from the Drama of European Literature* (New York, 1959).

2. *Chief Pre-Shakespearean Dramas,* edited by Joseph Q. Adams (Cambridge, 1924), p. 23.

3. Adams, p. 24.

4. The name of the early Christian communion "changed from *Eucharista,* which means thanksgiving, to *Missa,* which means (or was thought to mean) the dismissal of the unworthy." Erik Erikson, *Young Man Luther* (New York, 1962), p. 142.

5. Adams, pp. 51–54.

6. Adams, p. 87.

7. In *The Medieval Stage* (Oxford, 1930), E. K. Chambers reports a decree of the Synod of Worms in 1316 which "orders that the 'mystery of the resurrection' shall be performed before the *plebs* comes into the church, and gives as a reason the crowds caused by a prevalent superstition that whoever saw the crucifix raised would escape [death] for that year." In his admirable study *Religion and the Decline of Magic* (New York, 1971), K. V. Thomas details the "parasitical" popular beliefs which made the medieval Church appear "as a vast reservoir of magical power, capable of being deployed for . . . secular purposes. . . . Almost any object associated with ecclesiastical ritual could assume a special aura in the eyes of the people. Any prayer or piece of the Scriptures might have a mystical power waiting to be tapped" (p. 45). Thomas provides invaluable examples of the subtle persistence of many such beliefs in Shakespeare's time.

8. This is the contention of Ann Righter (*Shakespeare and the Idea of the Play* [London, 1962]), who holds that "no idea could have been more foreign to medieval dramatists than the Renaissance conception of the essentially self-contained play. . . . While the performance lasted, audience and actors shared the same ritual world, a world more real than the one which existed outside its frame" (p. 21).

We cannot always trust our impressions of mental processes so remote from us in time. A different account of the same drama is V. Kolve's *The Play Called Corpus Christi* (Stanford, 1966), which views the cycles in terms of festival performances. Kolve, however, tends to deemphasize their ritualistic character, documenting in detail the plays' conscious artfulness.

9. Stage directions from *The Trial of Christ*, in Adams, pp. 185–86.

10. See the self-serving but otherwise believable accounts in Thomas Beard's *Theatre of God's Judgments* (London, 1631), pp. 206ff. Chambers recounts admonitory tales of how horrors mimicked by actors miraculously became real. In Elizabethan England a widespread story described the appearance of an extra devil onstage during a performance of *Doctor Faustus*.

11. Just this tradition of ecclesiastical hostility informs Sonnet 105 (see chapter one) and the protestations of magic's lawfulness at the close of *The Winter's Tale* (5.3.105 and 111).

12. Roland August, *Cruelty and Civilzation* (London, 1972), p. 103.

Index

Abel, Lionel, *Metatheatre: A New View of Dramatic Form*, 4 n, 59 n, 169 n
Adams, Joseph Quincy, 226 n, 227 n, 228 n
Alighieri, Dante, 57
Aretino, Pietro, 58 n
Arthos, John, 199 n
Auerbach, Erich, *Scenes from the Drama of European Life*, 56 n, 157 n, 226 n
August, Roland, *Cruelty and Civilization*, 229 n
Augustine, Saint, 118; *On Christian Doctrine*, 157 n, 160

Bacon, Francis, *Novum Organum*, 30 n
Barber, C. L., 61 n; *Shakespeare's Festive Comedy*, 61, 70 n, 104 n, 110 n, 159 n
Beard, Thomas, 228 n
Benson, John, 6 n
Berry, Francis, 197 n
Bethell, S. L., *The Winter's Tale: A Study*, 57 n
Blanpied, John W., 222 n
Booth, Stephen, 167 n, 176 n; *Essay on Shakespeare's Sonnets*, 12 n
Bradbrook, M. C., *The Growth and Structure of Elizabethan Comedy*, 50 n
Bradley, A. C., *Shakespearean Tragedy*, 174 n
Burckhardt, Sigurd, *Shakespearean Meanings*, 4 n, 14 n, 62 n, 68 n, 148, 150, 158 n, 186 n, 222 n
Burke, Kenneth, 4 n, 68 n

Calderwood, James L., *Shakespearean Metadrama*, 4 n, 62, 79 n, 114 n, 222 n
Campbell, Joseph, *The Masks of God*, 38, 39
Campbell, Lily B., *Shakespeare's Tragic Heroes*, 35 n
Cassirer, Ernst, *Language and Myth*, 11 n
Chambers, E. K., *The Medieval Stage*, 100 n, 228 n
Charney, Maurice, 141 n; *Shakespeare's Roman Plays*, 191 n
Cirillo, Albert, 70 n, 186 n
Clemen, Wolfgang, *English Tragedy Before Shakespeare*, 140 n; *The Development of Shakespeare's Imagery*, 167 n
Coghill, Neville, 220 n
Coleridge, Samuel Taylor, 4, 68, 124
Cope, Jackson I., *The Theater and the Dream*, 39 n
Cunningham, J. V., *Woe or Wonder*, 190 n

Davison, Francis, *The Masque of Proteus*, 40–45, 49–52, 76 n, 81, 90, 118 n
Doran, Madeleine, *Endeavors of Art*, 4 n

Edwards, Philip, *Shakespeare and the Confines of Art*, 4 n, 73 n

249